English Reading Comprehension

정재문 지음

신아사

머리말

이 책은 영어 독해 능력을 기르려는 목적으로 만들어진 책입니다. 그런데 영문의 뼈대를 이루는 구문에 대한 확실한 이해 없이는 영문을 제대로 이해할 수 없습니다. 그래서 이 책에서는 먼저 영문의 가장 중요한 뼈대를 이루는 구문들을 제1부 단문 독해에서 정리하여 되풀이 연습시켜 완전히 익히게 한 다음, 제2부 중문 독해에서는 상당히 복잡한 문장들을 다룸으로써 제1부에서 익힌 것들을 응용할 수 있는 능력을 기를 수 있게 했고, 제3부 장문독해에서는 국가직 9급과 7급의 영어독해 기출문제들을 다룸으로써 취업에도 대비할 수 있게 했습니다.

영어독해 능력은 결코 하루아침에 향상되지 않습니다. 부지런히 단어와 숙어를 암기하고, 구문을 이해한 다음 반복 학습하여 완전히 자기 것으로 만들고, 좋은 글을 많이 읽음으로써 향상되는 것입니다.

이 책의 장점을 살려 부지런히 학습함으로써 여러분의 독해 능력이 향상된다면 저자에게 이보다 더 큰 기쁨과 보람은 없을 것입니다. 학습자 여러분의 건승을 빕니다.

2014. 01

정재문

CONTENTS

제1부 단문 독해

제1장 부정사

제2장 동명사

제3장 분사

제4장 관계대명사와 관계부사

제5장 가정법

제6장 접속사

제2부 중문 독해

제3부 장문 독해

제1부 단문 독해

제1장

부정사(Infinitive)

동사 본래의 기능을 가지고 있으면서 다른 품사의 구실을 하는 동사형을 준동사라고 한다.

준동사에는 부정사, 동명사, 분사의 3 종류가 있다.

부정사 : to + 원형동사 ; 명사, 형용사, 부사의 구실을 한다.
동명사 : 원형동사 + ~ing(현재분사와 같은 꼴) ; 명사의 구실을 한다.
분사 : 현재분사, 과거분사 ; 형용사, 부사의 구실을 한다.

부정사는 일반적으로 'to + 동사원형'의 형태를 취하지만 to 없는 부정사도 있다. to 없는 부정사, 즉 동사원형을 원형부정사라고 한다. 부정사는 동사 본래의 성질을 가지고 있으므로 부정사로 쓰인 동사의 종류에 따라 목적어, 보어를 취하기도 하고 부사(구)의 수식을 받기도 하면서, 문장 속에서는 명사, 형용사, 부사의 구실을 한다. 또한 시제, 태의 구분이 있으며, 의미상의 주어도 있다. 부정사의 부정은 to 앞에 not나 never를 두면 된다.

단순부정사 : to do(능동), to be done(수동), to be doing(진행)
완료부정사 : to have done(능동), to have been done(수동),
to have been doing(진행)

영어독해

1 명사적 용법

• 부정사가 명사처럼 주어, 보어, 목적어로 쓰일 때로서, 보통 '~하는 것, ~하기'와 같이 번역한다.

[1] 주어로서의 용법

1. To err is human, to forgive divine.
2. To see is to believe.
3. To work is the duty of everyone.
4. To do everything is to do nothing.
5. To love and to be loved is the greatest happiness on earth.

❖ 가주어 It을 쓰고 진주어인 부정사를 뒤에 두는 형식.

6. To read this book is interesting.
   =It is interesting to read this book.
7. It is difficult to master English in a few years.
8. It is not hard to finish the work.
9. It isn't nice to have a dirty house.
10. It is pleasant to play basketball.

[2] 보어로서의 용법

(1) 주격보어

1. To see is to believe.
2. To see her is to love her.

3. His job is to mend shoes.
4. The best thing is to try it again.
5. My delight is to travel around the world.

(2) 목적격보어

1. I asked him to open the window.
2. I want you to stay with me.
3. I ordered him to come back.
4. I believe her to be honest.
5. Her father never allows her to go out in the evening.

[3] 목적어로서의 용법

(1) 타동사의 목적어

❖ S+V+부정사(목적어)

1. I want to go there tomorrow.
2. I like to swim in the lake.
3. I don't like to go out late at night.
4. I began to understand him.
5. I finally decided to go abroad.

❖ S+V+it(가목적어)+OC+부정사(진목적어)

6. I found it interesting to read the novel.
7. Science made it possible to go to the moon.
8. I found it easy to climb a tree.
9. I think it wrong to tell a lie.

10. He felt it necessary to pay the price first.

(2) 전치사의 목적어

❖ except, but, save, about

1. He desired nothing but to succeed.
2. You have no choice but to accept the fact.
3. The bus was about to start.
4. I will do anything except (to) resign.

[4] 명사와 동격인 용법

1. Her ambition to become the world swimming champion was understandable.
2. Both alternatives, to advance and to retreat, seemed equally dangerous.
3. She has only one aim in life, to succeed.

[5] 의문사+to 부정사

1. What to do is the question.
2. The question is what to do.
3. Whom to send there is the question.
4. She learned how to ride a horse.
5. I don't know what to do [which to choose, when to leave, where to go, how to dance].
6. Tell me whether to trust him or not.
7. I wondered whether to write or phone.

영어독해

2 형용사적 용법

• 부정사가 명사나 대명사를 직접 혹은 간접적으로 수식하는 용법

[1] 한정 용법(직접수식): ~할, ~해야 할, ~하는

(1) 주어 관계: 수식되는 말이 부정사의 의미상의 주어

1. He is the very man to do the work.
2. He was the only one to survive the crash.
3. She loves parties; she is always the first to come and the last to leave.
4. He is the second man to be killed in this way.
5. It was the best play to be performed that year.

(2) 목적어 관계: 수식되는 말이 부정사의 의미상의 목적어

1. I have no food to eat.
2. I want something to eat for lunch.
3. There are many sights to see in Seoul.
4. Does he get enough to eat?

(3) 전치사의 목적어: 수식되는 말이 부정사구 안의 전치사의 목적어

1. I want something to write on. (=I want something on which to write.)
2. I want something to write with. (=I want something with which to write.)
3. I need a chair to sit on. (=I need a chair on which to sit.).

4. He has no house to live in.
5. I have no pen to write with.

(4) **형용관계:** 수식되는 명사는 추상명사.

1. There is no other way to do it.
2. What is the best way to learn English?
3. He made an attempt to stand up.
4. Failure to obey the regulations may result in disqualification.
5. She was annoyed by his unwillingness to do his share of the work.

영어독해

3 부사적 용법

• 부정사가 동사, 형용사, 부사를 수식하는 용법

(1) **목적:** ~하기 위하여

1. I came here to see you.
2. I save my money to buy a computer.
3. We eat to live, not live to eat.
4. You must study hard not to fail in the test.
5. Man is born to live, not to prepare for life.
6. He studied hard in order to pass the examination.
7. The people stood up so as to see the parade better.
8. I hurried so as to be in time for class.
9. He works hard in order to support his family.

10. He kept quiet so as not to disturb his father.

Cf. go, come, try 등

1. Come to see me. = Come and see me. = Come see me.
2. Go to see her. = Go and see her. = Go see her.
3. Go to get it. = Go and get it. = Go get it.

(2) **결과**: ~한 결과, ~해서 마침내 …하다.

❖ 무의지동사(live, succeed, grow up, awake 등)+부정사

1. He lived to be ninety years old.
2. He grew up to be a famous scientist.
3. I awoke one morning to find myself famous.
4. He worked hard only to fail.
5. He went to China, never to return.
6. He opened the door only to find the room empty.
7. I did my best only to fail in the examination.
8. Shelley left England never to return.
9. They parted never to see each other again.
10. The good old days have gone never to return.

(3) **감정의 원인**: ~하여, ~하게 되어

❖ 감정을 나타내는 동사(smile, regret, weep, grieve 등), 감정을 나타내는 형용사(sorry, glad, happy, surprised, pleased, delighted, shocked, angry, ashamed, disappointed, astonished, proud 등)+부정사

1. I am very glad to hear that.

2. I was surprised to hear the news.
3. I was lucky to be there at that moment.
4. I am sorry to hear that.
5. He smiled to see her.

(4) 판단의 근거: ~하다니

❖ 흔히 must be ~, cannot be ~, 감탄문 등에서

1. He must be a fool to do such a thing.
2. He cannot be poor to buy such a large house.
3. How foolish he is to do such a mean thing!
4. What have I done to be treated like this?
5. You must be hungry to eat three hamburgers at once.

(5) 조건: 만일~한다면(가정법의 구문에서)

1. To hear him speak English, you would take him for an American.
2. I should be happy to be of service to you.

(6) 감탄, 소망

a) To think~! 따위의 형태로 '~하다니'라는 놀람이나 의의의 뜻을 표현. To think that I was once a billionaire!
b) Oh, to be in England! (=I wish I were in England.)

(7) 형용사 수식

a) hard, difficult, easy, dangerous 등의 뒤에서

1. Chinese is hard to learn. (=It is hard to learn Chinese.)
2. Your question is difficult to answer.
3. This lake is dangerous to swim in.
4. The building was easy to find.
5. This novel is very easy to read.

b) pretty, jolly, sad 등의 뒤에서

1. The mountain is pretty to look at.
2. Some children are jolly to watch when they run.
3. The story was sad to listen to.

c) sure, certain, likely 등의 뒤에서

1. The girl is certain to appear. (=It is certain that the girl will appear.)
2. The girl is sure to appear.
3. The girl is likely to appear.

d) slow, quick, long 등의 뒤에서

1. The boy is slow to learn.
2. The girl is quick to sympathize with the poor.
3. He was not long to discover her guilt.

e) good, bad, unfit 등의 뒤에서

1. This apple is good to eat.
2. This water is bad to drink.

3. She is unfit to work.
4. He is qualified to teach English.
5. He is worthy to be honoured.

f) eager, anxious, inclined, ready 등의 뒤에서

1. The woman is eager to please.
2. The woman is anxious to know the truth.
3. The woman is inclined to take offence easily.
4. The woman is ready to die.
5. The woman is shy to begin her speech.

(8) too, enough를 수식

❖ too+형용사/부사+to부정사~: 너무 …해서 ~할 수 없다. ~하기에는 너무 …하다.
❖ 형용사/부사+enough+to부정사~: 매우(충분히) …해서 ~하다. ~할 정도로 (충분히) …하다.

1. You are old enough to know better.
2. You are young enough to marry.
3. You are not young enough to dress in that showy way.
4. You are too young to marry.
5. This water is too hot to drink.
6. This stone is too heavy for me to lift (it).
7. This problem is too difficult for me to solve (it).
8. He walks too fast for me to keep up with (him).

cf.

1. The man is too anxious to know the result.
2. The man is too ready to find fault.

3. The man is too apt to do so.
4. The man was only too delighted to accept her invitation.
5. The scenery was too beautiful for words.

(9) so ~ as, such ~ as, as much as, as if 등의 뒤에서

❖ so+형용사/부사+as to~: 매우 …하여 ~하다. ~할 정도로 그렇게(매우) …하다.

1. He was so kind as to drive me to the station.
2. The skirt was so long as to touch the floor.
3. His eloquence was such as to move her audience to tears.(such as=so great as)
4. The monkey chattered as if to say(=as much as to say) "I'll catch you now".

비교 연습

1. The boy is too young to understand it.
2. The boy is old enough to understand it.
3. The boy is so old as to understand it.
4. You are too young to drive a car.
5. You are old enough to drive a car.
6. You are so old as to drive a car.
7. He is too busy to eat lunch.
8. She is kind enough to help me.
9. She is so kind as to help me.
10. He is too weak to carry the heavy bag.
11. He is strong enough to carry the heavy bag.

12. He is so strong as to carry the heavy bag.
13. I got up early enough to catch the first train.
14. I got up so early as to catch the first train.
15. I got up too late to catch the first train.

영어독해

4 독립부정사

• 문장의 다른 부분으로부터 독립하여 문장 전체를 수식하는 부정사. 일종의 관용구

1. To tell the truth, I don't like her. (사실을 말하면)
2. Strange to say, Hamlet wasn't afraid of his father's ghost. (이상한 말이지만)
3. Needless to say, health is above wealth. (말할 필요도 없이)
4. He is, so to speak[say], a walking dictionary. (말하자면)

중요한 독립 부정사

To tell the truth: 사실을 말하면
To be frank[honest] with you: 솔직히 말하면
To speak frankly: 솔직히 말하면
To be brief: 간단히 말하면
To be sure: 확실히
To be exact: 정확히 말해서
To make matters worse: 설상가상으로
Strange to say: 이상한 말이지만

So to speak: 말하자면
To do (him) justice: 공평하게 말해서
To say nothing of~: ~은 말할 것도 없고
Not to mention[speak of]~: ~은 말할 것도 없고
not to say~: ~라고는 말할 수 없지만
to begin[start] with: 우선, 첫째로
to do one's best: 최선을 다 했지만
lucky to say: 다행하게도
to make[cut] a long story short: 간단히 말하면
to say the least: 줄잡아 말해도
to sum up: 요약하면
to conclude: 결론적으로
to come to the point: 요컨대

영어독해

5 분리부정사

- To와 동사원형 사이에 부사가 들어 있는 형태의 부정사를 분리부정사라고 한다. 이것은 부사가 부정사를 수식한다는 것을 명확히 나타내기 위한 용법이다.

1. He failed to entirely avoid it.
   Cf. He failed to avoid it entirely. He failed entirely to avoid it.
2. I cannot find words to sufficiently express my gratitude to you.
3. To clearly understand it was impossible.
4. For the first time she seemed to really know and feel the sort of lives they led.

6 대부정사

- 같은 말이 반복되는 것을 피하기 위해 부정사의 본체를 생략하고 to만을 남기는 경우가 있는데 이것을 대부정사라고 한다. 일종의 생략법으로 구어에서 많이 쓴다.

1. You can stay here if you want to.(want to = want to stay here)
2. I'll help you whenever you want me to. (to=to help you)
3. I don't know him, and I don't want to.

7 원형부정사

- to가 붙지 않은 부정사를 원형부정사라고 한다. to 없는 부정사 또는 동사원형이라고도 한다. 원형부정사는 다음과 같이 비교적 한정된 경우에 쓰인다.

(1) 조동사 뒤에서

a) 의문문, 부정문을 만드는 조동사 do [does, did] 뒤에서

1. Did you like her?
2. He does not like her.

b) 그 밖의 조동사(can, may, must, will, shall 등)의 뒤에서

1. He can dance well.
2. May I help you, sir?

(2) 지각동사의 목적보어일 때: 지각동사 + 목적어 + 원형부정사(목적보어)

❖ 지각동사: see, hear, feel, watch, behold, observe, notice, perceive 등

1. I saw him swim in the lake.
   Cf. He was seen to swim in the lake by me.
2. Did you hear her sing in her room?
3. Must I watch the sheep sleep and eat?
4. I felt the earth tremble.
5. They observed the car stop.

(3) 사역동사의 목적보어일 때: 사역동사 + 목적어 + 원형부정사(목적보어)

a) make, have, let의 경우

1. My mother made me clean my room.
   Cf. I was made to clean my room by my mother.
2. My mother let me clean my room.
   Cf. I was allowed(permitted) to clean my room by my mother.
3. My mother had me clean my room.
4. I would like to have him attend school.
5. He had his wife die suddenly.

원형부정사 익히기 연습

1. I saw the girl play the piano.
2. He let me take a rest.
3. I heard Tom play the guitar.
4. I saw him draw a picture of a dog.
5. She made him do the work.
6. I saw two cats fight.
7. I heard a bird sing in the garden.
8. Can you make the car go faster?
9. Let her come in.
10. He let his son go swimming.
11. I had him write the letter.
12. I had him paint the house.
13. He made me enter the room.
14. I felt his hands tremble.
15. I never saw him laugh.
16. I had him cut my hair.

❖ let은 관용적으로 let go[drop, fall, fly, slip]과 같은 구를 이룬다.

1. Don't let go the rope.= Don't let the rope go.
2. Let go my hand.
3. Don't let slip the golden time.
4. She let fall some of the most unpleasant remarks I have ever heard.

❖ let, make, hear, help 등 다음에 목적어(others, someone, people 등)가 생략되는 경우.

1. Live and let live.
2. He made believe that he was an Indian.
3. I have heard say that your country is very beautiful.
4. They all helped lay the table for tea.

b) help의 경우: help + 목적어 + (to)부정사, help + (to)부정사

1. I helped him (to) do the work.
2. This medicine will help (to) relieve your headache.
3. Help me (to) lift it.

c) bid의 경우: bid+목적어+(to)부정사

1. I bade him (to) do the work. (문어적 표현)
2. Bid him go.

(4) 원형부정사를 쓰는 관용 구문

Had better, had best, had rather, had sooner, had as soon, would rather, can but, cannot but, do nothing but

a) had better + 원형부정사: ~하는 것이 좋다.

❖ You had better go now.
You'd better ~. (구어)
You better ~. (구어)
Better ~. (구어)

1. You had better not go now.
2. Hadn't you better go now? (지금 가는 것이 더 낫지 않을까?)
3. We had better take off our shoes, hadn't you?
4. You'd better hurry up if you want to get home before dark.
5. I better try again later.

b) had best+원형부정사: ~하는 것이 제일 좋다.

1. We had best consult a doctor.
2. You had best go home.
3. You had best start at once.

c) had rather[had sooner, had as doon]+원형부정사=would rather[would sooner, would as soon]+원형부정사: 차라리 ~하는 것이 낫다. 차라리 ~하겠다. 차라리 ~하고 싶다.

1. I had rather stay here alone.
2. I would rather stay here alone.
3. Would you rather stay here alone?
4. I would rather not stay here alone.
5. I had as soon go as stay.
   =I had rather go than stay.
   =I had sooner go than stay.
   =I would as soon go as stay.
   =I would rather go than stay.
   =I would sooner go than stay.
6. I would sooner die at once than live in this agony.

d) but의 뒤에서

❖ cannot but 동사원형=cannot choose but 동사원형=cannot help but 동사원형=have no choice but to 동사원형=have no alternative but to 동사원형=cannot help 동명사=~하지 않을 수 없다.
❖ do nothing but+동사원형=~하기만 하다.

1. I cannot but obey you. (but=except)
   Cf. I can but obey you. (but=only)
2. I cannot but accept your offer.
3. None can but pity him.
4. She did nothing but smile.
5. She does nothing but complain of her husband's shortcomings.

e) All[what, the only thing] …do is (to) v~. 과 같은 형식의 문장에서 (be동사의 주어가 되는 부분에 do가 들어 있는 경우가 많다. 미국 구어 표현에 특히 많음)

1. The only thing to do is (to) write to him.
2. All we can do is write to him.
3. What we can do is write to him.

영어독해

8 be동사+to부정사

• be to가 하나의 조동사와 비슷한 역할을 하면서 다음과 같은 의미를 나타낸다

(1) 예정(계획)(~할 예정이다=be due to, be scheduled to): 흔히 미래 표시 부사(구) 동반

1. He is to go to America next week.
   Cf. His plan is to go to America next week. (명사적 용법)
2. We are to meet him at five.
3. The concert is to be held this evening.
4. She is to make a speech tonight.
5. The prime minister is to make a statement tomorrow.
   Cf. The prime minister to make a statement tomorrow. (신문, 잡지의 표제)

(2) 의무(~해야 한다=must, should)

1. We are to obey our parents.
2. Passengers are to observe these regulations.
3. We are to clean our room every day.
4. Such people are to be pitied rather than despised.
5. This fact is not to be forgotten.

(3) 의도(~하고자 하다=intend to): 주로 조건절에서

1. If we are to succeed, we must work hard.
2. If you are to have good friends, you must be good.
3. If you are to be there before noon, you must be quick.

(4) 가능(~할 수 있다=can): 주로 수동태, 부정문, 의문문에서

1. No cloud was to be seen in the sky.
2. Nothing is to be attained without labour.
3. The book was not to be found anywhere.
4. How am I to pay such a debt?

(5) 운명(~할 운명이다=be destined to, be doomed to)

1. She was never to return home.
2. She was never to see her country again.
3. They said good-bye, little knowing that they were never to meet again.

영어독해

9 부정사의 의미상의 주어

- 부정사의 동작을 하는 주체를 그 부정사의 의미상의 주어라고 한다.

(1) 부정사의 의미상의 주어=문장의 주어

1. I want to succeed.
2. I have something to do.
3. She will come to see you.

(2) 부정사의 의미상의 주어=문장의 목적어

1. I want you to succeed. (나는 네가 성공하기를 바란다.)

2. I told her to wash her hands.
3. I asked her to clean my room.

(3) 부정사의 의미상의 주어 = 일반사람

1. To tell a lie is wrong. ([누구든지] 거짓말하는 것은 나쁘다.)
2. It is important to learn English.

(4) 부정사의 의미상의 주어 = "for+목적격"

부정사의 의미상의 주어가 문장의 주어나 목적어, 또는 일반인이 아닐 때: "for+목적격"으로 나타내며, to 부정사 바로 앞에 둔다.

1. There is some work for you to do. (네가 해야 할 일이 좀 있다.)
2. It is easy for her to read this book.
3. I stepped aside for her to pass by.

(5) 부정사의 의미상의 주어="of+목적격"

It is …to~(~하는 것은 …하다)의 구문에서 is 뒤에 사람의 성질을 나타내는 형용사(kind, nice, good, foolish, wise, clever, brave 따위)가 오면 to 부정사의 의미상의 주어는 "of+목적격"으로 나타낸다.

1. It is kind[nice, good, foolish, wise, clever] of you to invite me to the party.
   (당신이 저를 파티에 초대해주셔서 감사합니다.=You are kind to invite me to the party.)
2. It is very nice of you to come here.

부정사의 주어 익히기 연습

1. It is kind of you to say so.
2. It was foolish of him to do such a thing.
3. It is difficult for her to answer the question.
4. It was easy for Tom to speak English.
5. It is very important for me to read newspapers everyday.
6. It is very important to read newspapers everyday.
7. I want to dance.
8. I want her to dance.
9. I told him to sit down.
10. I believe him to be honest.
11. I found him to be honest.
13. Tell me when to start.
14. She asked me to help her.
15. My mother asked me to wash the dishes.
16. My mother allowed me to go out.

영어독해 10 부정사의 시제

- 단순부정사(to+동사원형)는 대부분 술어동사와 같은 시제를 나타내지만, 소망, 기대, 예정 등의 의미를 나타내는 동사와 결합하면 술어동사보다 미래의 일을 나타낸다.
- 완료 부정사(to have+과거분사)는 술어동사보다 하나 앞선 시제를 나타낸다. 단, 소망, 기대, 예정 등의 의미를 나타내는 동사의 과거시제와 완료 부정사가 결합하거나, 또는 소망, 기대, 예정 등의 의미를 나타내는 동사의 과거완료시제와 단순부정사가 결합하면, 소망, 기대, 예정 등을 했으나 이룩하지 못한 것을 나타낸다.

1. The man seems to be sick.
   = It seems that the man is sick.
2. The man seemed to be sick.
   = It seemed that the man was sick.
3. The man seems to have been sick.
   = It seems that the man was(또는 has been) sick.
4. The man seemed to have been sick.
   = It seemed that the man had been sick.
5. I expect the man to be a doctor.
   = I expect that the man will be a doctor.
6. I expected the man to be a doctor.
   = I expected that the man would be a doctor.
7. I promise to study hard.
8. The man intended[wished, hoped, expected, was] to have come here.
   = The man had intended[wished, hoped, expected, been]

to come here.

= The man intended[wished, hoped, expected, was] to come here, but he couldn't.

부정사의 시제 익히기 연습

1. The man seemed to work hard. = It seemed that the man worked hard.
2. The man seemed to have worked hard. = It seemed that the man had worked hard.
3. Ten years seemed to have passed since then.
4. The man is said to have been a famous singer.
5. The man was reported to have been killed.
6. Some discoveries are said to have been made by accident.
7. The man believes it to have been a mistake.
8. The man was to have gone with her.
9. The man expected to have come on time.
10. The man wished to have persuaded her that she was in the wrong.

영어독해

11 부정사의 부정

• 부정사를 부정하려면 부정사 앞에 not을 두면 된다.

1. I always try not to tell a lie.
   (나는 거짓말하지 않으려고 항상 노력한다.)

2. It is impolite not to say "Excuse me."

부정사의 부정 익히기 연습

1. I told him not to swim in the river.
2. Take care not to catch cold.
3. He pretended not to listen.
4. I turned off the radio in order not to disturb him.
5. I asked him not to go there.
6. I asked her not to dance.
7. He tried not to smile. / He didn't try to smile.

영어독해

12 동사+to부정사의 관용적인 의미

- come[get, learn] to V: ~하게 되다.
- grow to V: 서서히 ~하게 되다.
- chance[happen] to V: 우연히 ~하게 되다.
- have only to V: ~하기만 하면 된다.
- be too ready[likely, apt, liable, prone] to V: 너무나 ~하기 쉽다. 걸핏하면 ~한다.
- only too~to V=매우 ~해서 ~하다.

1. The man happened to meet her at the station.
2. The man chanced to sit beside her in the theater.
3. The man came to like dogs.
4. How did the man get to know it?
5. They learned to restrain themselves as they get older.
6. The man will learn to love it.
7. London seldom fails to impress visitors from abroad.
8. Don't fail to let the man know.

9. It turned out to be valuable.
10. The result turned out to be satisfactory.
11. The document proved to be a forgery.
12. The man managed to get back to the tent.
13. The man managed to be in time.
14. That remains to be seen.
15. We sought to come to an agreement.
16. I should not care to be seen with her.
17. It threatened to rain.
18. You have only to do your duty.
19. At the worst the man will have only to lose a month's salary.
20. To understand it you have only to read this book.
21. The man is seriously ill. You have only to look at him to see it.
22. She is too ready to cry.
23. I am to blame. (=I am to be blamed.)
24. This is a room to let. (=This is a room to be let.)

영어독해 13 so as to; so～as to

so as to; so～ as to 익히기 연습

1. The man got up early so as to be in time for the first train.
2. The man got up so early as to be in time for the first train.
3. The man stood up so as to see better.
4. We must save so as to provide for future needs.
5. Make haste so as not to be late for school.

6. The man listened attentively in order not to miss a single word.
7. The man was so kind as to show me the way.
8. The man was so fortunate as to escape.
9. The man was so angry as to be unable to speak.
10. The man is so young as to look like a child.
11. Be so good as not to forget my name.
12. A man must so train his habits as to rely upon his own powers.

제2장

동명사(Gerund)

동사의 원형에 -ing를 붙여 "~하는 것, ~하기"라는 명사적 의미를 나타내는 것을 동명사라고 한다. 동명사도 부정사, 분사와 마찬가지로 동사의 성질을 그대로 지니고 있으므로 그 자체의 목적어, 보어를 취하기도 하고 경우에 따라서는 부사(구)의 수식을 받기도 하며, 또한 의미상의 주어, 태(능동동명사, 수동동명사), 시제(단순동명사, 완료동명사)를 가진다. 결국 동명사는 동사의 성질을 유지하면서 명사의 구실을 하는 것이다. 동명사는 명사의 구실을 하므로, 문장에서 주어, 목적어, 보어의 구실을 한다. 동명사의 부정은 "not+동명사"이다.

1 명사적 용법

- 명사와 마찬가지로 문장의 주어, 보어, 목적어로 쓰인다.

1. Learning French is not easy. (주어)
2. My hobby is collecting coins. (보어)
3. The man has just finished writing a letter. (타동사의 목적어)
4. The man enjoyed swimming in the pool. (타동사의 목적어)
5. The man is sure of succeeding. (전치사의 목적어)

6. The man went away without saying good-by. (전치사의 목적어)
*The man is sure of to succeed, 또는 without to say ~라고는 못함.

동명사 익히기 연습

1. He is good at playing the violin.
2. I am fond of listening to music.
3. He went away without saying good-bye.
4. I am sure of succeeding.
5. I am sure of passing the test.
6. He is proud of having a smart son.
7. I succeeded in solving the problem.
8. Eating is an important part of life.
9. Playing basketball is fun.
10. Taking a walk in the morning is good for health. = It is good for health taking a walk in the morning.
11. I don't mind working at night.
12. I like swimming in the sea.
13. I stopped smoking.
14. His hobby is reading books.
15. His business is making shoes.
16. His job is teaching how to drive a car.
17. I finished doing my homework.
18. They began talking.
19. Seeing is believing.
20. Collecting stamps is fun.
21. She is tired of staying alone.
22. Thank you for coming to help me.
23. I take a bath after playing basketball.

영어독해

2 형용사적 용법

- 〈동명사+명사〉 형으로 일종의 복합명사를 만들 때 동명사는 뒤의 명사를 수식하는 구실을 한다. 이때 동명사는 〈용도, 목적〉 관계를 나타낸다.

1. a lodging house (하숙집=a house for lodging)
2. a sleeping car (침대차=a car for sleeping)
   cf. a sleeping baby (잠자고 있는 아기)
3. a walking stick (도보용 지팡이=a stick for walking)
4. a smoking room
5. a waiting room
6. a swimming pool
7. the reading room
8. a dancing hall
9. the living room

❖ 현재분사와 동명사

- 현재분사+명사: 현재진행중인 동작이나 상태(~하고 있는)를 나타낸다.
- 동명사+명사: 용도나 목적(~를 위한, ~로 사용되는)을 나타낸다.

a sleeping baby (잠자고 있는 아기) (현재분사)
a sleeping car (잠자기 위한 차, 즉 침대차) (동명사)
a sleeping bag (침낭) (동명사)
a smoking man (담배를 피우고 있는 남자)
a smoking room (담배피우기 위한 방, 즉 흡연실)
a waiting girl (기다리고 있는 소녀)
a waiting room (기다리기 위한 방, 즉 대기실)

동명사와 현재분사 구별 익히기 연습

❖ 다음을 번역하고, 동사원형+ing가 현재분사인지, 동명사인지를 말하시오.

1. Look at the smoking man.
2. Please smoke in the smoking room.
3. Look at the sleeping baby.
4. I bought a sleeping bag.
5. I bought some drinking water.
6. I need a frying pan.
7. I bought him a pair of running shoes.
8. Look at the swimming boys.
9. The boys are swimming in the swimming pool.

영어독해 3 동명사의 의미상의 주어

(1) 동명사의 의미상의 주어는 보통 소유격을 동명사 앞에 두어 그 동명사의 의미상의 주어로 삼는다. 그러나 구어에서는 소유격 대신 목적격으로 나타내는 경우가 많다.

1. I don't like his[him] coming here.
   (나는 그가 여기에 오는 것을 좋아하지 않는다.)
2. I don't like your[you] going out.
3. I am sure of his[him] succeeding.
4. I am sure of his father's[father] succeeding.

❖ 무생물이 의미상의 주어일 때는 항상 목적격으로 나타낸다.

1. I never heard of this happening before.
2. I am proud of my house having a beautiful garden.

❖ 주어로 쓰이는 동명사의 의미상의 주어가 대명사일 때는 보통 소유격으로 나타낸다.

His coming is uncertain. Him coming is uncertain. (드묾)

(2) 동명사의 의미상의 주어가 문장의 주어 또는 목적어와 같거나, 동명사의 의미상의 주어가 일반인일 때는 의미상의 주어를 생략한다.

1. I don't like coming here.
   cf. I don't like his[him] coming here.
2. I don't like going out.
   cf. I don't like your[you] going out.
3. I am sure of succeeding.
   cf. I am sure of his[him] succeeding.
4. Thank you for helping me with my work.
5. I scold him for being lazy.
6. Eating is an important part of life.
7. Playing basketball is fun.
8. Taking a walk in the morning is good for health.

동명사의 의미상의 주어 익히기 연습

1. His going there is uncertain.
2. He does not doubt her being able to do it.
3. There is no hope of my succeeding.
4. There is no reason for your refusing to do it.
5. He is sure of its being she.
6. There is little danger of the rule's being broken.
7. I talked to him about everything's depending upon his own exertions.
8. I object him(=his) coming here.
9. I hated him being made so unhappy.
10. It is no use him staying here.
11. What is the use of us talking about respect?
12. She comes to my island without me knowing about it.
13. He is proud of the lady being a scientist.
14. He insists on John going there.
15. All this talk about the business being a waste of your life is rather stupid.
16. I have no doubt of this being true.
17. In spite of those three telling the same story, I could not believe it.
18. Have you heard of Peter the carpenter being injured?

영어독해

4 동명사의 시제

(1) 단순동명사

단순동명사는 원칙적으로 술어동사의 시제와 같은 때를 나타낸다. 그러나 술어동사에 따라서는 술어동사보다 이전의 때를 나타내기도 하고 이후의 때를 나타내기도 한다.

1. The man is proud of being a Korean. 〈술어동사와 같은 때〉
   =The man is proud that he is a Korean.
2. The man is sure of her coming. 〈술어동사보다 이후의 때〉
   =The man is sure that she will come.
3. The man remembers seeing her before. 〈술어동사보다 이전의 때〉
   =The man remembers that he saw[has been] her before.
   * remember, forget+동명사〈(과거에) ~한 것을 기억하다(잊다)〉
   * remember, forget+부정사 〈(앞으로) ~할 것을 기억하다(잊다)〉
4. The man remembers meeting them.=The man remembers that he met them.
5. The man remembers to meet them.=The man remembers that he should meet them.

(2) 완료동명사(having+과거분사): 술어동사의 시제보다 하나 앞선 시제를 나타낸다.

1. The man regrets having done so.
   =The man regrets that he did so.

2. The man is sure of her having been idle.
=The man is sure that she was[has been] idle.

동명사의 시제 익히기 연습

1. The witness denied having seen the accused.
2. The man never minds having failed in the examination.
3. The man repents of having been idle in his youth.
4. The man regrets having told it to her.
5. The man regrets having been careless of his health in his youth.
6. The man could not bear being treated in that manner.
7. The man doesn't like being asked to make a speech.
8. The man never heard of such a thing having been done.
9. The man objected to being treated like that.
10. There is no hope of the man being saved.
11. The man cannot stand things not being kept in their proper places.
12. The man is sure of its having been done by her.

영어독해

5 동명사와 명사적 용법의 부정사

• 둘 다 "~하는 것, ~하기"의 뜻으로 명사적 구실을 한다. 그러나 서로 바꿔 쓸 수 있는 경우와 그렇지 못한 경우가 있다.

(1) 서로 바꾸어 써도 되는 경우

1) 주어, 보어일 때

1. To play basketball is fun. = Playing basketball is fun. (주어)
2. My hobby is to collect stamps. = My hobby is collecting stamps. (보어)

2) begin, start, continue, like, hate, love, prefer 따위의 동사의 목적어로는 부정사, 동명사 양쪽을 다 쓸 수 있고 의미도 거의 차이가 없다.

1. He began to write a letter. = He began writing a letter.
2. He continued reading(=to read) the book.
3. He likes reading(=to read) books.

(2) 동사가 그 목적어로 준동사를 취할 때 동명사와 부정사를 가려 쓰는 경우

1) 동명사만을 목적어로 취하는 동사: enjoy, finish, mind, stop, give up, avoid, postpone 등

1. I enjoyed hunting.
   cf. I enjoyed to hunt.(x)
2. I finished eating lunch.

2) 부정사만을 목적어로 취하는 동사: want, wish, hope, expect, decide, plan, learn 등

1. I hope to see you soon.
   cf. I hope seeing you soon. (x)
2. I want to go to America.

3) 동명사와 부정사를 쓸 때 뜻이 달라지는 경우

❖ remember[forget]+동명사: 과거에 ~한 것을 기억하다[잊다]
remember[forget]+부정사: 미래에 ~할 것을 기억하다[잊다]
try+동명사: 시험 삼아 ~해보다.
try+부정사: ~하려고 애쓰다.
stop+동명사: ~하는 것을 멈추다[그만두다] (동명사=stop의 목적어)
stop+부정사: ~하기 위해 (걸음[일]을)멈추다 (부정사=stop을 꾸미는 부사적용법)
want[need]+~ing: ~되어질 필요가 있다. 〈수동의 의미〉
want[need]+to 부정사: ~하기를 원하다. 〈능동의 의미〉

1. I remember[forget] seeing her.
   (나는 그녀를 과거에 만난 것을 기억한다[잊고 있다].)
2. I remember[forget] to see her.
   (나는 그녀를 미래에 만날 것을 기억한다[잊고 있다].)
3. I stopped smoking. (그는 담배를 끊었다.)
4. I stopped to smoke.
   (그는 담배를 피우려고 걸음[또는 하던 일]을 멈추었다.)
5. I tried opening the big door.
6. I tried to open the big door.
7. My watch wants mending.

=My watch needs to be mended.
cf. The man wants to go with you.

동명사와 명사적 용법의 부정사 익히기 연습

❖ (　) 안에 있는 동사를 동명사나 부정사로 바꾸고 번역하시오.

1. I enjoyed (read) novels.
2. I don't want (play) the piano.
3. She finished (make) a doll.
4. He hopes (be) a doctor.
5. He likes (skate).
6. She started (work).
7. I stopped (see) the game.
8. I remember (mail) the letter.
9. It stopped (rain) two hours ago.
10. He stopped (talk) with his friends.
11. (see) is (believe).
12. She began (run).
13. His job is (make) toys.
14. He planned (travel) all over the world.
15. (drive) a new car is fun.
16. (rise) early is good for the health.
17. It began (rain), so they stopped (play) football.
18. I remember (see) her before.
19. He decided (write) a letter to her.
20. He wished (go) to America.
21. He gave up (look) for the book.
22. They postponed (go) on a picnic this week.

23. He avoids (talk) to the boss.
24. He remembered (be) there.

영어독해

6 동명사의 관용적 용법

① It is (of) no use [good] ~ing 〈~해도 소용없다〉
② cannot help ~ing = cannot but + 원형부정사 〈~하지 않을 수 없다〉
③ There is no ~ing = It is impossible to-부정사 = We cannot+동사원형 〈~할 수 없다〉
④ feel like ~ing 〈~하고 싶은 기분이다〉
⑤ be worth ~ing 〈~할 가치가 있다〉 = It is worth while to ~
⑥ on[upon] ~ing 〈~하자마자〉 = as soon as + 주어 + 동사
⑦ of one's own ~ing 〈자신이 ~한〉
⑧ never[cannot]··· without ~ing 〈~하면 반드시 ···하다〉
⑨ be far from ~ing 〈결코 ~하지 않다〉

1. It is (of) no use crying over spilt milk.
(엎질러진 우유를 보고 울어도 소용없다.)
*It은 형식 주어 ~ing(동명사)가 진주어.

2. The man could not help laughing.
=The man could not but laugh.
(그 남자는 웃지 않을 수 없었다.)

3. There is no denying the fact.
(그 사실을 부정할 수 없다.)

4. The man feels like crying.
(그 남자는 울고 싶은 심정이다.)

5. This novel is worth reading.
=It is worth while to read this novel.
(이 소설은 읽을 가치가 있다.)

6. On seeing me, the man ran away.
=As soon as the man saw me, he ran away.
(나를 보자마자 그 남자는 도망쳤다.)

7. This is a dress of her own making.
=made by herself
(이것은 그녀 자신이 만든 옷이다.)

8. I never see the man without thinking of his mother.
(나는 그 남자를 보면 반드시 그의 어머니 생각이 난다.)

9. The man was far from being satisfied.
(그 남자는 결코 만족하지 않았다.)

10. He is above telling a lie.

11. What do you say to eating out?

12. The old man is on the point of dying.

13. I make a point of attending such meetings.

14. He came near being run over by a car.

15. It goes without saying that honesty is the best policy.

16. He went fishing.

17. Be careful in crossing the road.

18. He is busy preparing for his homework.

동명사의 관용표현 익히기 연습

1. It goes without saying that health is above wealth.
2. It goes without saying that the proposal will not be accepted.
3. There is no denying the fact.
4. It is no use trying to persuade the man.
5. Is it any use expecting the man to be on time?
6. It is no good making an excuse for that.
7. There is no going out in such bad weather.
8. There is no standing still in this life ; one must advance or fall back.
9. This museum is worth visiting.
10. It is worth considering what it is that makes people happy.
11. A book which is worth reading at all is likely to be read more than once.
12. His hair wants cutting.
13. My shoes need mending.
14. The man didn't feel like dancing then.
15. The man didn't feel like going out then.
16. The man cannot help laughing at the idea.
17. The man cannot help respecting her for her act of kindness.
18. The man cannot help believing what she says.
19. On leaving school, I was obliged to go into business against my will.
20. On hearing the news she burst into tears.
21. On his getting into the train, it began to move.

22. Those gloves are of her own knitting.
23. That is the picture of my own painting.
24. The man makes a point of having a cup of coffee every morning.
25. The man makes a point of attending such a meeting.
26. The man was on the point of breathing his last.
27. It began to rain when the man was on the point of going out.
28. Illness prevented the man from going on the trip.
29. The urgent business prevented the man from starting.
30. The heavy snow kept the man from coming to the meeting.
31. It goes without saying that honesty is the best policy.
32. It goes without saying that right is might.
33. The man looks forward to her visiting him.
34. Your composition is far from (being) satisfactory.
35. So far from reading the letter, the man did not open it.
36. The man devoted himself to finishing the work.
37. The man is above doing such a mean thing.
38. Did the man object to her going there alone?
39. The man came near forgetting it.
40. The man could hardly keep from smiling.
41. The man did it with a view of saving her trouble.
42. The man is used to getting up early in the morning.
43. Nothing worth having can be had without labor.

제3장

분사(Participle)

분사에는 현재분사(동사원형+ing)와 과거분사(동사원형+ed, 또는 불규칙적인 것)가 있으며 〈be동사+현재분사(-ing)〉는 진행형을, 〈be동사+타동사의 과거분사(p.p)〉는 수동태를, 〈have동사+과거분사(p.p)〉는 완료형을 만든다. 또한 분사는 형용사 역할을 하기도 하여 형용사처럼 명사를 수식하거나(한정용법), 주격보어, 목적격보어로 쓰인다(서술용법). 또한 분사구문에 사용되어 부사 역할을 하기도 한다.

영어독해

1 현재분사의 한정적 용법

- 현재분사는 동명사와 같은 〈동사원형+-ing〉의 형태이지만 동명사가 명사의 역할을 하는데 반하여, 현재분사는 형용사처럼 명사를 수식한다. 이 때 현재분사는 〈~하고 있는〉의 의미, 즉 능동진행의 의미를 나타낸다. 그러므로 "동사원형+ing"가 "~하고 있는"의 의미를 가지고 있으면 현재분사이고 "~하는 것"의 의미를 가지고 있으면 동명사이다.
- 현재분사가 단독으로 명사를 수식할 때는 명사 앞에서 수식하고, 목적어·보어를 취하거나 부사(구)의 수식을 받을 때는 이들 어구와 함께 명사 뒤에서 수식한다. 뒤에서 수식할 때는 「관계대명사+be동사」가 생략된 것으로도 볼 수 있다.

1. The sleeping boy is his son.
2. A rolling stone gathers no moss.
3. The boys playing basketball over there are my friends.
   =The boys who are playing basketball over there are my friends.
4. The boy talking to Ms. Mary is my brother.
   =The boy who is talking to Ms. Mary is my brother.
5. The boy sitting on the sofa was my friend.
   =The boy who was sitting on the sofa was my friend.

현재분사의 한정적 용법 익히기 연습

1. I saw a singing bird.
2. The crying boy is my brother.
3. The boy sitting on the chair is my brother.
4. The boy playing the violin is my brother.
5. The boy standing over there is my brother.
6. I know the girl sitting on the bench.
7. I know the man walking in the garden.
8. I know the singing boys.
9. I know the boys singing in the room.
10. The singing boys are all Koreans.
11. Look at the girl playing the piano.
12. The boy sitting behind her began to sing.
13. This baby has shining eyes.
14. Barking dogs never bite.
15. I am afraid of barking dogs.
16. I am afraid of dogs barking at people.
17. Look at the sun rising above the mountain.

18. The girl speaking to the man is Miss Jane.
19. The man sitting at the piano is her uncle.
20. Look at the sleeping baby.
21. Look at the baby sleeping in the cradle.
22. A watched pot never boils.
23. A word spoken is an arrow let fly. (let fly an arrow:화살을 발사하다)
24. The man looked down upon a stream winding its way through the meadows.
25. The man was awed by the grandeur surrounding him.
26. A man continually complaining is never listened to.
27. Coming events cast their shadows before.

영어독해

2 현재분사의 서술적 용법

• 현재분사가 주어의 상태나 동작을 설명하여 주격보어로 쓰이기도 하고, 목적어의 상태나 동작을 설명하여 목적격보어로 쓰이기도 한다.

(1) 주격 보어로 쓰일 때: 〈주어+불완전자동사+현재분사~〉(주어가 ~하면서 …하다〉

1. The man sat reading a book.
2. The man was standing trembling.
3. The man lay whistling on the grass.
4. A dog came running after the man on his way back home.

❖ 현재분사를 보어로 취할 수 있는 동사는 sit, stand, lie, keep, remain(계속 ~하다) 등의 상태 동사와 go, come, run 등의 동작 동사들로서 현재분사와 결합하여 2형식을 만든다.

현재분사의 서술적 용법 익히기 연습

1. The man sat waiting on the sofa.
2. The man stood watching an approaching train.
3. The man sat looking at the album.
4. It is annoying to be interrupted in my talk.
5. The man stood trembling at the sight.
6. The man came back stealing on tiptoe.
7. The man stood at the gate smiling on me.

(2) **목적보어로 쓰일 때:** 〈주어+불완전타동사+목적어+현재분사~〉(목적어가 ~하는 것을 …하다〉

1. The man kept me waiting for an hour.
2. The man heard his dog barking at the gate.
3. The man saw a boy running.
   cf. The man saw a boy run.
4. The man found her standing under the tree.
5. The man left the baby crying.
6. The man set the clock going.

❖ 흔히 지각동사(see, hear, find, feel 등) 및 keep, leave, start, set 등의 목적격보어로 쓰인다. 지각동사는 목적보어로 원형부정사나 현재분사를 쓸 수 있는데, 이 때 현재분사는 원형부정사보다 진행의 뜻이 더 강하다.

현재분사의 서술적 용법 익히기 연습

1. I saw a bird singing merrily.
2. I saw a bird sing merrily.
3. I saw a lot of girls skating on the pond.
4. I saw a lot of girls skate on the pond.
5. I saw him watching TV.
6. I saw him watch TV.
7. I watched the man working in the field.
8. I heard the bell ringing.
9. I saw him cooking something.
10. I saw the smoke coming out of the house.
11. I found the boys running away.
12. The man saw the girl coming to him.
13. The man saw her getting off the bus.
14. Please start the clock going.
15. The man caught her stealing apples from his garden.
16. The next morning the man awoke early and found breakfast waiting for him again.
17. The man heard her coming slowly up the steps as if under a heavy load.
18. The man kept her waiting so long.

영어독해

2 과거분사의 한정적 용법

- 과거분사도 형용사처럼 명사를 수식한다. 이 때 타동사의 과거분사의 의미는 〈~되어진, ~된〉의 의미, 즉 수동의 의미를 나타낸다. 과거분사가 단독으로 명사를 수식할 때는 명사 앞에 오고, 다른 말(수식어구·보어·목적어)과 함께 쓰인 과거분사는 수식받는 명사 뒤에 오는데 이 때 명사와 과거분사 사이에는 「관계대명사+be동사」가 생략된 것으로도 볼 수 있다.

1. It was a crowded bus.
2. The man is planning to buy a used car.
3. The man saw a sealed envelope.
4. There were no printed books in those days.
5. Here are some books printed in those days.
   = Here are some books which were printed in those days.
6. There are a lot of goods made in China.
   = There are a lot of goods which were made in China.
7. The man lived on the money given to him by his uncle.
   = The man lived on the money which was given to him by his uncle.
8. The television set made in Korea is excellent.
   = The television set which was made in Korea is excellent.
9. The man has never read a book written by her.
   = The man has never read a book which was written by her.

과거분사의 한정적 용법 익히기 연습

1. A watched pot never boils.
2. The man was like one enchanted.(대명사 수식)
3. To understand world commerce we must first know the part played by the ocean.
4. The man acted like one overwhelmed.
5. What effects a word lightly spoken can produce!
6. The soldiers took a rest at previously chosen points.
7. Soon the man came to a crowded street, a very wide street crowded with all sorts of vehicles.

❖ 자동사의 과거분사는 수동의 뜻을 나타내는 것이 아니라 완료된 상태를 나타낸다.

- The risen sun(떠오른 태양), fallen leaves(낙엽), grown-up children(성장한 아이들), the departed guest(떠나버린 손님), a returned traveller(돌아온 여행객)

❖ 〈the+현재분사[과거분사]〉가 복수 보통명사로 「사람들」의 뜻을 나타내기도 한다.

- the living(살아 있는 사람들)
- the dying(죽어 가는 사람들)

1. The wounded were many, but the missing were a few.
2. The conquered raised a flag of truce.

영어독해

2 과거분사의 서술적 용법

- 과거분사도 현재분사와 마찬가지로 주격보어(주어+불완전자동사+과거분사)로도 쓰이고, 목적격보어(주어+불완전타동사+목적어+과거분사)로도 쓰인다.

(1) 주격보어로 쓰일 때

1. An old man sat surrounded by his grandsons.
2. The man came home utterly exhausted.
3. She could hardly drag one foot before the other, as she went upstairs, and sank down on her bed exhausted.

과거분사의 서술적 용법 익히기 연습

1. The man seemed quite satisfied with the answer.
2. The man left satisfied with my answer.
3. The man appears satisfied with the result.
4. The man remained unmarried all his life.
5. The man got excited at the sight.
6. The man lay there wounded.
7. The man looked pleased when he got a present.
8. The man look tired.
9. The man became acquainted with her.
10. The man got married last year.

(2) 목적격보어로 쓰일 때

1. The man heard his name called.
2. The man wants it finished by next Friday.
3. The man had his watch stolen.
4. The man felt himself touched on the shoulder.
5. The man saw her beaten by a man.
6. The man found her killed in the wood.

❖ 〈have[get] + 목적어(사물) + 과거분사〉는 주어에게 유리한 것은 〈~시키다〉로 해석하고, 불리한 것은 〈~당하다〉로 해석한다.

7. The man had [got] the baggage carried by her.
   cf. The man had her carry the baggage.
   cf. The man got her to carry the baggage.
8. The man had[got] his watch fixed.
9. The man had[got] his wallet stolen.

과거분사의 서술적 용법 익히기 연습

1. The man wants it finished by next Monday.
2. The man had his watch mended by her.
3. The man got his purse stolen in the bus.
4. The man had a position offered to him.
5. Some of the houses had their windows broken by the explosion.
6. We must make ourselves respected.
7. The man found her surrounded by many children.
8. The man wishes it finished by next Thursday.
9. The man had his purse stolen.

10. The man had his computer repaired.
11. Nobody likes to get his words doubted.
12. Some of the houses had their windows broken by the explosion.
13. The man had his eyes tested and fitted with glasses.
14. It is one thing to know truth about oneself; it is quite another thing to have it told one by somebody else.
15. The man had [got] his watch mended by her.
16. The man wishes it finished by Wednesday.
17. The man made himself respected.
18. The man has never seen a woman hanged.
19. The man heard his name called behind him.
20. The man could not make himself understood in English.
21. I should like to see a tiger caught.
22. The man left no work unfinished.
23. The man had his house burnt down in the late fire.
24. The man went to have his photograph taken.
25. Where did the man get his visiting cards printed?
26. The man had his hat blown off by the strong wind.

영어독해

3 분사구문(Participial Construction)

(1) 분사구문이란?

1) 분사구문이란 때, 이유, 조건, 양보 따위를 나타내는 부사절을 분사로 시작하는 부사구로 간결하게 나타내는 구문을 말한다. 즉, 종속절(부사절)의 「접속사+주어」가 생략되고 동사가 분사(현재분사·

과거분사)로 바뀐 문장을 말한다. 종속절의 주어가 주절의 주어와 같고 시제가 같으면 접속사와 주어를 생략하고 동사에 -ing를 붙여서 분사구문을 만든다. 결국 분사구문은 주절을 수식하는 부사구의 역할을 한다. 요약하면 〈접속사+주어+동사 ~〉를 〈분사 ~〉로 나타내는 것이 분사구문이다.

1. As the man was poor, he couldn't buy a car.
   = (Being) poor, the man couldn't buy a car.
2. Though the boy lives near the school, he is often late for school.
   =Living near the school, the boy is often late for school.

* 분사구문에서 Being이나 Having been을 생략하기도 한다.

2) 분사구문은 일반적으로 주절 앞에 두는 경우가 대부분이지만, 삽입구로 문장 중간에 두거나 문장 뒤에 둘 수도 있다.

Walking along the street, the man met a friend of his.
= The man, walking along the street, met a friend of his.
= The man met a friend of his, walking along the street.

3) 어떤 문장에서 분사구문이 나오면 앞뒤 관계를 보고 생략된 접속사(의미하는 접속사)가 무엇인가를 판단하고 시제는 언제나 주절의 시제에 맞추어서 생각하면 된다. 대체로 분사구문에서 생략된 접속사는 시간, 원인, 이유, 양보, 조건, 연속 동작, 부대 상황 등이다.

(2) 분사구문의 의미

1) 때(when, as, while, after 등)를 나타내는 경우

1. Walking in the park, the man met his uncle.
   =When[While] the man was walking in the park, he met his uncle.
2. Opening the door, the man found her reading.
   =When the man opened the door, he found her reading.
3. Seeing the policeman, the man ran away.
4. Finishing his work, the man went out.

2) 원인·이유(because, as, since)를 나타내는 경우

1. Living in a remote village, the man has few visitors.
   =Because the man lives in a remote village, he has few visitors.
2. Written in haste, her letter was very hard to read.
   =As her letter was written in haste, it was very hard to read.
3. Having no money, the man could not buy the car.
4. Being sick, the man stayed at home.

3) 양보(though, although, even if)를 나타내는 경우

1. Knowing that the man is idle, I still like him.
   =Though I know that the man is idle, I still like him.
2. Admitting what the man said, I still think he was wrong.
   =Though I admit what the man said, I still think he was wrong.

3. Living next door, the man seldom sees her.

4) 조건(if)을 나타내는 경우

1. Turning to the right, you will find the station.
   = If you turn to the right, you will find the station.
2. Weather permitting, we'll start tomorrow.
   = If weather permits, we'll start tomorrow.

5) 연속동작(and)을 나타내는 경우

1. The man started early this morning, arriving there before dark.
   = The man started early this morning and arrived there before dark.
2. The man got to the airport at five, seeing his friend off.
   = The man got to the airport at five and saw his friend off.
3. Going up to the man, she asked who he was.

6) 부대상황을 나타내는 경우: 주절의 동작과 동시에 일어나는 경우

1. The man watched television, drinking a glass of wine.
   = The man watched television, as[while] he drank a glass of wine.
2. Walking along the street, the man read the letter.
3. Smiling brightly, the man extended his hand.
4. The man ate breakfast, reading the morning paper.

7) 독립분사구문: 주절의 주어와 분사구문의 주어(의미상의 주어)가

일치하지 않을 때엔 분사구문의 주어를 생략하지 않고 분사 앞에 두는데, 이것을 독립분사구문이라고 한다. 분사가 주어를 가져 하나의 독립된 절과 같은 역할을 하므로 독립분사구문이라는 명칭을 사용한다.

1. As it was fine yesterday, the man went on a picnic.
   =It being fine yesterday, the man went on a picnic.
2. School being over, he went home.
   =When school was over, he went home.
3. Night coming on, the man started for home.
   =As night came on, the man started for home.
4. The sun having set, the man came down the hill.

독립분사구문 익히기 연습

1. This done, I quietly awaited the result. (=This having been done.)
2. The village being small, the man had no difficulty in finding the house.
3. Night coming on, the man started for home.
4. The sun having set, the man started for home.
5. It being fine, the man went out for a walk.
6. The man sat on the sofa, his eyes closed.
7. The man went out, his heart full of hopes.
8. The job done, the man was sent over to London.
9. Mother being ill, he had to look after his little brothers.
10. He stood against the wall, pipe in mouth.

❖ 〈with + 독립분사구문〉.

부대상황을 나타내는 독립분사구문에는 with를 붙인 것이 많다. 따라서 부대상황을 나타내는 〈with + 명사 + 분사 ~〉 구문의 대부분은 with를 없애면 독립분사구문이 된다고 할 수 있다.

1. The man was standing with his arms folded.
   =The man was standing folding his arms.
2. The man was standing with his eyes closed.
   =The man was standing closing his eyes.

〈with + 독립분사구문〉 익히기 연습

1. The man listened to the music with his eyes closed.
2. The man sat in the chair with his eyes closed.
3. The man sat reading the newspaper with his wife knitting beside him.
4. The man stood with his back leaning against the wall.
5. The man stood with his face turned away from her.
6. The man was sleeping with his feet on the pillow.
7. The man looked straight in front of him with brows knit.
8. With an eye bandaged, the man could not write properly.
9. The man was standing with his son on his back.

(4) **무인칭 독립분사구문(관용적인 독립분사구문)**: 분사구문의 주어가 일반 사람을 가리키는 we, you, they, people 따위일 때엔 주절의 주어와 일치하지 않더라도 분사구문의 주어를 생략하는데 이것을 무인칭

독립 분사구문이라고 한다. 보통 숙어처럼 사용되는데 주로 조건이나 양보를 나타낸다.

1. honestly speaking (=if we speak honestly) (정직히 말하면)
2. generally speaking (일반적으로 말하면)
3. frankly speaking (솔직히 말하면)
4. considering~ (~을 고려해 보면)
5. judging from~ (~로 판단해 보면)
6. speaking of~ (~에 관해 말할 것 같으면, ~로 말하면)

(5) 완료분사구문(having+과거분사)은 주절의 시제보다 분사구문의 시제가 하나 앞섬을 나타낸다.

1. The sun having risen, the man started.
   =As the sun had risen, the man started.
2. Having finished his homework, he has nothing more to do.
   =As he has finished his homework, he has nothing more to do.
3. Having been idle in my youth, I must work hard in my old age.

(6) 수동형 분사구문(being+과거분사~ 또는 having been+과거분사~)에서 being 또는 having been을 생략하는 것이 보통이다.

1. (Being) Written in an easy style, the novel has many readers.
   =As the novel is written in an easy style, it has many readers.
2. (Being) United, we stand; (being) divided, we fall.
   =If we are united, we stand; if we are divided, we fall.

3. (Being) Wounded in the legs, the man could not walk.
4. Left alone, the man began to read a book.
5. Tired from the work, the man went to bed earlier.
6. (Having been) Written in haste, the book has many faults.

   cf. (Being) Angry at her words, the man made no reply.
   Dinner (being) over, the man went out for a walk.
   (Being) A man of social instincts, the man had many acquaintances.

(7) 분사구문의 부정: 부정의 분사구문은 〈not[never]+−ing〉이다.

1. As the man didn't know what to say, he remained silent.
   =Not knowing what to say, the man remained silent.
2. Not being rich, the man cannot buy a car
3. Not receiving any answer, the man wrote her again.

(8) 접속사+분사구문: 분사구문의 의미를 명확하게 하기 위해 분사구문 앞에 접속사를 두기도 한다.

1. While staying in New York, the man lost his child.
2. Though living so near his house, I can't see him.
3. After finishing the work, the man went home.

(9) 분사+as+주어+동사[be, do]~

1. Standing, as it does, on a hill, his house commands a fine view.
2. Hidden as it was among the trees, the tomb was not easily found.

3. Living as he does in a remote village, the man rarely has visitors.
4. Surrounded, as they were, by the enemy, they could not march forward.

분사구문 익히기 종합 연습

1. Arriving at the station, the man found the train already gone.
2. Having nothing to do, the man went fishing.
3. Turning to the left, you will find the house.
4. Admitting what you say, I still think you are wrong.
5. Smiling brightly, the man held out his hand.
6. Judging from the look of the sky, it will rain in the afternoon.
7. Having finished the work, the man went out.
8. Defeated repeatedly, the man had no courage to fight again.
9. Taking all things into consideration, this plan is impracticable.
10. Living,as he does, so remote from the town, he rarely has visitors.
11. Looking up, the man saw a white cloud in the sky.
12. Living in a remote village, the man rarely has visitors.
13. Turning to the left, you will find the post office.
14. Admitting what you say, I still think I am right.
15. Walking on tiptoe, the man approached the window.
16. Seeing me, the man smiled a warm welcome.
17. Being tired out, the man lay down to rest.
18. Coming tomorrow, you will be able to see the man.

19. Living near her house, the man seldom see her.
20. Smiling brightly, the man held out his hand.
21. Attacked as I was on all sides, I could not resist.
22. Having finished his assignment, he has nothing to do now.
23. Left to himself, he began to weep.
24. Written in haste, the book has some faults.
25. The man spoke excellent English, having studied at Oxford.
26. Praised by the teacher, the boy felt very happy.
27. Built about five thousand years ago, these pyramids still remain nearly perfect.
28. Some books, read carelessly, will do more harm than good.
29. The scene, once seen, can never be forgotten.
30. Generally speaking, women live longer than men.
31. Strictly speaking, this sentence is not correct.
32. Judging from his accent, the man seems to be an Italian.
33. Taking all things into consideration, his lot was a happy one.
34. Talking of the TV, what program do you like best?
35. Granting that the man was drunk, that is no excuse for his conduct.
36. Democracy is, historically speaking, something very recent.
37. The world may, broadly speaking, be full of sorrows, but it contains a million things in which we can find the joys of life.

제4장

관계대명사와 관계부사

관계대명사란 접속사의 역할과 대명사의 역할을 겸하면서 한 문장을 앞 문장의 명사나 대명사에 연결시키는 역할을 하는 낱말이다. 즉, 관계대명사는 「접속사 + 대명사」의 구실을 하면서 형용사절을 이끈다. 이때 관계대명사가 이끄는 형용사절의 수식을 받는 앞 문장의 명사나 대명사를 관계대명사의 선행사라고 한다. 관계대명사는 선행사의 종류에 따라 달라지고 그 역할에 따라 주격·소유격·목적격으로 구분된다.

* 두 문장을 관계대명사로 연결하기 위해서는 두 문장에서 동일한 대상을 가리키는 명사와 대명사를 파악하고, 뒤의 대명사를 앞의 (대)명사(즉, 선행사)의 성격과 문장에서의 역할(주격·소유격·목적격 역할)에 따라 적절한 관계대명사로 바꾸어야 한다.

* 관계대명사가 이끄는 형용사절은 선행사의 바로 뒤에 오는 것이 원칙이다.

영어독해

1 관계대명사 who(주격), whose(소유격), whom(목적격)의 용법

- 선행사가 사람인 경우에 사용되며, 관계대명사가 관계사절에서 주어 역할을 하면 who, 소유격 역할을 하면 whose, 목적어 역할을 하면 whom이 사용된다.

1. Tom is a boy. + He writes well. (a boy=He)
   → Tom is a boy who writes well. 〈주격〉 (선행사=a boy)
   (탐은 글을 잘 쓰는 소년이다.)
2. The boy who is playing on the ground is Tom. 〈주격-주어가 선행사〉
   = The boy is Tom. + He is playing on the ground.
   (운동장에서 놀고 있는 소년은 탐이다.)
3. Do you know the boy who is reading a book?
   (너는 책을 읽고 있는 소년을 아니?)
4. Tom is a boy. + His heart is true to all. (His=The boy's)
   → Tom is a boy whose heart is true to all. 〈소유격〉
   (탐은 모든 사람에게 마음이 진실한 소년이다.)
5. I know a boy whose name is Tom.
6. A child whose parents are dead is called an orphan.
7. Tom is a boy. + I met him yesterday. (a boy=him)
   → Tom is a boy whom I met yesterday. 〈목적격〉
   (탐은 내가 어제 만난 소년이다.)
8. I know a boy who(m) we call Tom.
9. Tom is the boy with whom I went there. 〈전치사의 목적어〉
   =Tom is the boy who(m) I went there with.
   =Tom is the boy. + I went there with him.

(탐은 내가 그곳에 함께 갔던 소년이다.)

10. The boy who(m) I spoke to was very handsome.
    = The boy to whom I spoke was very handsome.

❖ 목적격 관계대명사 whom 대신에 구어에서는 who를 쓰기도 한다. 그러나 바로 앞에 놓인 전치사의 목적어인 경우에는 whom을 쓴다.

영어독해

2 관계대명사 which(주격), whose[of which](소유격), which(목적격)의 용법

• 선행사가 동물이나 사물인 경우에 쓴다. 주격과 목적격은 which이고, 소유격은 whose나 of which이다.

1. The book is yours. + It is on the chair. (The book = It) (선행사 = The book)
   → The book which is on the chair is yours. 〈주격〉
   (의자 위에 있는 책은 네 것이다.)
2. This is the cat which caught the mouse.
3. I saw a building which stands on the hill.
4. The book which she lost yesterday was mine. 〈타동사의 목적격〉
   = The book was mine. + She lost it yesterday.
5. I like the picture which she painted.
6. This is the house in which I was born. 〈전치사의 목적격〉
   = This is the house which I was born in.
   = This is the house. + I was born in it.

7. The house whose roof we see is my uncle's. 〈소유격〉
   =The house of which the roof we see is my uncle's.
   =The house the roof of which we see is my uncle's.
   =The house is my uncle's. + We see its roof [the roof of it].

8. The house whose roof is red is my uncle's.
   =The house the roof of which is red is my uncle's.
   =The house of which the roof is red is my uncle's.
   =The house is my uncle's. + Its roof[The roof of it] is red.

9. The book whose cover is red is mine.
   =The book the cover of which is red is mine.
   =The book of which the cover is red is mine.

10. She said a word whose meaning I don't know.
   =She said a word the meaning of which I don't know.
   =She said a word of which I don't know the meaning.
   =She said a word which I don't know the meaning of.
   =She said a word (생략) I don't know the meaning of.

❖ 소유격은 〈whose+명사〉, 〈the+명사+of which〉, 〈of which the+명사〉 중 어느 것을 써도 상관없다.

영어독해

3 관계대명사 that의 일반 용법

- 선행사가 사람·사물·동물의 어느 경우에도 사용될 수 있으며, 주격과 목적격이 같은 형태이고 소유격은 없다. 따라서 who, whom, which를 대신해서 쓸 수 있다. 전치사의 목적어로 쓰일 때 〈전치사+that〉으로는 쓸 수 없고 반드시 전치사를 뒤에 두어야 한다. 제한적 용법에만 쓰이고, 계속적 용법에는 쓰이지 않는다.

1. This is the letter that [which] was written by me. 〈주격〉
   =This is the letter. + It was written by me.
2. Tom likes the camera that [which] she bought for him. 〈목적격〉
   =Tom likes the camera. + She bought it for him.
   cf. This is the house in that our teacher lives.(x)

영어독해

4 관계대명사 that의 특별 용법

- that는 who나 which보다 한정적인 뜻이 강하여 계속적 용법이 없고, 또한 선행사에 형용사의 최상급, 서수, the only(same, very), all, any, every, no 등이 있는 경우에는 주로 that이 쓰인다. 선행사가 〈사람+동물〉, 〈사람+사물〉인 경우와 선행사가 의문대명사인 경우 그리고 의문사가 있는 의문문에서는 반드시 that를 쓴다.

(1) 선행사가 형용사의 최상급이나 서수에 의해 수식되는 경우에는 관계대명사 that를 쓴다.

1. Shakespeare is one of the greatest playwriters that ever lived.
2. This is the most expensive stamp that he has collected.
3. It was the last building that was destroyed.

(2) 선행사가 the only, the very, the same에 의해 수식되는 경우에는 관계대명사 that를 쓴다.

1. Man is the only animal that can speak .
2. This is the same bag that I have lost. (동일물)

(3) 선행사가 all, any, every, no에 의해 수식되는 경우에는 관계대명사 that를 쓴다.

1. All that glitters is not gold.
2. None can get everything that they need.
3. No man that is wise believes it.

(4) 선행사가 〈사람+동물〉, 〈사람+사물〉인 경우에는 관계대명사 that를 쓴다.

1. Look at the boy and the dog that are coming this way.

(5) 의문사가 있는 의문문이나 의문사가 선행사일 경우에는 관계대명사 that를 쓴다.

1. Who that knows her will trust her?
2. But what did she say that so discouraged you?

❖ 선행사에 that, those가 있는 경우에는 관계대명사 that를 안 쓴다.

3. That kite which he made is very big.
4. Heaven helps those who help themselves.

영어독해 5 관계대명사 what의 용법

(1) 관계대명사 what은 그 자체에 선행사를 포함하고 있는 관계대명사로서 명사절을 이끌며 그 의미는 다음과 같다.

① the thing(s) which~: ~하는 것(들)
② all that~: ~하는 것은 모두
③ anything that~: ~하는 것은 무엇이나

(2) 관계대명사 what이 이끄는 절은 명사절이므로 문장에서 주어, 보어, 목적어 역할을 한다.

1. What [=The thing which] you say is always true. 〈주어〉
2. What he said is not true.
3. What is beautiful is not always good.
4. He spends what [=all that] he earns. 〈목적어〉
5. I don't believe what she says.
6. We must do what is right.
7. Do you understand what I say?
8. There is some truth in what [=the thing that] he says. 〈전치사의 목적어〉
9. This is what [=the thing that] I wanted to say. 〈보어〉
10. This is what we need.

(3) 관계대명사 what의 관용적 표현

1) What one is : 〈현재의 그 사람, 그 사람의 사람됨〉
What one was [used to be] : 〈과거의 그 사람, 그 사람의 사람됨〉

1. He is no more what he was.
   = He is no more the man (that) he was.
   (그는 이제는 과거의 그가 아니다.)
2. I am not what I was[used to be].
3. Seoul is not what it used to be.

2) What is (still) +비교급 : 〈더욱 더 ~한 것은〉

He is rich, and, what is better, he is intelligent.

3) A is to B what[as] C is to D : 〈A와 B의 관계는 C와 D의 관계와 같다〉

1. Water is to fish what air is to man.
   (물과 물고기의 관계는 공기와 인간의 관계와 같다.)
2. Leaves are to the plant what lungs are to the animal.

4) What is called (= what we [you, they] call) : 〈소위, 이른바〉

1. She is what is called a 'modern girl'.
   (그녀는 소위 '현대여성'이야.)
2. He is what we call a walking dictionary.

영어독해

6 관계대명사와 전치사

(1) 관계대명사가 전치사의 목적어가 되는 경우 전치사는 관계대명사의 앞에 두는 것이 보통이나 뒤에도 둘 수 있다.

This is the house in which I live.
= This is the house which I live in.

(2) beside, beyond, during, except, opposite, outside, round 등의 전치사는 언제나 관계대명사 앞에 온다.

I turned to the door outside which my brother was waiting.

(3) all of, both of, half of, many of, most of, none of, one of, some of 등은 관계대명사 앞에 온다.

I had a lot of friends, all of whom were teachers.

영어독해

7 관계대명사의 생략

(1) 목적격 관계대명사의 생략

제한적 용법에서 타동사나 전치사의 목적어인 목적격 관계대명사 whom, which, that은 생략할 수 있다. 그러나 〈전치사+목적격 관계대명사(whom, which)〉의 경우에는 관계대명사를 생략할 수 없다. 따라서 전치사의 목적어로 쓰인 관계 대명사가 생략되면 전치사는 반드시 뒤에 두어야 한다.

1. She is the woman I met yesterday. 〈타동사의 목적어〉
2. She is the woman I spoke to yesterday. 〈전치사의 목적어〉
   = She is the woman to whom I spoke yesterday.

(2) 주격 관계대명사의 생략

주격관계대명사는 일반적으로 생략할 수 없다. 그러나 다음과 같은 경우에는 생략할 수 있다.

1) 관계대명사가 be 동사의 보어일 때

He is not the man he was.

2) There is[was], Here is[was]로 된 문장의 주어를 수식하는 주격관계대명사

1. There is a man wants to see you.
2. There was nobody could do that.

3) It is[was] ~ that[who, which] …의 강조구문에서

1. It is you told it to him.
2. It isn't everybody can do it.

4) 관계 대명사절에 there is[are, was, were]가 있을 때

He is one of the greatest scholars there are in the world.

영어독해

8 관계대명사의 제한적(한정적) 용법과 계속적(연속적) 용법

(1) **제한적 용법:** 관계대명사 앞에 코마(,)가 없는 경우로서 관계대명사절은 선행사를 수식하여 제한한다.

He had two sons who became teachers. (아들은 둘 이상)
(그에게는 교사가 된 두 아들이 있었다.)

(2) **계속적 용법:** 관계대명사 앞에 코마(,)가 있는 경우로서 관계대명사절은 선행사를 보충, 설명한다.

He had two sons, who became teachers. (아들은 둘뿐)
(그에게는 두 아들이 있었는데, 그들은 교사가 되었다.)

(3) **계속적 용법의 관계대명사는 문맥에 따라 〈and, but, for [because], though+대명사〉로 바꾸어 쓸 수 있다.**

1. I met the boy who did not tell the news.
2. I met the boy, who did not tell the news.
   =I met the boy, but he did not tell the news.
3. He said nothing which made her angry.
4. He said nothing, which made her angry.
5. I don't know the boy who lives near my house.
6. I don't know the boy, who lives near my house.

(4) **관계대명사 what과 that에는 계속적 용법이 없다.**

I cannot understand what she says.
cf. I cannot understand, what she says.(x)

(5) 계속적 용법의 which가 앞에 나온 절의 일부 또는 전체를 선행사로 받는 경우가 있다.

1. I tried to open the door, which(=but it) was impossible.
2. I lost my way, which(=and it) delayed me.

영어독해

9 유사관계대명사

• As, than, but 등은 원래 접속사이지만 다음에 오는 대명사가 생략된 결과 이들 접속사가 그 대명사의 역할을 겸하게 되어 관계대명사처럼 쓰이는 경우가 있는데 이것을 유사관계대명사라고 한다.

(1) As의 용법

1) such, the same, as와 상관적 형태로 쓰일 때

such A as B : 〈B하는 그러한 A〉

the same A as B 〈B와 같은 A〉 (같은 종류〉

as A as B : 〈B만큼 A한〉

1. I want to read such a book as you are reading now. 〈목적격역할〉
2. Choose such friends as will listen to you.
3. I don't like such people as praise you to your face.
4. This is the same watch as you lost yesterday. 〈목적격역할〉 〈동종물〉

cf. This is the same watch that you lost yesterday. 〈동일물〉

5. He goes to the same school as I do.
6. He is as great a man as ever lived. 〈주격역할〉
   = He is one of the most great man that ever lived.
7. We are given as much food as we can live on. 〈목적격역할〉

2) as가 주절 전체나 그 일부를 선행사로 할 때

1. She was very cheerful, as [which] is often the case.
   (그는 명랑했는데 그런 것은 흔히 있는 일이다.)
2. As is often the case with him, he was late for school.
3. The conditions are as follows.

(2) But의 용법

선행사에 부정어구가(no, never, few, scarcely 등) 있을 때 사용되며, that ~ not의 의미를 나타낸다.

1. There is no rule but has an exception.
   = There is no rule that has not an exception.
2. There is nobody but has his faults.
3. None came to him but were fed.
4. Who but knows it?
   = There is no one but knows it.

(3) than의 용법

선행사에 비교급이 포함되어 있는 경우에 많이 쓰인다.

1. He has more money than is needed. 〈주격역할〉
   = He has more money than he needs. 〈목적격 역할〉

(그는 필요 이상의 돈을 가지고 있다.)

2. There are more books than are needed.
3. I couldn't accept more money than I really needed.

영어독해

10 복합관계대명사

- 관계대명사(단, 관계대명사 that은 제외)에 -ever가 붙은 것을 복합관계대명사라고 한다. 따라서 복합관계대명사에는 whoever(주격), whose(e)ver(소유격), whomever(목적격), whichever(주격, 목적격), whatever(주격, 목적격)가 있다. 복합관계대명사는 그 자체에 선행사를 포함하고 있으며, 명사절 또는 양보의 부사절을 이끈다.

(1) 명사절을 이끄는 경우

복합관계대명사가 이끄는 절이 주어나 목적어 역할을 하는 경우에는 명사절을 이끄는데, 그 때의 복합관계대명사의 의미는 다음과 같다.

- whoever=anyone who~ (~하는 사람은 어느 누구나 다)
- whose(e)ver=anyone whose~ (~하는 사람은 어느 누구나 다)
- whomever=anyone whom~ (~하는 사람은 어느 누구나 다)
- whichever=any thing[one] that~ (~하는 것은 어느 것[쪽, 사람]이든 다)
- whatever=anything that ~ (~하는 것은 무엇이든 다)

1. Whoever [Anyone who] comes will be welcome. 〈주격〉
   (오시는 분은 누구나 환영합니다.)

2. Bring whoever wants to come.
3. Whoever leaves the office last should switch off the light.
4. He flatters whose(e)ver [anyone whose] position is high. 〈소유격〉
   (그는 지위가 높은 사람은 누구에게나 아첨한다.)

5. Give it to whomever [anyone whom] you like. 〈목적격〉
   (네가 좋아하는 누구에게나 그것을 주어라.)
   cf. Give it to whoever wants it.

6. I will employ who(m)ever you recommend.
   * 구어에서는 whomever 대신 whoever를 쓰기도 한다.

7. You may take whichever [any thing that] you like. 〈목적격〉
   (너는 네가 좋아하는 것을 어느 것이나 가져도 좋다.)

8. You can have whichever you like.
9. You may give it to whichever comes first.
10. Do whatever [anything that] you like. 〈목적격〉
    (네가 좋아하는 것은 무엇이든 해라.)

11. Whatever has a beginning also has an end. 〈주격〉

(2) 부사절을 이끄는 경우

복합관계대명사가 부사절을 이끌면 다음과 같은 양보의 의미를 나타내는 절이 된다.

- whoever = no matter who~ (누가 ~할지라도)
- whose(e)ver = no matter whose~ (누구의 ~할지라도)
- whomever = no matter whom~ (누구를 ~할지라도)
- whichever = no matter which~ (어느 것을[이] ~할지라도)
- whatever = no matter what~ (무엇을[이] ~할지라도)

1. Whoever says so, he is a liar. 〈부사절〉
   = No matter who says so, he is a liar.
   (누가 그렇게 말할지라도, 그는 거짓말쟁이다.)
   cf. Whoever says so is a liar. 〈명사절〉
   = Anyone who says so is a liar.
   (그렇게 말하는 사람은 누구나 거짓말쟁이다.)
2. Whoever [No matter who] may object, I will go there.
   (누가 반대한다고 할지라도 나는 거기에 가겠다.)
3. Whoever may say so, I don't believe it.
4. I will have the house, whosever(=no matter whose) it may be.
   (그것이 누구의 것일지라도 나는 그 집을 갖겠다.)
5. Whomever(=No matter whom) you may ask, he will say so.
   (네가 누구에게 물어볼지라도 그렇게 말할 것이다.)
6. Whichever [No matter which] you decide, I will back you up.
   (네가 어느 쪽을 결정하더라도, 나는 너를 후원하겠다.)
7. Whichever you may choose, it will become you.
8. Whatever[No matter what] you may do, do it well.
   (네가 무엇을 하더라도 그것을 잘 해라.)
9. I won't leave you whatever happens.
10. Whatever they said to him, he would not change his mind.

영어독해 11 관계부사(Relative Adverb)

• 관계 부사는 〈접속사+부사〉의 구실을 하는 말로서 뒤의 문장을 앞의 선행사에 연결시킨다. 따라서 관계부사가 이끄는 절은 형용사절이 된다. 주의해야 할 점은 관계부사가 이끄는 절은 관계대명사가 이끄는 절의 경우와는 달리 문장의 주요소(주어·목적어·보어) 중 어느 것도 빠져 있는 것이 없다는 점이다. 관계부사에는 where, when, why, how가 있으며, 선행사에 따라 그 중에서 선택하여 쓴다. 관계부사는 〈전치사+관계대명사〉로 바꾸어 쓴 것과 같다.

영어독해 12 관계부사 when

• 선행사가 대개 the time, the day, yesterday, tomorrow, next [last] week[month, year] 등과 같이 시간을 나타내는 말일 때 쓰며, 〈at [on, in] which〉로 바꿔 쓸 수 있다.

1. I know the day. +He was born then
→ I know the day when he was born.
(나는 그가 태어난 날을 알고 있다.)

2. I don't know the day. + He will come back on the day.
→ I don't know the day which he will come back on.
=I don't know the day on which he will come back.
=I don't know the day that he will come back on.
=I don't know the day when he will come back.

3. I told her the exact time when [at which] I would arrive here.
4. I don't know the time when she came home.

영어독해 13 관계부사 where

• 선행사가 대개 the place, the house, the town 등과 같이 장소를 나타내는 말일 때 쓰며, 〈at [on, in] which〉로 바꿔 쓸 수 있다.

1. This is the house. + He lives there.
   = This is the house where he lives.
   (이것이 그가 사는 집이다.)
2. This is the house. + He was born in the house.
   = This is the house which he was born in.
   = This is the house in which he was born.
   = This is the house that he was born in.
   = This is the house where he was born.
3. The park where we planted pine trees belongs to the city.
4. I would like to live in a country where it never snows.

영어독해 14 관계부사 why

• 선행사가 the reason(이유)일 때 사용하며, 〈for+which〉로 바꿔 쓸 수 있다.

1. I don't know the reason. + She was absent for the reason.
   = I don't know the reason which she was absent for.
   = I don't know the reason for which she was absent.
   = I don't know the reason that she was absent for.
   = I don't know the reason why she was absent.
   (나는 그녀가 결석한 이유를 모른다.)
2. The reason why she did it is obscure.
3. Do you know the reason why the sky is blue?

영어독해

15 관계부사 how

- 선행사가 the way(방법)이지만 선행사 the way나 관계부사 how 중 하나만을 쓴다. 따라서 the way how라고는 하지 않는다. 〈the way in which〉로 바꿔 쓸 수 있다.

1. I will show you the way. + You can do it in the way.
   = I will show you the way which you can do it in.
   = I will show you the way in which you can do it.
   = I will show you the way that you can do it in.
   = I will show you the way you can do it.
   = I will show you how you can do it.
   (나는 네가 그것을 할 수 있는 방법을 보여 주겠다.)
2. This is how she always treats me.

영어독해 16 관계부사를 대신하는 that

• 관계부사 when, where, why, how 대신 that을 쓸 수 있다.

1. Do you know the time that(=when) the train leaves?
2. This is the way that(=how) I study English.

영어독해 17 관계부사 및 선행사의 생략

• 선행사가 the place, the time, the reason 등인 경우 이들 선행사는 생략될 수 있다. 선행사가 생략되면 관계부사가 이끄는 절은 명사절이 된다. 또한 그 뜻을 분명히 알 수 있는 경우에는 관계부사를 생략하기도 한다.

1. This is the place (where) I met him yesterday.
2. This is where I met him yesterday.
3. Sunday is the day (when) she is busiest.
4. Sunday is when she is busiest.
5. I don't know the reason (why) she hates him.
6. I don't know why she hates him.
7. That is the way (how) he does it.
8. That is how he does it.
9. The best time of his life is when all the family get together.
10. Something exploded a few meters away where we were standing.
11. The museum is where I spend most of my time.

12. This is how the evening with the young people went.
13. He arrived on the day she married.

영어독해

18 관계부사의 계속적 용법

- 관계대명사와 마찬가지로 관계부사 when, where에도 제한적 용법과 계속적 용법이 있다. 그러나 관계부사 how, why에는 제한적 용법만 있고 계속적 용법이 없다. 계속적 용법의 경우에는 보통 관계부사 앞에 코머(,)가 있으며 선행사나 앞 문장 전체에 대한 부가적인 설명을 하는 글을 이끈다. 계속적 용법의 경우에는 글의 내용에 따라 보통 다음과 같이 〈접속사+부사〉로 바꾸어 해석한다.

- where = and there(그리고 그곳에서), but there(그러나 그곳에서), for[because] there(왜냐하면 그곳에서)
- when = and then(그리고 그때), but then(그러나 그때), for[because] then(왜냐하면 그때)

1. I was in bed till noon when he came. 〈제한적 용법〉
   (나는 그가 온 정오까지 자리에 누워 있었다.)
2. I was in bed till noon, when(=and then) he came. 〈계속적 용법〉
   (나는 정오까지 자리에 누워 있었는데, 그때 그가 왔다.)
3. He went to the library, where(=and there) he read a lot.
4. You had better call at ten, when(=for then) I'll be at home.
5. Please come at ten, when(=for then) I will be free.

영어독해

19 복합관계부사

• 관계부사 where, when, how에 -ever를 붙인 것을 복합관계부사라고 하는데, 선행사를 그 자체에 포함하고 있다. 시간이나 장소의 부사절을 이끌거나(whenever와 wherever의 경우) 양보의 부사절을 이끈다.

(1) 시간이나 장소의 부사절을 이끄는 경우의 의미

❖ whenever = at any time when~ (~할 때는 언제나)
❖ wherever = at[in] any place where~ (~하는 곳은 어디에나), to any place where~ (~하는 곳은 어디로나)

1. You may sit wherever(=at any place where) you like.
   (네가 좋아하는 곳은 어디에나 앉아도 좋다.)
2. Whenever I visited her, she was not at home.
3. Come whenever it is convenient for you.

(2) 양보의 부사절을 이끄는 경우의 의미

❖ whenever = no matter when~ (언제 ~할지라도)
❖ wherever = no matter where~ (어디에서 ~할지라도)
❖ however = no matter how~ (아무리 ~할지라도, 어떻게 ~할지라도)

1. Whenever(=No matter when) you (may) come, you'll be welcomed.
   (네가 언제 올지라도, 너는 환영받을 것이다.)
2. Wherever(=No matter where) you (may) go, I'll follow you.

(네가 어디를 갈지라도, 나는 너를 따라가겠다.)

3. However much she eats, she never gets fat.
4. Wherever he is, he must be found.

영어독해

20 관계형용사

• 관계사가 그 뒤에 명사를 수반하여 형용사적으로 쓰이는 것을 관계형용사라고 한다. 관계형용사에는 whose, which, what, whatever, whichever 등이 있다.

1. The man whose house we have just passed is a famous poet.
2. You may take which servant(=either servant or any servant that) you like.
3. I stayed there for a week, during which time(=and during that time) I visited my old friend.
4. I gave her what money(=all the money that) I had.
5. I sold what few books(=all of the few books that) I had.
6. You may read whatever book(=any book that) you like.
7. Whatever book(=No matter what book) you may read, read it carefully.
8. Whatever excuse she makes will not be believed.
9. You have to go on, whatever difficulties come up.
10. You may use whichever dictionary you like.
11. Whichever TV channel I turned on, I saw nothing but westerns or mysteries.

관계사 익히기 연습

1. Thank you very much for the present you sent.
2. He was dancing with a student who had a slight limp.
3. She was looking after some children who were terribly spoilt.
4. This is the house I was born in.
5. He is the teacher they love best.
6. What is that building the roof of which we see over there?
7. I know a boy, whose father is a doctor.
8. They imitate what they see.
9. He told the story to whoever would listen.
10. The man who is playing soccer on the ground is my father.
11. This is a lady whose son is a pianist.
12. She is the leader we have chosen.
13. She is the most beautiful woman who came to the meeting.
14. Romeo and Juliet were two lovers whose parents hated each other.
15. The bed I sleep on has no mattress.
16. What is that building whose window we see over there?
17. He has lost the watch I bought for him last year.
18. This is the girl whose mother you met yesterday.
19. Jane, who is poor, is always happy.
20. Everybody likes the boy, who is kind and honest.
21. He was not in the train which arrived just now.
22. She saves what he earns.
23. She said she had seen him before, which was a lie.
24. He is so sincere that he succeeds in whatever he undertakes.
25. He is a man I am looking for here.
26. That is a gentleman who I think can speak English.
27. He is not the idle man he used to be.

28. There is a lady wants to see you.
29. There are many books, most of which are novels.
30. This is the story I am interested in.
31. He has a son he is very proud of.
32. That's one of the reasons I hate you.
33. He told me how he escaped the danger.
34. He knows the day I was born.
35. He went back to the city, where he spent his holidays.
36. Whenever you may come, you can't get it without money.
37. He told me the exact time he would arrive here.
38. We went to America, where we stayed for a month.
39. I don't know why his father failed.
40. We stayed at the hotel for a week, when we received a letter.
41. He arrived on the very day her son went to Seoul.
42. Is that the reason she did not come?
43. This is where they walked about on the park yesterday.
44. Wherever you may go, you will never find a place like home.
45. I was just going to answer, when the bell rang.
46. I went to Los Angeles, where I met her.
47. Whenever I coughed, I felt a lot of pain.
48. Wherever she is, I will find her.
49. I don't know the city we met before.
50. Is that the reason she was absent?
51. However strong you may be, you cannot finish it by tomorrow.
52. He died in 2000, when his second daughter was born.
53. The day we had a term examination was fine, but very cold.

54. I met a boy, who showed me the way to the station.
55. My uncle, whose house was burnt down last night, came to live with us.
56. I did not know him, whom I had not seen before.
57. I will lend you this book, which is interesting.
58. He likes fish, which he eats every day.
59. He has two sons who became teachers.
60. He has two sons, who became teachers.
61. I, who am your friend, tell you so.
62. We who are his friends cannot believe this.
63. She is a woman who knows how to express herself.
64. Heaven helps those who help themselves.
65. The book of which the cover is black is mine.
66. The dog the tail of which is long is mine.
67. The building whose roof is red is the library.
68. He wanted to come, which was impossible.
69. He lost his health, which was the cause of his failure.
70. Tom said he was very sick, which was not true.
71. Some school children take no breakfast, which is not good for the health.
72. Students admire the professor, which I find natural.

* 선행사가 사람 그 자체가 아니고 그의 지위, 직업, 성격 등을 나타낼 경우에는 which를 쓴다. 이때 which는 보어로 쓰인다. that에도 이러한 용법이 있다.

73. He is not the man which his father wants him to be.
74. He is a gentleman, which his brother is not.
75. He looked like a lawyer _ which he was.
76. cf. Our father which art in heaven.(고문체)

77. This is the baby which needs inoculation.(선행사가 어린아이)
78. I want a man that can speak English.
79. This is the man that I met at the store.
80. I wish to read a book that is both easy and interesting.
81. He is the greatest poet that Korea has ever produced.
82. Man is the only creature that is gifted with speech.
83. This is the very thing that I want.
84. No man that has common sense can believe that.
85. The train ran over a boy and his dog that were just crossing the track.
86. Who is the man that is standing by the well.
87. Who that has sense of honor can do such a thing?
88. That kite which Tom made is very big.
89. It is time that(=when) we start.
90. This is not the way that(=how) we came .
91. He came back from abroad on the very day that(=when) his father died.
92. I have five elder sisters, none of whom is married yet.
93. He has hundreds of books, most of which he has read.
94. This is the gentleman that I spoke of.
95. That rich man is great who does not think himself great because he is rich.

* 이중한정

96. There is nothing (which) you could do which I had not already done.
97. There is no one (that) I know of who deserves to love you.
98. Is there any thing you want which I can get for you?
99. Can you mention any one that we know who is as talented as he?

100. He gave me what I wanted.
101. He did not know what I wanted.
102. What is done cannot be undone.
103. What you say is true.
104. What is beautiful is not always good.
105. Do you understand what I say?
106. I know what you want.
107. I will do what I can do for you.
108. I owe what I am to him.
109. I have done what I could.
110. He saves what he earns.
111. He has made me what I am.
112. I am sorry for what I have done.
113. This is what I need.
114. She is not what she used to be.
115. He is what you call a self-made man.
116. Leaves are to the plant what lungs are to the animals.
117. We are very tired, and what is worse, became very hungry.
118. He is handsome, clever, and what is the best of all, rich.
119. She is not the woman she was.
120. He behaved like the brave soldier he always was.
121. There is someone at the door wants to see you.
122. It was you told it to me.
123. There is a boy wants to see you.
124. Who was it broke the window?
125. This is the best dictionary there is in this library.
126. He is one of the greatest scholars there are in the world.
127. At last he had done all there was to be done.
128. (Those) Whom the gods love, die young.(시나 격언에서는

that, those, he, one과 같은 선행사가 생략되기도 한다.)

129. Who steals my purse, steals trash.
130. Who never climbs will never fall.
131. Whoever says so is a liar.
132. Bring whoever wants to come.
133. He wants to shoot whoever comes near him.
134. He told the story to whoever would listen to.
135. He told the story to whomever he met.
136. You may meet whomever you like.
137. You may give it to whomever you meet.
138. He flatters whosever relation is rich.
139. Choose whichever you like.
140. Do whatever you like.
141. Whatever is worth doing at all, is worth doing well.
142. Whosever it may be, I want to have it.
143. Whomever it may offend, I will speak the truth.
144. Whichever you may take, I will not object to it.
145. Whatever happens, we must do it.
146. Whatever he may undertake, he succeeds in it.
147. He is as diligent a man as ever lived.
148. She is as good-natured woman as ever breathed.
149. As many girls as came were admitted into the school.
150. They paid as much respect as they could.
151. I have bought the same watch as you have.
152. This is the same watch that I have lost.
153. Such boys as are strong may join the party.
154. Don't read such books as will defile your mind.
155. His conduct is not such as I can admire.
156. He was a foreigner, as you perceived from his accent.
157. He was absent, as is often the case.

158. The conditions are as follows.
159. You have more money than I have.
160. The house cost much more than I could afford.
161. There are more books than are needed.
162. There was no man but admired him.
163. No body knew her but loved her.
164. The letter was written in French, which language he could not understand.
165. He stayed there for ten days, during which time he visited his friends.
166. I gave him what money(=all the money that) I had.
167. I gave him what help I could.
168. I will offer what service is in power.
169. He has sold what few books(=all of the few books that) he had.
170. Let him have what little pleasure he can.
171. Take whichever book(=either of the books, or any of the books, that) you like.
172. Whichever book you may read, you will find it interesting.
173. You may read whatever book(=any book that) you like.

제5장

가정법(Subjunctive Mood)

문장의 내용에 대한 말하는 사람의 심적 태도를 보여주는 동사의 어형변화를 법(Mood)라고 하는데, Mood에는 사실을 사실 그대로 표현하는 직설법과 상대방에게 명령하고 요구하는 명령법, 그리고 어떤 일을 가정해서 말하는 가정법이 있다. 가정법에는 가정법 과거, 가정법 과거완료, 가정법 현재, 가정법 미래가 있다.

He opened the door.(그는 그 문을 열었다.) [직설법]
Open the door.(그 문을 열어라.) [명령법]

영어독해

1 가정법 과거

• 가정법 과거는 현재의 사실과 반대되는 가정을 나타내는데 쓰는 표현이다.

형식: If + 주어 + 동사의 과거형~[조건절], 주어 + would(should, could, might) + 동사의 원형…[귀결절]
(만약 ~한다면[조건절], …할텐데[귀결절])

❖ 가정법 과거에서 조건절의 be동사는 인칭에 관계없이 were를 쓰는 것이 원칙이나 1·3인칭 단수일 때 was를 쓰기도 한다.

❖ 가정법에서 주절에 사용해야 하는 조동사의 과거형(would, should, could, might)은 상황에 따라 선택하여 사용한다. would, should는 조동사의 용법에 맞춰서, could는 〈~할 수 있다〉는 능력에, might는 〈~해도 좋다〉는 허락에 쓰면 좋다.

1. If I knew his address, I would write to him.
   (=As I don't know his address, I don't write to him.)
   만일 내가 그의 주소를 안다면, 그에게 편지를 쓸 텐데.
   (=나는 그의 주소를 모르기 때문에, 그에게 편지를 쓰지 못한다.)

2. Because she isn't taller, she isn't a champion.
→ If she were taller, she'd be a champion.

3. As she doesn't have a doll, she won't give it to me.
→ If she had a doll, she would give it to me.

4. If she were(was) honest, I would employ her.
5. If I knew, I could tell you.
6. If he didn't get up late, he'd have plenty of time.

영어독해

2 가정법 과거완료

• 과거의 사실에 반대되는 일을 가정하는데 사용하는 표현이다.

형식: If + 주어 + had + 과거분사~, 주어 + would[should, could, might] have + 과거분사 …
(만일 ~했었더라면, …했을 텐데)

1. He didn't study hard, so he failed.
→ If he had studied hard, he would not have failed.
2. As he didn't come five minutes later, I wasn't out.
→ If he had come five minutes later,I should have been out.
3. If I had been there, I might have been wounded.
4. If you had worked harder, you would have succeeded.
5. If he had not helped me, I could never have succeeded.
6. What would have happened if I hadn't smelled the gas?

영어독해

3 혼합가정

- if절(조건절)과 귀결절의 시제가 다를 수도 있는데 이것을 혼합가정이라고 한다.

1. If he had not broken his leg, he would be skiing here now.
   = As he broke his leg, he is not skiing(cannot ski) here now.
2. If he were alive now, he would have written to me earlier.
3. If he were in this museum, I should have recognized him.

영어독해

4 가정법 현재

- 현재 또는 미래의 불확실한 일을 가정하는 표현이다.

형식: If+주어+동사원형[또는 직설법 현재동사]~, 주어+will[shall, can, may]+동사원형 …
(만일 ~라면, …할 것이다.)

❖ if절에 동사원형을 쓰는 것이 원칙이나 현대 영어에서는 직설법 현재동사를 쓰는 것이 보통이다.

1. If he be[is] honest, I will employ him.
2. If it rain[rains] next Sunday, the game will be put off.

* 기원문도 일종의 가정법 현재이다.

(May) God bless you! 〈동사원형〉

(그대에게 신의 가호가 있기를!)

cf. God blesses you.

(May) Lord preserve us!

(주여 우리를 지켜 주소서!)

❖ 주장, 요구, 명령, 제안, 의도 따위를 나타내는 that 절에서 가정법 현재 즉 동사원형을 사용한다. 이 경우 미국에서는 동사원형을, 영국에서는 should+동사원형을 사용하는 것이 보통이다.

1. I suggested that he go[should go] there.
2. I insist that he be allowed his freedom.
3. I propose that the matter be put to vote at once.
4. I move that the case be adjourned till tomorrow.

영어독해

5 가정법 미래

• 현재 또는 미래의 비교적 실현 가능성이 없는 일을 가정할 때 쓰는 표현이다.

형식: If+주어+should[were to]+동사원형~, 주어+would[should, could, might, will, shall,can,may]+동사원형…
(만일 ~한다면, …할 것이다.)

1. If I should fail, I will try again.
2. If he should call me, tell him he can come at any time.
cf. If he would work harder, he could succeed.
(더 열심히 공부하려고 한다면,그는 성공할 것이다.) 〈would는 주어의 의지〉
* If I would, I could.
* If I could, I would.

❖ were to+동사원형 : 〈be to+동사원형〉의 가정법 과거형이지만, 미래의 실현 가능성이 매우 희박한 것을 가정할 때 주로 사용한다. 주절에서는 보통 과거형 조동사가 쓰인다.

1. If the sun were to go out, all living things would die.
2. If the Pacific Ocean were to dry up, my father would never change his mind.

❖ 가정법 현재와 가정법 미래의 비교
가정법 현재 : 미래에 대해서 불확실한 가정
가정법 미래 : 미래의 가능성이 희박하거나 거의 불가능한 것을 가정

1. If it be[is] fine tomorrow, I will have a picnic.
(내일 날씨가 (맑을지 흐릴지 불확실하지만) 만일 맑다면, 소풍을 갈 것이다.)

2. If it should be fine tomorrow, I will go on a picnic.
(내일 날씨가 (맑을 리 없지만) 만일 맑다면, 소풍을 갈 것이다.)

영어독해

6 I wish + 가정법

- 현재에 실현하기 어려운 소망이나, 과거에 실현하지 못한 소망을 나타낼 때 주로 동사 wish를 쓴다.

(1) 주어+wish+(that)+가정법 과거

❖ 현재 또는 미래에 실현하기 어려운 소망(~라면 좋을 텐데)을 나타냄.
❖ 주절과 종속절의 시제가 같을 때 사용

1. I wish my sister were a boy.
=I am sorry my sister is not a boy.

2. I wish the rain would stop.
=I am sorry the rain will not stop.

3. I wished I were there.
=I was sorry I was not there.

4. I wish you would help me.

(2) 주어+wish+(that)+가정법과거완료

❖ 과거에 실현하지 못한 소망(~였었더라면 좋을 텐데)을 나타냄.
❖ 주절보다 종속절의 시제가 앞설 때 사용.

1. I wish I had never seen him.
   =I am sorry I saw him.
2. I wished I had never seen him.
3. I wish I had been there.
4. I wished I had been there.
   =I was sorry I had not been there.
5. I wish I had not gone there.
6. I wished I had not gone there.

영어독해

7 as if[though]+가정법

(1) as if[though]+가정법 과거: 〈마치 ~인 것처럼〉

❖ 주절과 종속절의 시제가 같을 때 사용.

1. She acts as though she were a millionaire.
2. She acted as though she were a millionaire.
3. He talks as if he were somebody.
4. He talked as if he were somebody.

(2) as if[though]+가정법 과거완료: 〈마치 ~이었던 것처럼〉

❖ 주절보다 종속절의 시제가 앞설 때 사용.

1. He looks as if he had seen a ghost.
   (그는 마치 유령을 보았던 것 같은 표정이다.)
2. He looked as if he had seen a ghost.
   (그는 마치 유령을 보았던 것 같은 표정이었다.)
3. She cared for me as if I had been her baby.
   (그녀는 내가 그녀의 애기였던 것처럼 돌보았다.)
4. He looks as if he had known nothing.
5. He looked as if he had known nothing.
6. He entered the room as though nothing had happened.

영어독해

8 It is time + 가정법 과거

- It is time (that)+가정법 과거~: 〈(이제) ~해야 할 시간이다〉
  (=It is time for+의미상의 주어+to+동사의 원형)

1. It is time you started [should start].
   (이제 네가 출발해야 할 시간이다.)
2. It's time he were studying English.
   → It's time for him to study English.
3. It's time you went to bed.
4. It was high time that they came to a conclusion.

영어독해

9 if의 생략

• If 절에서 접속사 if를 생략하면 〈조동사(동사)+주어 ~〉의 도치구문이 된다.

1. If I had had much money, I could have gone abroad.
→ Had I had much money, I could have gone abroad.
2. If I knew the result, I could tell it to you.
→ Did I know the result, I could tell it to you.
3. Were I a bird, I would fly to you.
4. Should she come, tell her about it.
5. Had she a child, she would be happy.
6. Had they been careful, this could not have happened.

영어독해

10 if절(조건절)의 생략

• 귀결절만으로 가정의 표현을 하는 경우로서, 내용의 전후관계와 조동사의 과거형으로 판단한다.

1. I could have come yesterday.
(=If I had wanted to come, I could have come yesterday.)
((오기를 원했다면) 어제 올 수 있었는데.)
2. A gentleman would do such a thing.
3. You might have come to say good-bye.
4. You would have stopped me.

영어독해 11 If 이외의 조건을 나타내는 어구들

(1) With ~ = 〈~가 있다면〉

- ❖ But for ~ = Without ~ = 〈~가 없다면〉 = If it were not [had not been] for ~
- ❖ Otherwise = 〈그렇지 않으면〉 앞 사실에 반대되는 가정
- ❖ Unless ~ = If ~ not … = 〈만약 ~않는다면〉
- ❖ But (for the fact) that ~ = 〈~만 않는(않았)다면〉: that 이하에는 직설법을 쓴다.

1. With his help I would have succeeded.
2. But for your help, I couldn't have swum across the river.
   = If it had not been for your help, I couldn't have swum across the river.
3. Without water, nothing could grow.
4. Had it not been for you, our project wouldn't have succeeded.
5. Without appropriate software, a computer would be a mere box.
6. I worked hard, otherwise I would have failed.
   = I worked hard. If I had not worked hard, I would have failed.
7. Unless she goes back home early, she will be punished.
   = If she does not go back home early, she will be punished.
8. But (for the fact) that he is a prince, he would be free.

(2) 접속사 if를 대용하는 어구: suppose, supposing, provided, providing, granted, granting, in case

1. Suppose[Supposing] (that) you had five million dollars, what would you do?
2. I will stay here provided[providing] the climate agrees with me.
3. Granted[Granting] that he were a child, he could answer the question.

(3) 부정사와 분사에 가정의 의미가 포함되어 있는 경우

1. I would be glad to win the prize.
   = I would be glad if I won the prize.
2. To hear him speak English, you would take him for a American.
   = If you heard him speak English, you would take him for a American.
3. Turning to the right, you will find the museum.
   = If you turn to the right, you will find the museum.

영어독해

12 가정법의 관용적 표현

(1) as it were = so to speak: 말하자면

He is, as it were, a walking dictionary.
(그는 말하자면 걸어 다니는 사전(만물박사)이시다.)
cf. ~ as it is: 있는 그대로

He put the book as it was.
(그는 그 책을 있는 그대로 놓았다.)

(2) had better+동사원형: ~하는 게 낫다.

He'd better not go to college.

(3) would rather [sooner]+동사원형 than+동사원형: 차라리 ~하겠다.

I would rather die than live in dishonor.

(4) would [should] like to+동사원형: ~하고 싶다.

I would like to drink milk.

(5) might as well+동사원형: ~하는 것이 낫다.

You might as well give it up.

(6) if ever: 설령 ~해도

He seldom, if ever, goes to church.
(그는 설령 교회에 간다 해도 좀처럼 가지 않는다.)

(7) if any: 설령 ~있다 해도

There is little, if any, water in the bottle.
(설령 병에 물이 있다 해도 거의 없다.)

(8) What if : ~이면 어떻게 될까?; ~해도 아무 상관 없다.

What(would happen) if he should come?
(혹시 그가 오면 어떻게 될까?)

What(does it matter) if you fail this time?
(이번에 실패한들 어때?[실패해도 상관없다.])

(9) O that~!=Would that~=I wish~

O that my father were living!
(아, 아버님이 살아 계신다면 좋으련만!)

Would that I were young again!
(다시 한번 젊어졌으면!)

Ah, would that it had been true!
(아, 그것이 사실이었더라면 좋으련만!)

가정법 익히기 연습

1. If she does it, she will be punished.
2. If I were(was) a bird, I could fly to her.
3. If man had never found metals, he would have remained in a savage state.
4. If I had taken his advice, I should be happy now.
5. The commander ordered that the deserter (should) be shot to death.
6. Long live the King!
7. If the sun were to come nearer to us, it would scorch us to death.

8. If she should fail to come, I will have to go without her.
9. Were I you, I should confess everything to her and ask her pardon.
10. Did he not know for certain, he would not say so.
11. Were I asked, I would tell him all the fact.
12. Had they been more careful, such a calamity would not have befallen them.
13. He would go even to the North Pole for her sake, should it be necessary.
14. Were I to tell you the whole story, it would take more than two hours.
15. Should we fail again, what should we do?
16. If it were not for your idleness, you would be a good student.
7. Newspapers could not be sold so cheaply, were it not for the immense income derived from advertising.
18. But for his care, she should have died.
19. Had it not been for your aid, I could not have succeeded.
20. Without the light of the sun we couldn't see anything.
21. I should have gone out for a walk but that it rained.
22. But for this fault of yours, I would employ you.
23. Supposing (that) it snows tomorrow, what shall I do?
24. Suppose I were your husband, what would you want me to do?
25. In case you fail, you must have something to rely upon.
26. I will do it on condition that you help me.
27. So that it is done, it matters not how.
28. Providing that you admit your faults, I will pardon you.

29. An honest man would not do such a thing.
30. I could have done it with your help.
31. To attempt such a thing would be crazy.
32. Anyone who should do such a thing would be laughed at.
33. In your place I would act differently.
34. The cloudy sky spoiled what would else have been a magnificent view.
35. He would be a poor writer who were careless in the choice of subjects.
36. The branches were so near his window that he could have picked off the blossoms. (if he had wished to do so)
37. What poor creatures we are and how great we might be! (if we would)
38. You might post this letter for me.
39. Don't! If anybody should come! (what would be the result?)
40. What if we are poor?(What does it matter if we are poor?)
41. What if I should fail in the examination?
42. I wish it could be young again.
43. Oh! How I wish that I could meet her once more.
44. Would that I were young.
45. O, that it were not snowing!
46. He looks pale as if he had not slept last night.
47. He felt as though he should die of hunger.
48. You look as if frightened by something unseen.
49. Show me your companions, and I will tell you what you are.
50. One more word, and I will send you out of the office.
51. Laugh and the world laughs with you; weep and you weep alone.

52. Hold your tongue, or you will repent it.
53. One more such loss, and you are ruined.
54. One more effort, and you will finish it.
55. Let him study hard, and he will pass the examination.

제6장

접속사(Conjunction)

단어와 단어, 구와 구, 절과 절을 연결해 주는 역할을 하는 것을 접속사라 한다.

접속사처럼 연결을 하는 것으로는 관계사(관계대명사, 관계부사), 의문사(의문대명사, 의문부사)가 있다.

영어독해

1 접속사의 분류

(1) 기능에 의한 분류-문장에서 하는 역할에 따라서 나누는 것이다.

1) 등위〔대등〕 접속사: 단어, 구, 절을 문법상 대등한 관계로 연결시켜 주는 접속사로서 and, but, or, for, so 따위가 있다.

2) 종속접속사: 주절과 종속절을 연결시켜 주는 접속사로서 여기에는 명사절을 이끄는 것(that, whether, if 등), 부사절을 이끄는 것(when, because, as, while, if, though, 등), 형용사절을 이끄는 것(관계대명사, 관계부사)이 있다.

(2) 형태에 의한 분류: 접속사의 구성 요소에 따라서 나눈다.

1) 단순접속사 : 한 단어로 된 것. and, but, when, because, if 등

2) 구접속사: 두 개 이상의 낱말이 모여서 하나의 접속사 구실을 하는 것. as soon as, as if, even though, so far as, in order that 등

3) 상관접속사 : 두 개 이상의 낱말이 서로 관련되어서 하나의 접속사와 같은 구실을 하는 것. both A and B, either A or B, not only A but also B, no sooner ~ than … 등

영어독해

2 등위(대등)접속사 (Coordinate Conjunction)

• 등위접속사는 중문을 만들며 and, but, or, so, yet, both[at once] ~ and, as well as, not only ~ but (also), either ~ or, neither ~ nor, whether ~ or 등이 있다.

(1) and: 〈~와(과), 그리고〉가 기본적인 뜻이지만 「그런데, 그러자, 게다가」 따위의 뜻으로 쓰이기도 한다. 둘 이상의 사항을 나열할 때, 또는 순서적으로 발생하는 일을 나열할 때 쓴다.

1. You and I are brothers.
2. I met an old woman and she was my old teacher.

(2) 명령문+and~: 〈…하라, 그러면 ~할 것이다〉의 뜻으로서 다음과 같이 if를 사용하여 바꾸어 쓸 수 있다.

1. Work hard, and you will succeed.
   =If you work hard, you will succeed.

2. Go straight on, and you will come to the park.
3. Ask, and it shall be given; seek, and ye shall find; knock, and it shall be opened unto you.
4. Have confidence in yourself, and you can do anything.
5. One more effort, and you will succeed.
6. Make haste, and you will be in time.
7. One more word, and my story is done.
8. One more such loss, and we are ruined.
9. Let your mistakes be your lessons, and so you may make them stepping-stones to a better life.
10. Wait a little, and the tea will cool off.
11. Talk of the devil, and he will appear.

(3) **명사+and+명사**: 원칙적으로 복수이지만, 두 개의 명사가 and로 연결되어 하나의 물건(단일물) 혹은 하나의 개념을 나타낼 때는 단수취급을 하는데 이 때 and는 전치사 with로 바꿔 써도 뜻이 같은 경우가 있다.

Tom and John are good friends. 〈복수〉
Bread and[with] butter is served for dinner. 〈단수〉 (버터 바른 빵)
유예: soap and water(비눗물), a watch and[with] chain(줄 달린 시계), brandy and water(물을 탄 브랜디), whisky and soda(위스키 소다), curry and rice(카레라이스), all work and no play(공부만 하고 놀지 않는 것), trial and error(시행착오)

(4) **both[alike, at once] A and B**: A와 B 둘 다, A하기도 하고 B하기도 하다.

1. Both you and she are wrong.
2. It is alike good and cheap.
3. This book is at once interesting and instructive.

(5) 〈go, come, try, see, stay etc.+and+동사원형〉의 형식에서 and 는 to부정사의 to를 대신하기도 한다.

1. Come and see me tomorrow.
   =Come to see me tomorrow.
2. I'll come and see you soon. (곧 널 보러 갈게.)
3. Come and see me. (나를 만나러 와라.)
4. Go and help her. (그녀를 도우러 가라)
5. Try and do it. (그것을 해보아라.)
6. Mind and write to me. (잊지 말고 편지를 보내다오.)

(6) 〈형용사(fine, good, nice, rare)+and+형용사〉: 〈very+형용사〉의 뜻으로 뒤의 형용사를 강조한다.

1. It is nice and warm. = It is very warm.
2. This corner is nice and warm. (이쪽 구석은 기분좋게 따뜻하다.)
3. I am getting good and angry over the matter.

(7) A or B: ①〈A 또는 B〉, ②〈A 즉, B〉, ③부정문에서 〈A도 아니고 또한 B도 아니다〉

① Would you take tea or coffee?
② He weighs 132 pounds, or about 60 kilograms.
geology, or the science of the earth's crust (지질학, 즉 지각에 대한 학문)
It weighs a kilo, or just over two pounds. (그것은 무게가 1

킬로, 즉 2파운드를 약간 넘는다.)

③ I don't like her or won't.

(8) **명령문+or~:** …하여라, 그렇지 않으면 ~할 것이다.

1. Try hard, or you will fail in life.
   =If you don't try hard, you will fail in life.
2. Don't move, or I'll shoot.
3. Persevere, or you will fail.
4. Hold your tongue, or you will repent it.
5. Keep the rule well, or you may be hurt.

(9) **either A or B:** 〈A나 B 둘 중의 어느 한 쪽〉 [동사는 B의 인칭과 수에 일치시킴]

1. Either you or he knows.
2. Either you are lying, or I am dreaming.

(10) **(not) A nor B:** 〈A도, 또한 B도 ~않다〉
neither A nor B : 〈A도 B도 둘 다 ~아니다〉 [동사는 B의 인칭과 수에 일치시킴]

1. Not a man, nor a child, is to be seen.
2. Neither you nor he is in the wrong.
3. I have neither money nor job.

(11) **but:** 〈그러나〉 앞의 말과 반대 혹은 대조적인 내용을 연결
not only A but also B (=B as well as A): 〈A는 물론 B도 역시〉 [동사는 B의 인칭과 수에 일치시킴]

1. He is poor but honest.
2. It is not only beautiful, but also useful.
   = It is useful as well as beautiful.
3. Not only he but also I am wrong.
   = I as well as he am wrong.

* not only A but also B에서 only 대신 merely, alone, simply를 쓸 수도 있으며, also는 생략하기도 한다.

4. He not merely[only, alone, simply] smokes but drinks.
5. He is not only poor but sickly.
6. This means not only distance but also time.
7. He does not merely preach religion but lives it as well.
8. The Union must rest, not simply on shared interests, but on shared values.

(12) not A, but B : 〈A가 아니고 B이다〉

not that~, but that... : (= not because ~, but because ...)

〈 ~한 것(때문)이 아니고 …하다는 것(때문)이다〉

1. It is not a dog, but a wolf.
2. This book was written not by me but by my friend.
3. It is not that I dislike it, but that I cannot afford it.
4. Not because I dislike the task, but because I am unequal to it.
5. These things do not sell well not because their quality is bad, but because they are rather expensive.
6. Maybe it's not that we eat too much, but that we exercise too little.

(13) **for**: 〈왜냐하면 …이니까〉의 뜻으로 앞서 말한 것에 대하여 간접적으로 그 이유를 덧붙일 때 쓴다.

so: 〈그래서〉의 뜻으로 결과나 결론을 나타낼 때 사용한다.

for와 so는 절과 절만을 연결하는 접속사이다.

1. A fish cannot fly, for it has no wings.
2. Let me stay, for I am tired.
3. He must have been ill, for he was absent.
4. I have no money, so I can't buy it.
5. They cost a lot of money, so use them carefully.

❖ for와 because: for는 뒤에 생각난 이유를 설명하기 위해 쓰이는 등위접속사로 중문을 만들고, because는 처음부터 알고 있는 이유를 설명하는 종속접속사로 복문을 만든다.

(14) therefore: 〈그러므로〉

nevertheless [none the less]: 〈그럼에도 불구하고〉

1. He is healthy and diligent; therefore he will succeed.
2. He knew that he was in danger; nevertheless he would not stop marching.

영어독해 3 명사절을 이끄는 종속접속사: that, if, whether, 의문사

(1) that: 〈~이라는 것, ~하다는 것〉

that절은 주어, 보어, 목적어, 동격명사절 구실을 한다.

1. That he will come is certain. 〈주어〉
   =It is certain that he will come.
2. I think that he is honest. 〈타동사의 목적어〉
3. I know (that) it is impossible.
4. Her hope is that her husband will recover soon.
5. My point is that we have no power.
6. I heard the news that she was dead. 〈동격절〉
7. There is no hope that she will get well soon.
8. Everything was O.K. except that it was blowing hard. 〈전치사의 목적어〉
9. In that he killed Abel, he was a murderer.

❖ 동격절: fact[news, report, idea, opinion, rumour, knowledge etc.] that

❖ that절이 동사 say, believe, think, know 따위의 목적어일 때에는 접속사 that을 생략할 수 있다.

❖ 전치사 but, save, except, besides, beyond, in 이외의 전치사는 that절을 목적어로 취할 때 생략된다.

❖ except[but, save] that ~ : ~을 제외하고,

❖ in that ~ : ~라는 점에서

I am sure of his success.
I am sure that he will succeed.

* be afraid[amazed, angry, ashamed, aware, certain, convinced, delighted, disappointed, fortunate, glad, happy, impressed, lucky, pleased, proud, sad, shocked, sorry, sure, surprised, worried etc.] that

(2) if, whether: 둘 다 〈~인지 어떤지〉의 의미를 나타내는 명사절을 이끈다. if는 동사의 목적어절에만 쓰이며, whether는 or not을 동반하는 경우가 종종 있다.

1. Whether she is still alive is doubtful. 〈주어〉
   = It is doubtful whether she is still alive. 〈진주어〉
2. It is not certain whether he will come [or not].
3. The question is whether he will come [or not]. 〈보어〉
4. Nobody can tell if [whether] he will come. 〈목적어〉
5. I don't know whether or not he can swim.

(3) 간접의문문(의문사절)

의문문이 독립적으로 쓰이지 않고 다른 문장의 일부로 쓰인 의문문을 간접의문문 또는 의문사절이라고 한다. 즉, 의문문이 문장에서 종속절이 되는 것을 말한다. 간접의문문은 명사절로서 주어, 목적어, 보어의 역할을 한다. 간접의문문의 어순은 〈주어+동사〉의 어순이다. 의문사가 있는 의문문이 간접의문문인 경우에는 〈의문사+주어+동사~〉의 어순이 되고, 의문사가 없는 일반의문문이 간접의문문이 되는 경우에는 간접의문문 앞에 if나 whether를 둔 다음 〈if[whether]+주어+동사 ~〉의 어순으로 한다. if, whether = ~인지 아닌지

1) 의문사가 있는 간접의문문

❖ 간접의문문이 목적어 역할을 하는 경우

1. I know + Where does he live? 〉 I know where he lives.
   나는 안다 + 그가 어디에 사니? 〉 나는 안다 어디에 그가 사는지를

2. I don't know + Where does he live? 〉 I don't know where he lives.
3. I want to know + Where does he live? 〉 I want to know where he lives.
4. Do you know? + Where does he live? 〉 Do you know where he lives.
5. Can you tell me? + Where does he live? 〉 Can you tell me where he lives.
6. Please tell me + Where does he live? 〉 Please tell me where he lives.
7. I don't know who she is.
8. Tell me who did it.
9. I asked him what book he had read.
10. Did he hear what had happened?
11. He asked which was the best.

❖ 간접의문문이 주어 역할을 하는 경우

1. Who did it is a question to him.
2. It does not matter who did it.

❖ 간접의문문이 보어 역할을 하는 경우

1. The question is who did it.

❖ 간접의문문이 전치사의 목적어 역할을 하는 경우(전치사가 생략되는 경우가 많다)

1. There is no doubt as to who did it.
2. I had no knowledge what it really was.

2) 의문사가 없는 간접의문문

I don't know+Is she pretty? 〉 I don't know if[whether] she is pretty.
나는 모른다+그녀는 예쁘니? 〉 나는 모른다 그녀가 예쁜지 아닌지를.

❖ 간접의문문이 목적어인 경우

1. I don't know if[whether] it is correct.
2. Can you tell me if[whether] it is correct?
3. Ask her if[whether] it is correct.
4. Go and see if[whether] anyone is at the door.

❖ 간접의문문이 주어인 경우

1. Whether we shall go to him or he will come to us will not be much the matter.
2. It is no matter whether he is here or not.

❖ 간접의문문이 보어인 경우

1. The question is whether he will succeed or fail.

3) 의문사가 문장의 첫머리에 오는 간접의문문: Yes나 No로 답할 수 없는 do you think[suppose, believe, guess, imagine] 다음에 의문사가 있는 간접의문문이 목적어로 올 때엔 의문사가 문장의 첫머리에 온다.

Do you think? + Who is she? 〉 Who do you think she is?
(너는 그녀가 누구라고 생각하니?)

Who do you think she is? - I think she is Jane.
cf. Do you know who she is? - Yes, I do. She is Jane.

1. What do you suppose they should do?
2. How rich do you think he is?
3. Who do you believe did it?
4. What do you suppose she likes?
5. Which do you believe is the best?

＊ 비교(다음 각 문장에 대해 대답하시오)

1. Did she say what time she would arrive at the party?
2. What time did she say she would arrive at the party?

명사절 익히기 연습

1. That she loved him is evident.
2. Whether she is rich or poor is not important to me.
3. How great his labor was can be seen from the result.
4. It is not yet decided how they will start.
5. It happened that the man was not at home.(it happens that ~: 우연히 ~하다)
6. It follows from what you say that you are interested in the matter.(it follows that ~:당연한 귀결로서 ~이 된다)
7. Because you are good, it does not follow that you are wise.
8. If we posit that wage rises cause inflation, it follows that we should try to minimize them.
9. From your remarks, it follows that he has gotten involved in the affair.

10. It happened that he was present.
11. It happened that she was out when we called.
12. It so happened that I was out when he came by.
13. It penetrated into my mind that I had got into the wrong house.
14. It proved that they had so many difficulties.
15. It seems (that) you were lying.
16. It seems to me that you are not really interested in the question.
17. It chanced that I was absent from the meeting that day
18. It chanced that I was out when he called.
19. It appears unlikely that interest rates will fall further.
20. It appears (to me) that you are all mistaken.
21. It appears that he will arrive in time.
22. Her first impression is that he is handsome.
23. His excuse is that he did not know it.
24. The trouble is that you cannot speak English.
25. The truth is, I know nothing about it.
26. What I want to know is whether she is willing to join us or not.
27. The question is whether he will agree or not.
28. There is a chance that the boy will make progress.
29. Chances are that our team will win the championship.
30. Chances are good that he won't keep his promise.
31. Make the right choices and the chances are good that your kids will too.
32. Please let me know if you agree to my plan.
33. I thought it strange that she should leave without saying goodbye to me.

34. I take it for granted that he will come.
35. We took it for granted that he was the ringleader.
36. I owe it to his mother that I could finish the highschool course.
37. See to it that he do the job properly.
38. Please see to it that you keep covering the story.
39. Please see to it that the matter is worked out quickly.
40. There are several boxes on the loading dock that just came in. Would you see to it that they get distributed right away?
41. I was not aware that she was not interested in it.
42. Men differ from brutes in that they can think and speak.
43. The news that he died has proved false.
cf. The news that he brought has proved false. (that=관계대명사)
44. We have news that has just come in. (that=관계대명사)
45. Everybody was thrilled at the news that they won the gold medal.
46. She received the news that her father was near death.
47. I've just heard on the news that the airport is closed because of the fog.
48. She bemoans the fact that she did not finish high school.
49. The fact that the list didn't have his name struck me.
50. I like her except for the fact that she is over nice.
51. The fact that I said it is not true at all.
52. My heart aches at the thought that I can no longer see his warm heart or cute smile.
53. Console yourself with the thought that you did your best.
54. The thought occurred to me that I might be mistaken.
55. We cherish the hope that our country will be reunited.

56. I knocked loudly in the vain hope that someone might answer.
57. I have no idea who you're talking about.
58. You have no idea how much what you said just hurt my feelings.
59. He has no idea how anxious she has been.
60. He rejected the idea that beings can be ranked according to their relative value.
61. Empiricism is the idea that experience creates knowledge.
62. Antitrust is based on the idea that competition has a beneficial result on free markets, and should be encouraged.
63. So, the idea that children do not want healthy food is simply not true.
64. With nuclear power, there is always the fear that there will be an escape of harmful radiation.
65. I have no doubt that he is honest.
66. The question sometimes comes to my mind whether it is worth the effort.

영어독해

4 시간의 부사절을 이끄는 종속접속사

- when~ (~할 때에, ~하면)
- as~ (~할 때에, ~하면서, ~함에 따라)
- while~ (~하는 동안에)
- before~ (~하기 전에)
- It was not long before~ (오래지 않아 ~했다)
- It will not be long before~ (오래지 않아 ~할 것이다)
- It was long before~ (오래 있어야 ~했다)
- It will be long before~ (오래 있어야 ~할 것이다)
- after~ (~한 후에)
- till~ = until~ (~할 때까지)
- It is[was] not till[until] …that~.는 not~till[until] …의 강조구문.
- since~ (~한 이래로)
- whenever~=every time~=each time~ (~할 때마다, ~할 때면 언제나)
- as soon as~ = directly~ = immediately~ = the moment [instant, minute]~ = no sooner [scarcely, hardly] ~ than [before, when]~ (~하자마자)
- as[so] long as~ (~하는 동안은, ~하는 한)
- by the time~ (~할 때면, ~할 때까지는)
- the first time~ (처음 ~했을 때에)
- last time~ (지난번에 ~했을 때에)
- next time~ (다음번에 ~할 때에)

1. When it rains, he usually stays inside.
2. Strike while the iron is hot. 〈속담〉
3. Whenever [Every time, Each time] I am in trouble, I consult him.

4. He came up as I was speaking.
5. She talked as she was reading the paper.
6. I told him so as soon as he came.
   = No sooner had he come than I told him so.
   = Scarcely had he come before[when] I told him so.
   = Hardly had he come when[before] I told him so.

❖ 〈No sooner[Scarcely, Hardly] + had + 주어 + p.p. + than [before, when] ~〉은 〈주어+had+no sooner[scarcely, hardly] + p.p. + than [before, when)] ~〉의 도치구문으로 이 경우 시제가 과거완료로 되는 점에 주의해야 한다.

7. I will write the letter directly[immediately] I get home.
8. The moment[instant, minute] the earthquake shook the city, I hurried back to my home.
9. He shall never enter this house as [so] long as I live in it.
10. As [So] far as I know, he is clever.

❖ as [so] long as ~는 조건, 시간적인 것을 나타내고 as [so] far as ~는 정도, 한계적인 것을 나타낸다.

11. Where have you been since I saw you last?
12. He left after [before] I came.
13. Let's wait until [till] the rain stops.
14. By the time you get there, it will be dark.
15. He will not start by the time I come back.
16. It will not be long before spring comes.
17. It will be long before we meet again.
18. He didn't show up till the meeting was over.
19. We do not know the value of the health till we lose it.

20. The first time I saw her, she looked very happy.
21. Next time I see you, I will show you my new piano.
22. Last time I saw him, he talked about the examination.

시간의 부사절 익히기 연습

1. It was not long before she came.
2. It was not long before an island came in(to) sight.
3. It will not be long before this country has an oil deficit also.
4. My hope is that it will not be long before beef trade resumes.
5. It will not be long before my dream comes true.
6. It will be[not be] long before we know the truth.
7. He had gone some distance when he found his wallet stolen.
8. He had not waited long before the train came.
9. It was more than ten years before he met her again.
10. It was not until he got home that he missed his cell phone.
11. Not until yesterday did he realize the value of the documents.
12. It was not until the end of July that he got to London.
13. Not until his life was over did the seed which he had sown bear fruit.
14. It was not until I saw him that I was reminded of my promise.
15. As soon as the beans are cooking, begin adding the other ingredients.

16. People surged into the department store as soon as the doors were opened.
17. A man whipped off his coat, as soon as he came into the room.
18. As soon as he was put through to me, he put down the receiver.
19. He sleeps as soon as his boss' back is turned.
20. No sooner had I finished an elaborate car washing than the rain began to fall.
21. No sooner[Hardly; Scarcely; Barely] had I walked in the door than the phone rang.
22. No sooner had the President finished his speech before congress than they gave him a standing ovation.
23. No sooner had he arrived home than he was asked to start on another journey.
24. No sooner had he left home than he began to run for school.
25. He had hardly gone when[or before] they began to speak ill of him.
26. She had hardly come home when she started to complain.
27. I could hardly believe my luck when he said yes.
28. Scarcely did I awake when away flew the canon.
29. Scarcely had the game started when it began to rain.
30. He had scarcely put the phone down when the doorbell rang.
31. Scarcely had he entered, when the telephone rang.
32. Scarcely had the votes been counted, when the telephone rang.
33. Scarcely had he opened the door when a man rushed in.

34. I'll come directly I've finished the work.
35. We get up directly the bell rings.
36. Immediately she'd gone, I remembered her name.
37. Immediately he came, he told me so.
38. I want to see him the minute he arrives.
39. The ghost vanished the(very) moment(=as soon as) the cock began to crow.
40. A total lunar eclipse occurs whenever the moon passes through the earths' shadow.
41. You can visit me whenever you want.
42. He always says he doesn't love her whenever he is angry with her.
43. Every time he eats spicy food, he later has heartburn.
44. My little daughter, Remote, depends on me every time she watches TV.
45. Every time he meets me, he talks about money.
46. Please ask me each time you have questions.
47. Each time I phoned they said it would be done.
48. Each time I turned the television on, I heard someone talking about it.
49. His heart beats fast each time he meets her.
50. Each time the storyteller told about the encounter, she embellished the plot.
51. The first time I danced with a woman my face turned red.
52. Next time I hear something like that, I'm gonna kick their ass.
53. Next time someone leaves early, we'll dock their salary!
54. Next time you're at the office supply shop, please remember to pick up some envelopes and scissors.

55. Next time you're here let's have lunch together.
56. Last time I went there, I just walked along the beach.
    cf. The last time I saw Michelle was last summer.
    cf. The last time I saw him was fifty years ago during carnival season.
57. We're all so hungry by the time the lunch bell rings.
58. It'll be almost dark by the time we refuel.
59. By the time police arrived, though, the blond swimsuit model was in terrible pain.
60. By the time we reached the Air Force hospital in Germany, I had stayed up with that patient for 56 hours.
61. I promise by the time you're done eating it, you'll feel right as rain.
62. By the time I arrived, they'd all already cleared off.
63. Any book will do as long as it is interesting.
64. As long as you adopt an aggressive approach, nothing can stand in your way.
65. Let us part friends, as long as we are going to part anyway.
66. The colder the better, so long as it isn't frozen.
67. Anytime is fine, so long as you phone me today.
68. So long as you're organized, I think you're going to enjoy the flexibility this job affords you.
69. So long as he is able, age is nothing.
70. Any book will do so long as(= if only) it is interesting.

영어독해

5 장소의 부사절을 이끄는 종속접속사

- where ~ (~하는 곳에[으로, 에서])
- wherever ~ (~하는 곳 어디에서나)

1. Where there is a will, there is a way. 〈격언〉
2. Stay where you are.
3. They are where they should be.
4. Wherever you are, do your best.
5. Wherever I go, my heart turns to you.
6. She is hated wherever she goes.
7. I like to live where natives dwell. 〈종속 접속사〉
   cf. I like to live in the place where natives dwell. 〈관계 부사〉

영어독해

6 이유, 원인의 부사절을 이끄는 종속접속사

- because ~ ([왜냐하면] ~하기[이기] 때문에)
- as ~ (~하므로, ~하여)
- since ~ (~이니까)
- now (that) ~ (이제는 ~이니까)
- seeing[considering] that ~ (~이니까, ~을 고려하여)
- in that ~ (~이니까, ~라는 점에서)
- that ~ (~이니까, ~ 때문에)
- not that ~, but that … (~때문이 아니라, … 때문이다)

이유, 원인의 부사절 익히기 연습

1. She is happy because she is rich.

❖ not … because ~ : 〈~라고 해서 …인 것은 아니다〉라고 해석해야 할 때도 있다.

2. People despise him, because he is poorly dressed.
3. I did not come here, because I was sick.
4. Do not despise a man because he is poor.
5. Since you won't help me, I must do the job myself.
6. We didn't go, as it rained hard.
7. Now that you are tired, you must take a rest.
8. Now that the kids have left home we've got a lot of extra space.
9. Now you are here, I can go shopping.
10. Now I am a man, I think otherwise.
11. Seeing [Considering] (that) he doesn't work, he knows so little.
12. Seeing you don't know it, you had better keep silent.
13. Considering he doesn't work, he learns so little.
14. She was fortunate in that she had friends to help her.
15. Not that I loved Caesar less, but that I loved Rome more.
16. If I find fault, it is that I want you to do better in future.
17. Are you not glad that you are now able to speak English?
18. If I complain it is that I want to get justice.

❖ 이유를 나타내는 강도는 because, since, now that, as의 순이다.

영어독해

7 목적의 부사절을 이끄는 종속접속사

- that~ = in order that~ = so that~ = so~ (~하기 위하여, ~하도록)
- lest = for fear (that) = for fear lest (~하지 않도록, ~하면 안 되니까)

1. We eat that we may[can] live.
   = We eat in order that we may[can] live.
   = We eat so that we may[can] live.
   = We eat so we may[can] live. (구어에서는 that을 생략하기도 한다.)
2. He works hard so[in order] that he may succeed.
3. He worked hard lest he should fail.
   = He worked hard for fear that [lest] he should fail.
   = He worked hard so that he might not fail.

목적의 부사절 익히기 연습

1. Turn it that I can see it.
2. Come early that you may see him.
3. He went over to Paris that he might study arts.
4. Sit a little closer, so that we can have a talk.
5. Reader's Digest abridges long books so people can read them quickly.
6. Many parents deny themselves so their children can have the best.

7. All business should be carefully attended to so that it never fails.
8. Please bring him forward so that we can have a closer look.
9. Watch closely so that coconut does not burn.
10. He listened attentively in order that he might not miss a single word.
11. Go early in order that you may get a good seat.
12. She turned her head away lest he should see her tears.
13. Be careful lest you fall down.
14. We made haste lest we should be late.
15. I will note it lest I should forget (it).
16. They always speak quietly(= in a low voice) lest they should be overheard.
    cf. I am afraid lest I should miss the last train.(lest=~할까 봐[감정의 원인을 나타냄])
    cf. She was afraid lest she had revealed too much.
    cf. I fear lest he (should) die.
17. He fled lest he (should) be killed.
18. He is in constant fear lest the scandal (should) come to light.
19. She slipped out of the room for fear that she should(= lest she should) be seen by her father.
20. He is working hard for fear (that) he should fail.

영어독해

8 결과의 부사절을 이끄는 종속접속사

- so+형용사 또는 부사+(that)··· = such(+부정관사)(+형용사)+명사+that··· = so+형용사(+부정관사)+명사+that··· (매우 ~해서 ···하다; ···할 만큼 ~하다)
- such that··· = so great that··· (대단하여 ···하다)
- ···, so [that] ~(그래서[그런고로] ~하다)

* 구어에서는 that을 생략하기도 한다.

1. He is so kind (that) everybody likes him
   = He is such a kind man that everybody likes him.
   = He is so kind a man that everybody likes him.
2. He spoke so rapidly that we could not clearly understand him.
3. It was such a cold night that we stayed indoors.
   = It was so cold a night that we stayed indoors.
4. Her talent was such that she deserved to be famous.
5. Such was her anxiety that she couldn't stop trembling.
6. He was always idle,so [that] he failed in his examination.
7. We walked fast, so that we got there in time.

결과의 부사절 익히기 연습

1. She was so tired (that) she couldn't think straight.
2. He is not so poor that he cannot buy it.
3. He was so shabby-looking that at first I thought him a hobo.

4. It was such a lovely day that I went out for a walk.
5. It is such a tiny thing that it is little use to us.
6. The man has lied so often that no one will trust him.
7. There is no branch of knowledge so difficult that it cannot be conquered by perseverance.
8. The man was so sleepy he could not keep his eyes open.
9. There was such a crowd that they couldn't even get to the door.
10. The change in her looks was such that even her mother couldn't know her.
11. Her behavior was such that everyone disliked her.
12. The boys all went home in such an ecstacy of delight that they could hardly get a wink of sleep.
13. Such was his diligence that he made remarkable progress in his business.
14. Dogs work hard so that our lives are easier and safer.
15. His motions are swift as a greyhound so that you can hardly recognize them.
16. He stands his friend up so that he has no friends.
17. He enlisted as most young men were doing, so that they could protect Britain.

영어독해 9 양보의 부사절을 이끄는 종속접속사

- though = although ([비록] ~이지만)
- if = even if = even though (비록 ~일지라도)
- whether ~ or … (~이든지 …이든지 간에)
- whether ~ or not (~이든지 아니든지)
- 명사[형용사, 부사, 과거분사] + as[though]… (…일지라도, …이지만)
- 명령형 + 의문사절 (아무리 ~일지라도)
- 명령형 + as절 (아무리 ~일지라도)
- 명령형 + ever so + 형용사 (아무리 ~일지라도)
- 명령형 + A or B (A이건 B이건)
- A or B (A이건 B이건) *A와 B는 대조적인 낱말
- while (~임에도, 그럼에도, 그런데 한편)
- when (~에도 불구하고, 비록 ~이지만)

1. Though [Although] he is rich, he is not contented.
2. Even if [Even though] it is true, I can not believe it.
3. If [Even if] he is old, he is still strong.
4. Whether you like it or not, you must do it.
5. Dark as[though] it was, I was able to see the sign.
6. Child as[though] he is, he knows everything.
   cf. Though he is a child, he knows everything.
7. Wounded though he was, he fought and fought.
   cf. Honest as he was, he refused a bribe.
   (그는 정직했기 때문에 뇌물을 거절했다.)
8. He will not see her if he is at home. 〈양보의 부사절〉
   cf. He will see her if he is at home. 〈조건의 부사절〉

cf. I wonder if he is at home. 〈명사절〉

9. Come what may, I am prepared for it.
(무슨 일이 닥친다 할지라도 나는 그것에 대비되어 있다.)

10. Try as I may, I cannot move it.
(아무리 해봐도 그 돌을 움직일 수 없다.)

11. Be it ever so humble, there is no place like home.
(아무리 초라해도 내 집 같은 곳은 없다.)

12. Let a man be ever so rich, he should not live an idle life.
(사람이 아무리 부자라도 게으른 생활을 해서는 안 된다.)

13. Be it good or bad, it is my judgement.
(그것이 좋든 나쁘든 내가 한 판단이다.)

14. Rain or Shine, I will go there.
(비가 오든 개이든 나는 거기에 가겠다.)

15. Walking or sleeping, you are in my mind.
(자나 깨나 당신 생각뿐입니다.)

16. While I admit his good points, I can see his bad.
(그의 장점을 인정하지만 그의 약점도 안다.)

17. I have only two books when I need six.
(나는 6 권의 책이 필요하지만 2권 밖에 없다.)

양보의 부사절 익히기 연습

1. Though she seems happy, yet she is worried.
2. Even though they are so poor, they seem happy together.
3. She is believed to be a teacher even though she doesn't look like one.
4. Knuckle cracking will not cause arthritis, though it may lead to other problems.
5. The pearls are fake, although they look real.
6. Although they're twins, they are as different as night and day.
7. She is a foolish, if pretty, girl.
8. If he was not industrious in his youth, he now works very hard.
9. The existing order, if ever so slightly, must be altered.
10. If I am wrong, you are at least not absolutely right.
11. There'd be traffic jams, even if we had a lot of lanes!
12. Even if they fail, their determination lives on to inspire the rest of us.
13. I won't mind even if she doesn't come.
14. She is believed to be a teacher even though she doesn't look like one.
15. Even though it's new, this typewriter doesn't function properly.
16. Even though they spoke indirect it was very powerful.
17. Even though she was very upset herself, she never let it show.
18. Whether or not we're successful, we can be sure that we did our best.

19. Whether he comes or not, I'll go.
20. A habit is not easily shaken off, whether it is good or bad.
21. Rain, or shine, I will start tomorrow.(=Whether it will rain or shine, …)
22. Whether we enjoy being fallible or not, we are fallible.
23. Try as he might, he couldn't open the door.
24. Woman as she was, she was brave.
25. Poor as he was, he had won the general respect of the neighborhood.
26. Hero as he was, he shuddered at the sight.
27. Woman as she was, she was brave.
28. Incredible as it may seem, it is certainly true.
29. Dearly as he loved his native country, he loved liberty even more.
30. Woman as I am, I may be of help to you.
31. Young though he is, he has much sense.
32. Wounded as the soldier was, he did not wince at all.
33. You must go there, be the weather what it may.
34. Come when you will, you will find me in.
35. Please write him a letter, let it be ever so short.
36. Detest him as you may, you must acknowledge his greatness.
37. Be a life long or short, its completeness depends on what it was lived for.
38. While Tom's very good at science, his brother is absolutely hopeless.
39. While I admit that the problems are difficult, I don't agree that they cannot be solved.
40. The walls are green, while the ceiling is white.

41. Some are rich, while others are poor.
42. How can he succeed when he won't work?
43. He threatened to leave when he had no intention of leaving.
44. He walks when he might ride.
45. How can I convince him when he will not listen?

영어독해 10 조건의 부사절을 이끄는 종속접속사

- if (만일 ~라면)
- unless (만일 ~하지 않는다면)
- once (일단 ~하면)
- in case(that) (만약 ~인 경우에는)
- suppose = supposing(that) = providing(that) = provided(that) (만일 ~하면)
- as[so] long as (~하기만 한다면, ~하는 한)
- on condition that (~한다면, ~의 조건하에)
- so that (~하기만 하면, ~하면)

1. If it is fine tomorrow, I will go and see her.
2. If you have any questions, ask me.
3. Once you begin, you should end well.
4. Once you hesitate, you are lost.
5. Unless it rains, I go for a walk every day.
6. Unless you work harder, you will fail.
7. Who will succeed him in case he resigns?

8. In case she comes, tell her that I am not at home.
9. Suppose (=If) we are late, what will the teacher say?
10. Supposing (that) you are elected, what will you do?
11. I will go provided (that) (on condition that) my expenses are paid.
12. You may stay here so long as you keep quiet.
13. Any book will do as long as it is interesting.
14. So that it is done, it matters not how.
15. You can go there so that you come back in time.
16. She is indifferent to the means so that she accomplishes her purpose.

조건의 부사절 익히기 연습

1. We didn't know how we would cope once the money had gone.
2. Once he hesitates, we have him.
3. Once a beggar[thief], always a beggar[thief].
4. Once the way to proceed on is fixed upon, everything will be done accordingly.
5. Once within call, we are safe.
6. Once it is decided, it should never be changed.
7. Once you turn 18 you are officially considered an "adult".
8. The group is also talking over punitive measures in case incentives fail.
9. Just in case we needed to escape, we hired a car.
10. It also comes with a key override in case technology fails.

11. Suppose flights are fully booked on that day—which other day could we go?
12. Supposing (that) you are wrong, what will you do then?
13. Supposing it were true, what would happen?
14. Supposing you can't come, who will do the work?
15. We'll buy everything you produce, provided of course the price is right.
16. She will go, provided (that) her friends can go also.
17. You can go to the movies, providing (that) you finish your homework first.
18. He was with us for as long as I can remember.
19. Let us part friends, as long as we are going to part anyway.
20. Inflation is not going to abate for as long as this persists.
21. Drinking is all right as long as you don't do it to excess.
22. As long as you know how to think, I can teach you our business.
23. She will do it on condition that she is paid.
24. They agreed to lend us the car on condition that we returned it before the weekend.
25. I invested in his business on the condition that I would get 30 percent of the profits.
26. He spoke to reporters on condition that he was not identified.
27. This was granted on condition that the total project would be completed.
28. You may go where you like so that you are back by dinner time.
29. I have no objection providing(that) there is some reason for it.
30. In case you fail, you must have something to fall back upon.
31. Once you have made a promise, you should keep it.

영어독해

11 양태의 부사절을 이끄는 종속접속사

- as = like (~처럼, ~듯이, ~대로, ~함에 따라)
- as if[though] (마치 ~인 것처럼)
- It is in[with] A as in[with] B = As is in[with] B, so it is in[with] A = A is like B (A와 B는 같다)

1. Do in Rome as the Romans do.
2. Try and see things as they are.
3. As she grew older, she became wiser.
4. I'll do it like you do.
5. He looks as if he hadn't slept for a week.
6. He talks as if he knew everything.
7. It is in life as in a journey.
   = As it is in a journey, so (it is) in life.
   = Life is like a journey.
   (인생이란 여행과 같다.)

양태의 부사절 익히기 연습

1. They did as I had asked.
2. She lost it, just as I said she would.
3. Take things as they are.
4. It will be as you wish.
5. Do as I do.
6. As you sow, so shall you reap.

7. No one sings the blues like she did.
8. Like I said, you're always welcome to stay.
9. It is with nations as with individuals; right is might in the long run.
10. As is the husband, so is the wife.
11. As Dynamite is to the 19th century, so is Atomic power to the 20th century.
12. It is in studying as in eating; he who does it gets the benefits, and not he who sees it done.

영어독해 12 That의 정리

(1) 형용사(지시형용사)

1. [떨어져 있는 것[사람]을 가리켜] 저, 그

What is that loud noise?
(저 시끄러운 소리는 뭐야?)

2. [먼 때·곳을 가리켜] 저, 저쪽의, 그

at that time(그때(에)); in that country(그 나라에서는); that day[night, morning](그날[그날 밤, 그날 아침])

3. [this와 상관적으로] 저

He went to this doctor and that.
(그는 여기저기의 의사에게 진찰을 받았다.)

4. [대화자끼리 이미 알고 있는 것[사람, 양]을 가리켜] 저, 그

that car of yours (당신의 저 차)
That hundred dollars helped me greatly.
(그 백 달러는 크게 도움이 되었다.)

Have you listened to that tape (which) I gave you?
(내가 준 테이프 들어 봤니?)

(2) 대명사(지시대명사)

1. [this와 대조적으로 저쪽에 떨어져 있는 것을 가리켜] 그것, 저것

This is better than that.
(이것은 저것보다 좋다.)

This is my sister and that is my cousin.
(이쪽이 나의 누이이고 저쪽이 나의 사촌이다.)

That was the best time.
(그때가 가장 좋았다.)

2. [앞서 언급하였거나 서로 양해되어 있는 사물을 가리켜] 그 일, 그것

After that things changed.
(그 후 사정이 달라졌다.)

That'll be[That comes to] ten dollars.
(10달러 되겠습니다.)

That will do.
(그것이면 된다; 그만하면 됐다.)

3. [저편에 있는, 또는 화제에 오른 사람을 가리켜] 저 사람, 그 사람; 거기 있는 사람

That's Alice.
(저이는 앨리스다.)

4. [앞서 말한 명사의 반복을 피하기 위해] (…의) 그것

❖ one과는 달라서 the+명사(복수형은 those)의 대용이며 대개 전치사구가 따름.

The poison of the cobra is more deadly than that of the rattlesnake.
(코브라의 독은 방울뱀의 그것보다 더 치명적이다.)

A long time passed in a silence like that of the grave.
(무덤의 정적 같은 오랜 침묵이 흘렀다.)

This year's fashions are quite different from those of last year.
(올해의 유행은 작년의 것과는 전혀 다르다.)

His dress is that of a gentleman, but his manners are those of a clown.
(그의 복장은 신사(의 그것이)지만 그의 행동거지는 시골뜨기(의 그것이)다.)

The temperature here is higher than that of Seoul.
(여기의 기온은 서울(의 기온)보다 높다.)

Victim's own blood was of a different blood group from that found on the floor.
(피해자 자신의 혈액은 마루에서 발견된 혈액형과는 다른 것이었다.)

5. [앞의 진술(의 일부)을 강조적으로 되풀이하여] 그렇고말고; (and that의 형태로 강조하여) 더구나, 그것도.

   "Is Michael capable?"—"He's that."
   (마이클은 유능한가?—그렇고말고.) [Yes, he is.나 So he is.보다 강조적]

   He takes pictures, and that very well.
   (그는 사진을 찍는다, 그것도 아주 잘.)

   He did it, and that very well.
   (그는 그것을 했다, 그것도 아주 잘.)

6. [관계대명사 which의 선행사로] (…하는 바의) 것, 일

   ❖ that which는 what으로 바꾸어 쓸 수 있음; 단 there is 구문에서는 that과 which가 분리되는 수가 있음

   That which is bought cheaply is the dearest.
   ([속담] 싸구려를 사면 돈만 버린다.) (싼 것이 비지떡)

   There is that about him which mystifies one.
   (그에게는 무언가 사람을 미혹하는 부분이 있다.)

7. [this와 상관적으로] 전자(the former)

   Dogs are more faithful animals than cats; these attach themselves to places, and those to persons.
   (개는 고양이보다 충실한 동물이다. 후자는 장소에 애착을 갖고 전자는 사람에게 애착을 갖는다.)

   Work and play are both good for the health; this gives us rest, and that gives us energy.
   (일과 놀이는 다 같이 건강에 유익하다; 후자는 휴식을 주고 전자는 활력을 준다.)

(3) 관계사(관계대명사, 관계부사)

1. 관계대명사

He is the greatest novelist that has ever lived.
(그는 전대미문의 대소설가다.)

2. 관계부사

This is the reason that he came.
(이것이 그가 온 이유이다.)

(4) It is [was] … that … 형태의 강조구문

It was on this very spot that I first met my wife.
(내가 처음으로 아내를 만난 곳은 바로 이 장소이다.)

It is you that are to blame.
(나쁜 것은 너(희들) 쪽이다.)

(5) 부사(지시부사)

1. [수량·정도를 나타내는 말을 한정하여] 그만큼, 그렇게(so), 그 정도로

Are you sure she's that young?
(정말 그녀가 그렇게 젊다는 거냐?)

He only knows that much.
(그는 그 정도밖에 모른다.)

My arm doesn't reach that far.
(내 팔은 그렇게 멀리까지 닿지 않는다.)

2. [종종 all that으로; 대개 부정문에서] [구어] 그다지 (…않다),

그렇게까지 (…않다)

She isn't all that rich.
(그녀는 그렇게 부자는 아니다.)

The novel wasn't all that good.
(그 소설은 그렇게까지 우수한 것은 아니었다.)

(6) 접속사

1. [명사절을 이끌어] …이라는[하다는] 것

That Father did not scold me surprised me.
(나는 아버지께서 나를 꾸중하시지 않는 것에 놀랐다.)

It's true that we were a little late.
(우리가 조금 늦은 것은 사실이다.)

The trouble is (that) we are short of money.
(난처한 것은 우리가 돈이 모자란다는 것이다.)

I heard (that) you've been abroad.
(네가 외국에 갔다 온 것을 들었다.)

There was no hope that she would recover her health.
(그녀가 건강을 회복하리라는 희망은 전혀 없었다.)

The actress hid the fact that she was married.
(그 여배우는 결혼한 사실을 숨기고 있었다.)

2. [지각, 감정을 나타내는 형용사 자동사 등에 이어지는 절을 이끌어] …이라는[하다는] 것을; …하여서

I am afraid (that) she will not come.
(그녀는 오지 않으리라고 생각한다.)

I am very happy (that) you have agreed to my proposal.
(당신이 내 제의에 동의해 주어서 나는 매우 기쁩니다.)

I'm sorry that your father is sick.
(춘부장께서 아프시다니 안됐습니다.)

I am glad[or delighted] (that) I found you.
(너를 찾아내서 기쁘다.)

I am sorry[grieved] (that) he is gone.
(그가 가버려서 유감이다[슬프다].)

I was afraid (that) he might be late.
(그가 늦는 것이 아닐까 하고 걱정했다.)

I rejoiced that I had won a victory.
(나는 승리하여 기뻤다.)

I am sorry (that) I am late.
(늦어서 미안합니다.)

I'm glad [happy, pleased] (that) you (should) like it.
(마음에 들어 하니 기쁘다.)

We were informed that an epidemic had broken out in the next village.
(이웃 마을에 전염병이 발생했다는 통보를 받았다.)

3. [so[such] … that의 형태로 정도·결과를 나타내어] (너무) … 하므로, …할 만큼

❖ [구어]에서는 that이 흔히 생략됨.

The meeting became so disorderly that the speaker had to shout into the microphone.
(회의는 매우 무질서해져서 연설자는 마이크를 향해 큰 소리를 내야 했다.)

He is not so poor that he cannot buy it.
(그는 그것을 사지 못할 만큼 가난하지는 않다.)

There was such a crowd (that) we could hardly move.
(사람이 엄청 많아서 우리는 거의 움직이지 못했다.)

4. [(so) that, in order that의 형태로 목적을 나타내어] …하도록, …하기 위해

❖ that절 안에서 may[might]를 쓰는 것은 격식 차린 표현이며, can, will[could, would]이 쓰임; 또한 [구어]에서는 that이 흔히 생략됨.

Turn it so that I can see it.
(내가 볼 수 있도록 그것을 돌려주시오.)

He took a taxi so that he wouldn't be late.
(그는 지각하지 않기 위해 택시를 탔다.)

Come early in order that you may see him.
(그를 만날 수 있도록 일찍 오시오.)

5. [원인 이유] …이므로, … 때문에

I'm glad (that) you (should) like it.
(네가 마음에 든다니 기쁘다.)

If I complain it is that I want to get justice.
(내가 불평하는 것은 정당하게 대우 받기를 원하기 때문이다.)

They respected him the more that he was their rector.
(그들은 그가 그들 교구의 목사이기 때문에 그를 더욱 존경했다.)

Are you not glad that you are now able to speak English?
(이제 영어를 말할 수 있으니 기쁘지 않니?)

6. [that절 안에 종종 should를 써서 판단의 기준을 나타내어] …이다니, …하다니

You are crazy that you should lend money to him.
(그에게 돈을 꾸어주다니 너 미쳤구나.)

Who is he, that he should come at such an hour?
(이런 시간에 오다니 그는 도대체 어떤 사람이냐?)

What have you done to him, that he should be so disloyal to you?
(그가 너에게 그토록 불성실하다니, 네가 그에게 어떻게 했었니?)

Are you mad that you should say such a thing?
(그런 말을 하다니 너 미쳤니?)

7. [대개 부정어 뒤에서 제한하는 절을 이끌어] (…하는) 한에는, (…하는) 바로는

❖ 이 용법의 that은 그 자체는 관계대명사이며, 뒤의 타동사나 전치사의 목적어 구실을 함

There is no one like him that I can see.
(내가 보는 한에는 그이 같은 사람은 없다.)

No one knows anything about it, that I can find.
(내가 아는 한 아무도 그 일을 모른다.)

"Is she married? — Not that I know (of)."
(그녀는 결혼했나? — 내가 아는 바로는 안했어.)

8. [[감탄문을 이루어]] [that절 안에 should를 써서 놀람·분개를 나타내어] …하다니

That he should behave like this!
(그가 이 따위 짓을 하다니!)

That he should betray us!
(그가 우리를 배신하다니!)

9. [that절 안에 가정법 과거형을 써서 소원을 나타내어] …한다면 좋을 텐데

Oh, that I were in England now.
(아, 지금 잉글랜드에 있다면 좋을 텐데.)

Would (that) we were there!
(그곳에 있기만 한다면 (좋으련만)!)

O that I were a little younger!
(오, 내가 조금만 더 젊었으면 좋으련만.)

O that a rescue party might come soon!
(구조대가 빨리 와주었으면.)

Would that he were here with me!
(지금 그가 여기에 나와 함께 있다면 좋을 텐데.)

That he should go back on me at the critical moment!
(중대한 시기에 그가 나를 배반하다니.)

O that it were not so!
(그렇지 않으면 좋을 텐데.)

영어독해 13 but의 정리

(1) 대등접속사

1. [앞의 낱말·구·절과 반대 또는 대조되는 낱말·구·절을 이끌어] 그러나, 하지만, 그런데, 그렇지만

He is poor but cheerful.
(그는 가난하지만 명랑하다.)

2. [(it is) true, of course, indeed, may 등이 들어 있는 절 뒤에서 양보의 뜻을 나타내어] (과연) …지만

Indeed[True] he is young, but he is wise.
(과연[사실] 그는 젊기는 하지만 현명하다.)

You may not believe it, but that's true.
(네가 믿지 않을지 모르지만 그것은 사실이다.)

True, he is young, but he is well read.
(확실히 그는 젊지만 대단히 박학하다.)

You may change yours name, but you cannot change your fingerprints.
(너는 너의 이름을 바꿀 수는 있어도 지문은 바꿀 수 없다.)

True, it is a pity, but it cannot be helped.
(사실 그것은 애석하지만 어쩔 수가 없다.)

A home without love may be a castle or a palace, but it is not a home.
(사랑이 없는 집은 성이든 궁전이든 간에 가정은 되지 않는다.)

Indeed this flower is beautiful, but it bears no fruit.
(사실 이 꽃은 이름답긴 해도 열매를 맺지 않는다.)

3. [앞의 부정어·구·문과 대응하여] …이 아니고. not A but B로 「A가 아니고 B이다」의 뜻을 나타내는 표현; B가 앞에 올 때는 B and not A가 됨.

It is not red but black.
(그것은 붉은색이 아니고 검은색이다.)

Not that I loved Caesar less, but that I loved Rome more.
(시저를 사랑함이 덜해서가 아니고 로마를 더욱 사랑했기 때문이다.) ((Shakespeare작 Julius Caesar에서))

It is not I but you who are to blame.
(나쁜 것은 내가 아니라 너다.)

4. [감탄사나 감동 표현 등 뒤에 별 뜻이 없는 연결어로서]

Heavens, but it rains!
(이런, 비가 오잖아!)

"Why didn't you go?" — "Oh[Ah], but I did."
(왜 가지 않았지? — 아니야, 난 갔었어.)

Eh! But that's a queer story!
(뭐라고! 그것 참 기이한 이야기군!)

Good heavens, but she's beautiful!
(놀랐는걸, 대단한 미인이야!)

5. [놀람·뜻밖의 감정을 나타내어] 야, 어머나

"He has succeeded!" — " But that's great[amazing]!"
(그가 성공했대! — 야, 굉장하구나!)

But how lovely!
(어머나, 귀엽기도 해라!) (*이때 but은 부사로 볼 수도 있다.)

(2) 종속접속사

1. …외에(는), …을 제외하고(는)(except)

> ❖ 전치사의 전용(轉用)으로서 용례 속의 he, she를 각각 him, her로 하면 but은 전치사가 됨

All but he are present.
(그를 제외하고는 모두 참석하였다.)

Nobody but she knew it.
(그녀 외에는 아무도 그것을 몰랐다.)

There is no hope but through prayer.
(기도 외에는 희망이 없다.)

None but a fool would believe it.
(바보가 아닌 이상 아무도 그것을 믿지 않을 것이다.)

It is a game played nowhere but in Korea.
(그것은 한국 이외에서는 행해지지 않는 게임이다.)

Who could have done it but she?
(그녀가 아니고 누가 그것을 할 수 있었겠나?)

What can one call it but genius?
(그것을 천재라 하지 않으면 무엇이라고 불러야 한단 말인가?)

I know little of them but from hearsay.
(나는 소문으로밖에 그들을 잘 모른다.)

There is nothing for it but let it run its course.
(되어 가는 대로 맡기는 수밖에 도리가 없다.)

She did nothing but laugh.
(그녀는 웃고만 있었다.)

They had no other choice but (to) surrender.
(그들은 항복하는 이외에 달리 방법이 없었다.) (*but 다음에 명사·대명사가 와서 문장[절]이 끝날 경우에는 이 but은 전치사로 볼 수도 있다).

2. [부정문 뒤에서] [종종 but that으로 부정의 주절 중의 so 또는 such와 상관적으로] …못할 정도로 (이 but (that) 용법은 문어적임; 일반적으로는 that …not을 씀)

No man is so old but (that) he may learn.
(배울 수 없을 정도로 나이 든 사람은 없다, 아무리 나이가 많더

라도 배울 수 있다 = so old that he may not learn., [구어] No man is too old to learn.).

He is not such a fool but he knows it.
(그것을 모를 정도로 바보는 아니다 = that he does not know it).

He is not such a fool but he can tell that.
(그는 그것을 모를 정도로 바보는 아니다. = He is not such a fool that he cannot tell that.)

He is not such a fool but he knows it.
(그는 그것을 모를 만큼 바보는 아니다.)

3. [부정문 또는 의문문에 이어 필연적인 결과·부대 상황 따위를 나타내어]《뒤에서부터 번역하여》 …하지 않고서는 (…않다); 《앞에서부터 번역하여》 (…하면) 반드시 …하다.

It never rains but it pours.
([속담] 비가 오기만 하면 반드시 억수같이 내린다.; 화불단행(禍不單行), 엎친 데 덮친다.) (보통 나쁜 경우에 쓰지만, 좋은 경우에도 씀)

Scarcely a day passed but I met her.
(나는 그녀를 만나지 않는 날이 거의 없었다.) (Hardly a day passed without my meeting her. 쪽이 일반적임)

You cannot look into the index but you will find the word.
(색인을 찾아보면 반드시 그 말이 있을 것이다.)

He had never confided but he had been betrayed.
(그는 남을 믿고 속마음을 털어놓았다가는 꼭 배신당했다.)

I never pass there but I think of you.
(그 곳을 지나갈 때면 늘 자네를 생각하네.) (=without thinking of you).

Justice was never done but someone complained.

(공평히 판가름해도 반드시 누군가가 불평을 터뜨렸다.)

She never reads the paper in bed but she goes to sleep.
(그녀는 누워서 신문을 읽으면 꼭 잠들어 버린다.)

Not a day has passed but he talks about her.
(그가 그녀의 말을 하지 않는 날은 하루도 없다.)

He seldom goes to the park but he meets the beautiful woman.
(그는 공원에 가기만 하면 그 아름다운 여인을 만난다.)

They never meet but they quarrel.
(그들은 만나면 다툰다.)

No leader worthy of the name ever existed but he was an optimist.
(낙천가가 아니고서는 지도자라고 할 만한 지도자가 있어본 예가 없다.)

There was never a new theory but someone objected to it.
(새로운 학설이 나오면 반드시 누군가가 그에 반대했다.)

4. …하지 않으면, …이 아니(라)면(if…not, unless); …이라는 것이 없다면(*종종 that을 수반).

I would buy the car but I am poor.
(가난하지 않으면 차를 살 텐데 [=(구어) if I were not poor.]).

I would go abroad but that I am poor.
(가난하지만 않다면 해외여행을 할 텐데.)

But that I saw it, I could not have believed it.
(보지 않았다면 나도 믿지 못했을 거야.)

Nothing would satisfy him but he must go there.
(그는 그곳에 가지 않고서는 도저히 직성이 풀리지 않을 것이다.)

Nothing would do but that I should come in.
(내가 안에 들어가지 않으면 도저히 수습이 안 되겠네.)

What can I say but (that) I hope you may succeed?
(당신께서 성공하시기를 바란다는 것 외에 (더) 무엇을 말씀드릴 수 있겠습니까.)

5. [명사절을 이끌어서] 「주절에 doubt, deny, hinder, impossible, question, wonder 등 부정적인 뜻이 부정되어 있을 때」(but은 명사절을 이끌며 but that, 때로는 but what의 형태를 취하는데 뜻은 that과 같음) …하다는[이라는] 것(that).

I do not deny but (that) he is diligent.
(그가 부지런하다는 것은 부정하지 않는다.)

I don't doubt[There is no doubt] but (that) you will achieve it.
(당신이 그것을 해낼 것을 의심치 않는다.)

There was no question but that heart failure had caused his death.
(심장마비가 그의 죽음의 원인이었음은 의심의 여지가 없었다.)
(but에 선행하는 동사[명사]는 언제나 부정적 의미를 갖는 것에 주의)

Nothing will hinder but (that) I will accomplish my purpose.
(어떠한 것도 내가 목적을 달성하는 것을 방해할 순 없을 것이다.)

It was impossible but he should see it.
(그가 그것을 보지 않았을 리가 없다.)

How is it possible but that we should be discontented?
(우리가 어찌 불만을 품지 않을 수 있겠는가?)

There is no knowing but such an accident may happen.
(어쩌면 그 같은 사고가 일어날지도 모른다.)

I do not doubt but that you are surprised.
(아마 깜짝 놀라셨겠지요.)

I don't deny but that it is difficult.
(그것이 어렵다는 것은 부정하지 않는다.)

I shouldn't wonder but she wants to be a singer.
(나는 그녀가 가수가 되고 싶어한다 해도 별로 놀라지 않는다.)

There is no doubt but (that) he was murdered.
(그가 살해되었다는 것은 의심할 여지가 없는 사실이다.)

6. [명사절을 이끌어서] 「흔히 believe, expect, fear, know, say, think, be sure 따위의 부정문·의문문 뒤에 쓰이어」 (but 대신에 but that, but what을 쓸 때도 있는데 오늘날에는 that이 보통) —이 아닌[아니란] (것을), —않(는)다는 (것을) (that—not).

Never fear but I will go.
(꼭 갈 테니 걱정 마라.)

I don't know [I am not sure] but it is all true.
(아마 그것은 사실일 것이다.)

Who knows but that everything will come out all right?
(만사가 잘 될지도 모른다.) [문어적·수사적 표현]

Who knows but that he may be right?
(어쩌면 그가 옳을지도 모른다.) (옳지 않다는 것을 누가 알 것인가?)

(3) 전치사

❖ …을 빼고는[제외하고는], …밖에는; …이외의(except, save)
(*접속사와 구별하기 어려운 경우가 있다).

All but him were drowned.
(그 사람 외에는 모두 익사하였다.)

Nobody has heard of it but me.
(그 소문을 들은 것은 나 밖에 없다.)

It is nothing (else) but a joke.
(그것은 농담에 불과하다.)

Who but her would do such a thing?
(그녀 말고 누가 그런 짓을 하겠는가?)

No one replied but me.
(나 이외는 아무도 대답하지 않았다.)

There was no one left but me.
(남은 것은 나뿐이었다.)

I did not want to be anything but a writer.
(작가 이외에는 아무것도 되고 싶지 않았다.)

I want nothing but a little time.
(나는 그저 약간의 여가를 갖고 싶을 뿐이다.)

What is life but a search for a friend?
(인생이란 친구를 찾는 일이 아니고 무엇이랴?)

He is nothing but a student.
(그는 학생에 지나지 않는다)(nothing but=only).

Nothing remains but to die.
(죽음 외에는 길이 없다.)

They live next door but one.
(그들은 한 집 건너 이웃에 살고 있다.)

He was the last but one to arrive.
(그는 맨 끝에서 두 번째로 도착했다.) ([英, first, last, next 뒤에서] …을 빼고) (《美》 except)([the first[next, last] but one[two, three]의 형태로] 처음[다음, 끝]에서 두[세, 네] 번째의. the last house but one[two] (끝에서 두[세] 번째 집)

Nothing would please her but that we go along.
(함께 가주는 것 이외에 그녀를 기쁘게 해줄 길이 없으리라.) ([that(節)을 목적어로 하여] …이라는 것을 제외하고는, …이라는 것 이외에는)

I ask nothing from you but that you should come to see me once in a while.
(이따금 놀러와 달라는 것 이외에는 바랄 것이 없다.)

(4) 대명사(유사관계대명사)

❖ [부정을 수반한 말을 선행사로 하여] …이 아닌(that[who]…not). 종속절의 주어 또는 대명사의 목적어를 생략한 접속사라고도 볼 수 있다.

There is no one but wants to be happy.
(행복을 바라지 않는 사람은 없다.)

There is no one but knows it.
(그것을 모르는 사람은 아무도 없다.)

There is no rule but has exceptions.
(예외 없는 규칙은 없다.)

There is scarcely any man but loves his country.
(자기 나라를 사랑하지 않는 사람은 드물다.)

Nobody but has his faults.
(결점이 없는 사람은 없다.)

No one but errs.
(잘못을 저지르지 않는 사람은 없다, 원숭이도 나무에서 떨어질 때가 있다.)

There are few men but would risk all for such a prize.
(그러한 상을 위해서라면 모든 것을 내걸지 않을 사람이란 없다) (=who would not risk).

(5) 부사

❖ [문어] 그저, 오직, 단지, 오로지, 겨우(only).

He is but a child.
(그는 어린애에 지나지 않는다.)

There is but one God.
(신은 오직 하나뿐이다.)

His own work is but a tiny part in a vast process.
(그의 일은 거대한 공정 가운데 작은 한 부분일 뿐이다.)

This took him but a few minutes.
(그는 이것을 하는 데 단 몇 분밖에는 걸리지 않았다.)

Life is but an empty dream.
(인생이란 허무한 꿈에 지나지 않는다.)

She left but an hour ago.
(바로 한 시간 전에 떠났다.)

It happened but yesterday.
(그것은 바로 어제 일어난 일이다.)

I have but just seen him.
(방금 막 그를 만났다.)

I spoke but in jest.
(그저 농담으로 말했을 뿐이다.)

If I had but known!
(그저 알기만이라도 했으면.)

If I could but see him!
(그저 그 사람을 만나보기라도 했으면.)

Man can learn everything if he will but try.
(그럴 마음만 먹으면 사람은 무엇이든 배울 수 있다.)

제7장

비교(Comparison)

영어독해

1 원급을 이용한 비교

(1) **동등비교:** as+원급+as… (…만큼 ~한)

1. You are as beautiful as she (is beautiful).
(당신은 그 여자만큼 아름답다.)
2. Tom is as tall as Jim.
3. Does she study as hard as he?

(2) **동등비교의 부정:** not as[so]+원급+as… (…만큼 ~하지 않은)

1. You are not as beautiful as she (is beautiful).
(당신은 그 여자만큼 아름답지 않다.)
2. Tom is not as tall as Jim.
3. Does she not study as hard as he?

(3) **as+원급+as 주어 can:** as+원급+as possible (가능한 한 ~하게)

1. Run as fast as you can.=Run as fast as possible.
(될 수 있는 한 빨리 달려라.)

2. Get up as early as possible.

(4) 배수사+as+원급+as … (… 의 몇 배 ~한)

❖ 배수사: half(절반), twice(두 배), three[four, five, six…] times (3 [4, 5, 6…]배)

1. I am twice as tall as my little brother.
   (나는 내 남동생 키의 두 배이다.)
2. I have only half as many books as he does.

(5) not so much A as B: A라기보다는 차라리 B

1. He is not so much a scholar as a writer.
   (그는 학자라기보다 차라리 작가이다.)
2. He is not so much an actor as a singer.

(6) 원급을 사용한 관용표현

1. Get up as early as possible. (=as you can)
   (될 수 있는 한 일찍 일어나시오.)
2. He is as tall as any boy in his class. (=He is the tallest boy in his class.)
   (그는 그의 반에서 어느 누구 못지않게 〔가장〕 키가 크다.)
3. No other friend was so kind as he.
   (그 친구만큼 친절한 사람은 없었다. 〔그는 가장 친절한 친구다〕)
4. Nothing is as important as health.
   (건강만큼 중요한 것은 없다. 〔건강이 가장 중요하다〕)

5. He is as brave as ever lived.=He is as brave as any that ever lived.
(그는 고금을 통해서 누구 못지않게 용감하다.)

6. She is as pretty as ever.
(그녀는 여전히 예쁘다.)

7. Our teacher is a swimmer as well.
(우리 선생님은 또한 수영선수이시다.)

8. He is as good as dead.
(그는 죽은 것이나 다름없다.)

9. She left without so much as saying good-bye.
(그녀는 작별인사조차 없이 떠나갔다.)

10. He is as kind as honest.
(그는 정직하기도 하고 친절하기도 하다.)

11. She is as dull as her sister is witty.
(언니는 재치가 있는데 그녀는 둔하다.)

12. He is as happy as happy can be.=He is as happy as can be.
(그는 매우(더 할 나위 없이) 행복하다.)

13. I waited for five minutes but it seemed to me as many hours.
(나는 5분 기다렸다. 그러나 그것은 나에게 5시간이나 되는 듯 했다.)

14. He is respected, and his brother as much despised.
(그는 존경을 받지만, 그의 형은 그만큼 멸시를 받는다.)

15. They were swimming like so many frogs.=They were swimming as so many frogs.
(그들은 마치 개구리들처럼 수영하고 있었다.)

16. I looked upon it as so much labor lost.=I looked upon it like so much labor lost.
    (나는 그것을 그 만큼의 헛수고로 간주했다.)

17. As far as we knew, there was no cause for concern.
    (내가 아는 한은 염려할 이유가 없었다.)

18. We'll go so far as London.
    (우리는 런던까지 갈 거다.)

19. He cannot so much as write his name.
    (그는 이름조차 못쓴다.)

원급을 이용한 비교 표현 익히기 연습

1. You're as tall as your father.
2. She doesn't play as well as her sister.
3. He doesn't earn as much as me.
4. It's not as hard as I thought.
5. We'd like it as soon as possible.
6. I love you as much as she (does).
7. I love you as much as her.
8. This is twice[three times] as large as that.
9. He is not as young as he was[as he used to be].
10. He has as many books.
11. I am always as busy as (I am) now.
12. He has as many horses as you(do).
13. I will pay five times as much.
14. He meant no harm and I meant as little.
15. True reading lies not so much in how many books you have read, as in how many books you have understood.

16. It's not so much a remake as it is a reinvention.
17. Actually it is not so much a religion as a religion-social system.
18. This is not so much a question as just an illustration.
19. And often what they seek is not so much profound knowledge as quick information.
20. It's not so much a hobby as a career.
21. A man's worth lies not so much in what he has as in what he is.
22. I will help you as far as I am able.
23. He thought too much like so many philosophers.
24. Things had not gone as smoothly with me as I had planned.
25. He is as good as his word.
26. Snow lay as deep as two meters.
27. She looked as pale as he was jovial.
28. He has a face as kind and good-humored as a face can be.
29. He was as strange as anyone she had seen.
30. English is as fine a vehicle of thought as any.
31. He appeared as handsome a fellow as ever wore a military dress.
32. He disliked English more than ever.
33. She was always singing as merrily as any lark.
34. She worked harder than ever, but remained as poor as ever.
35. He was not in the least surprised, for he had expected as much.
36. I looked upon any time not spent in study as so much lost time.
37. Put three cups of water in the bottle, and then add as much whisky to it.

38. The wooden house flamed up like so many matchboxes.
39. He kept her present as long as he lived.
40. I will try as far as I can.
41. As far as I know, he is an honest man.
42. They were happy so long as they had health and enough to eat.
43. She went so far as to say that he was an impostor.

영어독해

2 비교급을 이용한 비교

(1) **우등비교 :** 비교급+than~ (~보다 더 …한[하게])

I am younger than he[him].
(나는 그보다 더 어리다.)

(2) **열등비교 :** less+원급+than~ (~보다 덜 ~한)

She is less happy than he.
(그녀는 그보다 덜 행복하다. 〉 그녀는 그만큼 행복하지 않다.)
= She is not as happy as he. = He is happier than she.

(3) **Which[Who]…비교급, A or B? (A와 B중 어느 쪽이[누가] 더 … 하니?)**

1. Who is older, she or he?
(그녀와 그 중에서 누가 더 나이가 많니?)

2. Which is faster, the train or the bus?

(4) **비교급의 강조:** 비교급 앞에 much, a good[great] deal, even, still, a lot, far, by far 등을 쓰면 "훨씬 더 ~한[하게]"의 의미가 되어 비교급이 강조된다.

1. He is much taller than I.
(그는 나보다 훨씬 더 키가 크다.)
2. He runs even faster than I.

(5) **get[become, grow]+비교급 and 비교급:** 점점 더 ~해지다.

1. She became prettier and prettier.
(그녀는 점점 더 예뻐졌다.)
2. He ran more and more slowly.

(6) **the+비교급 …, the+비교급~:** …하면 할수록 더욱더 ~하다.

1. The higher we climb, the colder it becomes.
(우리가 더 높이 올라가면 갈수록, 더욱더 추워진다.)
2. The more you eat, the more weight you will gain.

(7) **not~any longer[more]=no longer[more]:** 더 이상 ~이 아니다

She is not a child any longer.=She is no longer a child.
(그녀는 더 이상 어린애가 아니다.)

(8) **동일인(물)의 성질 비교:** 깊이, 높이, 길이, 넓이 등을 표시하는 단음절의 형용사(deep, high, long, tall, thick, wide)를 제외하고는 구분

없이 〈more[rather]+원급+than+원급〉을 쓴다.

1. She is taller than thin.
(그녀는 마른 것이기보다는 키가 크다.)

2. She is less beautiful than kind.
(그녀는 아름답기보다 오히려 친절하다.)

(9) 비교급의 관용표현

1. I like you better than he (likes you).
(그가 너를 좋아하는 것보다 내가 너를 더 좋아한다.)

2. I like you better than (I like) him.
(나는 그보다 너를 더 좋아한다.)

3. More than two weeks have passed since he died.(more than=~이상의)
(그가 죽은 지 두 주일 이상이 지났다.)

4. She is more than honest.(more than=very)
(그녀는 매우 정직하다.)

5. His marrying her is more than I can understand.(more than=what~not)
=His marrying her is what I cannot understand.
=His marrying her is beyond my understanding.
(그가 그녀와 결혼하는 것은 이해할 수가 없다.)

6. A whale is no more a fish than a horse is.
=A whale is not a fish any more than a horse is.
=A whale is not a fish, just as a horse is not (a fish).
(고래가 물고기가 아닌 것은 말이 물고기가 아닌 것과 같다.)

* A is no more B than C is D.=A is not B any more than

C is D.
(A가 B 아닌 것은 C가 D 아닌 것과 같다.)

7. I am no more a writer than you are.
(나도 너처럼 작가가 아니다.)

8. He is no more industrious than you (are).
=He is not industrious any more than you (are).
=He is not industrious just as you are not (industrious).
(그도 너처럼 근면하지 않다.)

9. He is not more industrious than you (are).
=He is less industrious than you (are).
=He is not so industrious as you (are).
(그는 (근면하긴 하지만) 너만큼 근면하지 않다.)

10. She is less beautiful than her sister.
=She is not so beautiful as her sister.
(그녀는 그녀의 여동생만큼 아름답지 않다.)

11. This dictionary contains no more than 30,000 words. (no more than=only, as few[little] as)
(이 사전에는 단지[겨우] 3만 단어가 수록되어 있을 뿐이다.)

12. This dictionary contains not more than 30,000 words. (not more than=at most)
(이 사전에는 많아야[기껏해야] 3만 단어가 수록되어 있다.)

13. This dictionary contains no less than 200,000 words (no less than=as many[much] as)
(이 사전에는 20만 단어(만큼이)나 수록되어 있다.)

14. This dictionary contains not less than 200,000 words. (not less than=at least)
(이 사전에는 적어도 20만 단어가 수록되어 있다.)

15. I am no more than an ordinary writer.
(나는 단지 평범한 작가일 뿐이다.)

16. No writer is more careful of words than he.
(그보다 어휘에 주의를 기울이는 작가는 없다.)

17. She is no less clever than he. (=just as+원급+as)
(그녀는 그만큼 영리하다.)

18. She is not less clever than he. (= probably+비교급+than)
(그녀는 그 못지않게 영리하다.)

19. I love her all the better for her faults.
(나는 그녀를 결점이 있기 때문에 더욱 사랑한다.)

20. I do not love her the less for her faults.
(나는 그녀가 결점이 있지만 여전히 사랑한다.)

21. He is none the happier for his wealth.
(그는 부자인데도 행복하지 않다.)

22. He has some faults, but I like him none the less.
=He has some faults, but I do not like him the less.
=I like him none the less for his faults.
=I do not like him the less because he has faults.
(그가 결점이 있다 해서 그를 덜 좋아하는 것은 아니다[여전히 좋아한다].)

23. He is the kinder of the two boys.
(그가 두 소년 중에서 더 친절하다.)

24. No less a dramatist than Shakespeare praised him.
(셰익스피어와 같은 위대한 극작가도 그를 칭찬했다.)

25. He is no less a personage than the king.
(그는 다른 사람 아닌 바로 왕 자신이다.)

26. He cannot so much as write his own name. (not so much as=not even)
(그는 자신의 이름조차 못쓴다.)

27. He is no better than a beggar. (no better than=as good as=~와 다름없는)
(그는 거지나 다름없다.)

28. If you must go there, much more must I. (much[still] more=한층 더 ~하다)
(만약 당신이 거기에 가야 한다면, 나야말로 더 한층 거기에 가야 한다.)

29. I don't know him, much less his brother. (much[still] less=한층 더 ~하지 않다)
(나는 그를 모르며, 그의 형은 한층 더 모른다.)

30. They were more or less excited. (more or less=다소)
(그들은 다소 흥분했다.)

31. Sooner or later the castle wall will fall to ruin. (sooner or later=조만간에)
(조만간에 성벽이 무너질 거야.)

비교급을 이용한 비교 익히기 연습

1. He is less clever than his elder brother.
2. He was less hurt than surprised.
3. It seemed much larger than I had expected.
4. I feel much better today.
5. She's even more intelligent than her sister.
6. You can do even better if you try.

7. If you can manage to get two tickets that's better still.
8. There are far more opportunities for young people than there used to be.
9. This is far better (than it was).
10. This book is far better than that.
11. I do not suspect him of equivocation, much less of lying.
12. The sky grew darker and darker.
13. The more you read it, the more interesting it will become.
14. The more excited you are, the less able you are to make the right decision.
15. The wiser one grows, the more modest one becomes.
16. The more excited we are, the less able we are to make the right decision.
17. The greater difficulties she meets with, the more energy she shows.
18. The more, the better.
19. It grows the colder, the higher you go up in the air.
20. I thought you and Phil were no longer friends after he took your girlfriend.
21. I have a career in air-conditioning repair, but that opportunity no longer exists.
22. I am no longer able to lie.
23. The judge censured Saddam, saying he was the accused and no longer president.
24. I no longer believe that that is so.
25. The law is no longer effective.
26. No less than one-hundred deaths resulted from influenza.
27. Wealth, no less than poverty, is a test of character.

28. As for my book on Ann Coulter, I received no less than 500 email messages.
29. No less than a thousand people came.
30. There was a balm in the air which soothed no less than it invigorated me.
31. The guide contains details of no less than 115 hiking routes.
32. The mishap cost him no less than his whole fortune.
33. Recreation is no less necessary than work.
34. There is room for no more than three cars.
35. The interview should take no more than 30 minutes.
36. She likes him all the better on account of his frankness.
37. He is none the happier for his wealth.
38. The meat cooks the better if we cook it slowly.
39. The work may be difficult, but none the less it must be done.
40. If we start at once, we will be back the sooner.
41. No period in human life is brighter, and more full of hope than student days.
42. You have already more than repaid me.
43. I know better than to do such a thing.
    (= I am not so foolish as to do such a thing.)
44. The man is never so happy as when he is busy.
45. Nothing is farther from his intention than to offend her.
46. It is well to live on yesterday's income, not today's and still less on that of tomorrow.
47. There is something more than we can understand in this book.
48. She had eyes as black as yours, and shoulders almost as beautiful.

49. A little breeze came up suddenly and as suddenly died away.
50. He treats the poor with no less justice than the rich.
51. Man, no less than the lower forms of life, is a product of evolution.
52. Liberty is no less important in the political sphere than in the sphere of ideas.
53. It is not less absurd than wicked to treat manual labor with contempt.
54. Action is no less necessary to you than thought.
55. Our weather may be fickle, but it is not more fickle than we are.
56. A home without love is no more a home than a body without a soul is a man.
57. Work is not of course, any more than play, the object of life.
58. She is not more economical than he is.
59. A journey of fifty miles can now be done in little more than an hour.

(10) 라틴 계통어의 비교급

라틴어에서 온 형용사는 비교급(-ior)만이 남아 있으며 이 때 접속사 than 대신에 전치사 to를 쓰는 점에 유의해야 한다.

❖ superior(더 우수한), senior(손위의), exterior(밖의), prior(보다 이전에), anterior(더 앞의), inferior(더 열등한), junior(손 아래의), interior(안의), posterior(더 뒤의)

1. This cloth is superior to that.
   =This cloth is better than that.
2. Tom is two years senior to me.
   =Tom is my senior by two years.
   =Tom is senior to me by two years.
   =Tom is two years older than I.
3. Foreign beef is inferior in flavor to home grown.

영어독해 3 최상급을 이용한 비교

(1) 최상급+of[in]~ : ~가운데서[~에서] 가장 …한

the+최상급+of+(대)명사의 복수 또는 the+최상급+in+장소[범위, 집단]명사. 내용을 알 수 있는 경우에는 〈of (in] ~〉은 보통 생략한다. of 대신에 among을 쓰기도 한다.

1. He is the tallest boy in the class.
   (그는 그 학급에서 가장 키가 크다.)

2. He is the tallest of all the boys.
(그는 모든 아이들 중 가장 키가 크다.)

3. She is the best singer among the five.
(그 여자는 다섯 명 중에서 가장 우수한 가수이다.)

(2) 절대최상급

〈(a) most(=very)+형용사의 원급〉은 「대단히〔매우〕 ~한」의 뜻으로서 다른 것과 구체적으로 비교하는 것이 아니라 강조의 의미를 나타낸다. most는 「대부분의, 대개의」 뜻으로 쓰이기도 한다.

1. He is a most brave man.
(그는 아주 용감한 사람이다.)

2. These dishes are most delicious.
(이들 요리는 아주 맛이 있다.)

3. Most people did not know the fact.
(대부분의 사람들은 그 사실을 모르고 있었다.)

(3) the가 없는 최상급

서술적으로 사용된 형용사와 부사의 최상급에는 the를 붙이지 않는다. 그러나 구어체에서는 부사의 최상급에 the를 붙이기도 한다.

1. This lake is deepest at this point.
(이 호수는 이 지점이 가장 깊다.)

cf. This lake is the deepest in Korea.
(이 호수는 한국에서 가장 깊다.)

2. I love her (the) best.
(나는 그녀를 제일 사랑한다.) 〈부사〉

(4) 최상급의 강조

최상급을 강조할 때는 최상급 앞에 much, (by) far, the very 등을 사용한다.

1. She is much [by far] the best singer in her class.
   = She is the very best singer in her class.
   (그녀는 학급에서 노래를 단연 제일 잘 한다.)
2. Your picture is by far the best of all in your class.

(5) 기타 주의해야 할 최상급

1) 최상급이 주어 또는 목적어의 자리에 있으면 〈 ~조차도, ~마저도 (=even)〉라는 양보의 의미를 나타내기도 한다.

1. The best student will blunder sometimes.
   (가장 우수한 학생이라도 때로는 실수하는 법이다.)
2. The most careful observation would not have revealed the mystery.
   (아무리 세심하게 관찰했더라도 그 신비를 밝히지 못했을 것이다.)
3. The wisest man may sometimes make a mistake.

2) the last : 〈결코 ~하지 않을(=most unlikely to)〉의 의미로 쓰이기도 한다. the 없는 last는 〈지난〉의 뜻이다.

1. He is the last man to make mistakes.
   (그는 결코 실수할 사람이 아니다.)
2. Breach of promise is the last thing that he is likely to commit.
   (약속 위반이라는 것을 결코 그가 할 것 같지 않다.)

3. He is the last man to tell a lie.
   cf. Mary was the last to get up this morning.
   (메어라는 오늘 아침 제일 나중에 일어났다. (= Mary got up last this morning.))

3) the+서수사+최상급 : 〈~번째로 ... 한〉

Pusan is the second largest city in Korea.
(부산은 한국에서 두 번째로 큰 도시다.)

4) the least+원급 : 〈가장 ~하지 않는〉

This is the least expensive.
(이것은 가장 돈이 들지 않는 방법이다.)

(6) 최상급을 나타내는 여러 표현

❖ the + 최상급(가장 ~한)
비교급 + than any other + 단수명사 (다른 어떤 …보다~)
비교급 + than all (the) other + 복수명사 (다른 모든 …보다~)
부정주어 + … as[so] + 원급 + as … (…만큼 ~한 것은 없다)
부정주어 + … 비교급 + than … (…보다 ~한 것은 없다)
as + 원급 + as any + (명사) (~에 못지않게 …하다)
as + 원급 + as ever + 동사 (~에 못지않게 …하다)

1. Seoul is the largest city in Korea.
   = Seoul is the largest of all the cities in Korea.
   = No (other) city in Korea is larger than Seoul.
   = No (other) city in Korea is so large as Seoul.

=Seoul is as large as any (other) city in Korea.
=Seoul is larger than any other city in Korea.

2. Nothing is so good as this.
   =Nothing is better than this.
   =This is better than anything else.
   =This is the best (thing).
3. This is the most beautiful sight that I have ever seen.
   =This sight is the most beautiful of all that I have ever seen.
   =This sight is more beautiful than any that I have ever seen.
   =No other sight that I have ever seen is more beautiful than this.
   =No other sight that I have ever seen is so beautiful as this.
   =This is as beautiful a sight as any that I have ever seen.
   =I have never seen a more beautiful sight than this.
   =I have never seen such a beautiful sight as this.

(7) 최상급을 사용한 관용표현

1. He is a fool at (the) best.
2. The flowers are at their best this month.
3. They were sincerely doing their best.
4. I think he is twenty at (the) most.
5. It will cost at least ten dollars.
6. It doesn't matter in the least.
7. You must make the most of your abilities.
8. He made the best of his small income.

제8장

특수구문

영어독해

1 강조

(1) It is+강조어구+that … 구문에 의한 강조

1. Tom broke the window here yesterday.
2. It was Tom that [who] broke the window here yesterday.
3. It was the window that[which] Tom broke here yesterday.
4. It was here that[where] Tom broke the window yesterday.
5. It was yesterday that[when] Tom broke the window here.
6. He was absent because he was sick.
7. It was because he was sick that he was absent.
8. What we earn does not make us rich, but what we save does.
9. It is not what we earn, but what we save that makes us rich.
10. One does not know how valuable health is until one gets ill.
11. It is not until one gets ill that one knows how valuable health is.

(2) do를 사용한 강조

⟨do[does, did]+동사원형⟩의 형태로 문장의 내용이 사실임을 강조하거나 명령의 뜻을 강조한다.

1. I do like dogs.
2. She does like dogs.
3. She did like dogs.
4. Do be careful.
5. Do tell me the reason.
6. Who did break the window?

(3) 반복에 의한 강조

1. He walked and walked towards the station.
2. She laughed and laughed until tears came into her eyes.
3. And everybody talked, talked, talked.
4. It is getting darker and darker.

(4) 부정문의 강조: whatever, in the least, at all, by any means(조금도 ~아니다) 등을 쓴다.

1. I know nothing whatever.
2. He was not surprised in the least.
3. I don't like him in the least.
4. I don't know her at all.
5. There is no doubt at all.
6. English isn't by any means(=is by no means) easy to master.
7. Your report is not satisfactory by any means.

(5) 의문문의 강조: ever, on earth, in the world(도대체) 등이 쓰인다.

1. Why ever didn't you go there?
2. What on earth do you mean by that?
3. How in the world did you do it?
   cf. Who was it that invented the telephone?

(6) 도치에 의한 강조

어떤 어구를 강조하기 위해 문장의 첫머리에 놓는다.

1. Great was our surprise when we saw the tiger. (보어강조)
2. Her name I still remember. (목적어강조)
3. Whether it is true or not I don't know.
4. Never did I dream that such a big building existed. (부사어구 강조)
5. Little did I dream of seeing you again.
6. Down fell the woman.
7. Down she fell.

영어독해

2 동격

- 명사(상당어구)를 다른 명사(상당어구)와 나란히 써서 그 명사(상당어구)를 보충 설명하는 것을 동격이라 한다.

(1) 명사 · 대명사 · 부정사가 동격어일 경우는 앞뒤에 코머(,)를 찍는 것이 일반적이다.

1. My sister, Mary, is pretty and smart.
2. Mr. Brown, our English teacher, is very handsome.
3. She has but one aim, to be a singer.

(2) 〈of+명사(상당어구)〉나 명사절이 동격어일 때는 코머(,)를 찍지 않는다.

1. The city of Busan is a famous port in Korea.
2. The thought of going abroad was in her mind.
3. The fact that she was innocent was well known.
4. They came to the conclusion that she had fled to a foreign country.
5. The question whether she would agree with us was discussed.

(3) 해설의 문구나 설명이 추가될 때는 대시(−)나 콜론(:)을 찍는다.

1. He saved the boys - a heroic act.
2. I find only one thing wrong with Tom : he is not very wise.

영어독해

3 삽입

(1) 삽입어구(절)은 앞뒤에 코머(,), 대시(–)를 넣어 구분하기도 한다.

1. She is, I think, over sixty years of age.
2. Your decision, it seems to me, is a wise one.
3. Do what you think is right.
4. He is, so to speak, a walking dictionary.
5. He knows little, if any, of the world.

(2) 주절이 삽입된 문장은 접속사 that를 이용하여 바꿔 쓸 수 있다.

1. He is, I believe, a brave man.
→ I believe that he is a brave man.
2. Your decision, it seems to me, is a wise one.
3. He is, I know, an experienced teacher.
→ I know that he is an experienced teacher.

영어독해

4 생략

• 문장을 간결하게 하고 불필요한 반복을 피하기 위해서 의미나 문법적으로 지장이 없는 범위 내에서 어구를 생략하는 것을 말한다. 문장의 전후관계나 상식적으로 생각해서 무엇이 생략되었는지 쉽게 알 수 있는 경우에 한한다.

(1) 생략해도 의미 파악이 되는 경우의 생략

1. (I wish you a) Good morning[afternoon, evening]. 〈인사말〉
2. (I wish you a) Merry Christmas.
3. Happy birthday.
4. What a fine day (it is)! 〈감탄문〉
5. (I) Got up at six. 〈일기문〉
6. It is just seven (O'clock). 〈시각〉
7. I am staying at my uncle's (house). 〈장소명사〉
8. What (would happen) if he should fail?
9. (I) Beg your pardon?
10. (I) Thank you.
11. (You) Look out!

(2) 반복되는 부분을 생략한다.

1. He gets up at six and (he) has breakfast at seven. 〈주어 〉
2. You may go if you want to (go). 〈동사〉
3. You may see him if you want to (see him). 〈동사와 그에 딸린 어구〉
4. He is brave and will be (brave). 〈보어 〉

5. Can he speak English? / Yes, (he can speak English) a little. 〈의문문의 대답〉
6. He is as strong as you (are strong). 〈비교구문〉

(3) 의미 파악이 분명히 되는 경우의 부사절(시간 · 이유 · 조건 · 양보)에서 「주어+동사」가 생략되는 경우가 많다.

1. While (I was) waiting for a bus, I was caught in a shower.
2. When (he was) a baby, he cried much.
3. If (it is) necessary, you may meet her.

(4) 광고문, 게시문, 격언에 관용적인 생략이 많다.

1. OLD FURNITURE (IS) FOR SALE.
2. (If a man is) Out of sight, (he will go) out of mind.
3. (What is) Well begun is half done.
4. (Take your) Hats off!
5. (Keep your) Hands off.
6. No smoking (is allowed).
7. No parking (is allowed).

특수 구문 익히기 연습

1. This I feel bound to mention.
2. What I am today I owe to my mother.
3. Great was the delight of the citizens when the hero returned.
4. Rarely in time of peace have people done so much to help one another.

5. Hate them perhaps you should not, but despise them you must.
6. He is, we hear, a great violinist.
7. Chicago, as everybody knows, is a big industrial city.
8. Who do you think that lady is?
9. Night fell and, what was still worse, it began to snow.
10. Necessity, it has been said from olden times, is the mother of invention.
11. She made an apology — I wonder if it were a sincere one — for having failed to come at the appointed time.
12. The book has few, if any, misprints in it.
13. George VI, King of England, died in 1952.
14. He forgot to take off his hat - a sure evidence of confusion.
15. Her house is next to Mr. White's, the florist.
16. He has no wish to be rich.
17. The accident happened only ten kilometers to the city of Rome.
18. The lady went away without a word, an act unimaginable for her age.
19. The discovery that coal could be burned made the industrial society possible.
20. He was a great novelist, that Hemingway.
21. One nation believes one way, and another another.
22. What about having a cup of tea?
    (=What do you think about having a cup of tea?)
23. Hate breeds hate; violence, violence.
24. Do you think it will rain tomorrow? Oh, I hope not.
25. The higher the tree, the stronger the wind.
26. By airplane we can make a faster journey, if not a cheaper one.

27. He was walking, pipe in mouth.
28. What if she is poor?
29. My physical energy is not and cannot be what it was.
30. We admit, though we often forget, the wonderful power of nature.
31. A man of virtue, and not of wealth, deserves our respect.
32. Man is not the creature, so much as he is the creator, of circumstances.

제2부 중문 독해

01. It is no sign of courage to try to escape from the unhappiness of others, caring little what happens to them.

02. Some people find it hard to make up their minds. They run to one and another to get advice. Perhaps it is regard to nothing more important than the color of a dress. Perhaps the bits of advice which they receive conflict with one another: then such people are worse off than they were before.

【Notes】 to one and another (차례로) 이 사람 저 사람에게로
regard to = about worse off 더 곤란해지다

03. England has been described as the paradise of the child; and certainly the English were the first people to realize that one of our first duties toward children is to give them an opportunity for having a happy time, and to let them have it in their own way.

【Notes】 paradise 낙원 in their own way 그들 좋을 대로

04. One cannot correct one's faults without knowing them, and I always looked upon those who told me of mine as friends, instead of being displeased or angry, as people in general are too apt to be.

【Notes】 correct 교정하다 look upon ~ as… ~을 …로 간주하다
instead of~ing ~하지 않고 people in general 일반사람들

05. I would have every student come to know, and the sooner the better, that there can be no thorough appreciation of the literature or culture without an exact knowledge of the language.

【Notes】 come to know 알게 되다 the sooner the better 빠르면 빠를수록 좋다 thorough 철저한 appreciation 감상 literature 문학 exact 정확한

06. No doubt it is an amazing miracle that man should have been able to overcome the animal conditions of his existence so far as to build the towering edifice of civilization and to construct rational order of scientific knowledge.

【Notes】 amazing miracle 놀라운 기적 overcome 극복하다 towering 우뚝 솟은 edifice 건물

07. The period of greatness of ancient Greece lasted five hundred years. Then that nation lapsed into a people of herdsmen, never again to regain its former glory.

【Notes】 lapse into~ ~으로 되다, ~으로 추락하다 herdsman(타인에게 고용되어 가축을 기르는)목축인 regain 도로 찾다

08. What you have to learn if you are to be a good citizen of the world is that though you will certainly dislike many of your neighbours, and differ from some of them so strongly that you could not possibly live in the same house with them, that does not give you the smallest right to injure them or even to be uncivil to them.

【Notes】 citizen 시민 possibly 아무리해도, 도저히 injure 상처를 입히다 uncivil 무례한

09. It is no good talking about the greatness of Korea, pretending to be proud of it, unless we who live in the country do something to make it great, and of which we, and those who come after us, have a right to be proud.

【Notes】 pretending to be proud 자랑하는 체 하면서 greatness 위대함 right 권리

10. When we read the lives of great men, we cannot but be struck by the manner in which all kinds of experiences that might in themselves seem to be random, or even disastrous, are turned to account in the long run.

【Notes】 lives [laivz] life (전기)의 복수 be struck 감동을 받다 in themselves 그것 자체, 본래 random 닥치는 대로의 disastrous 불행을 가져오는, 재난의 turn to account 이용하다 in the long run 결국

11. Mother decided that he had a cold. So she gave him some aspirin and hot lemonade. But Jimmy didn't feel like eating or drinking anything. He said that he had a sharp pain in the side. Mother called the doctor, who made an examination and said that it was appendicitis.

【Notes】 have a cold 감기를 앓다 have a pain in~ ~가 아프다 sharp (고통이) 심한 side 옆구리 take an examination 진찰하다 appendicitis 맹장염

12. Usually that which a man calls fate is a web of his own weaving, from threads of his own spinning.

【Notes】 fate 운명 web 직물, 피륙 weave (피륙을) 짜다 thread 실 spin (실을) 잣다

13. A virtue standing by itself is apt to fall into vice. It must be fortified by kindred virtues or be balanced by unrelated ones. Meekness unalloyed by fortitude, is liable to be weak. Bravery unmixed with docility, is prone to be rough. The dove's innocence must be coupled with the wisdom of the serpent.

【Notes】 fortify 강하게 하다 unalloyed 섞이지 않은 fortitude 꿋꿋함 docility 양순함 be prone to~ ~하기 쉽다

14. In his old age, Lessing became very absentminded. Coming home one night with his mind on some work he intended to finish, he found the door locked. In answer to his knock, a servant looked out of an upstairs window, and mistaking his master for a stranger, called out, "The professor is not at home." "Very well," Lessing answered meekly as he turned away, "Tell him that I'll call another time."

15. As he lay thinking, he saw a spider over his head, making ready to weave her web. He watched her toiling slowly and with great care.

16. There beats not a heart, however debased by sin, or darkened by sorrow, that has not its noblest impulse aroused, in view of a generous and kindly action.

【Notes】 debase 저하하다

17. Rivermouth is a very ancient town. In my day there existed a tradition among the boys that it was here Christopher Columbus made his first landing on this continent. I remember having the exact spot pointed out to me by an inhabitant. Rivermouth figures prominently in all the colonial histories.

【Notes】 figure 나타나다

18. Knowing so well that war is wrong, and fearing and hating it more than anything else, we seem compelled, in spite of ourselves, to go on waging it.

【Notes】 wage 전쟁을 행하다

19. Arriving at my hotel, I found to my surprise that my purchases had preceded me home, my instructions to send them having been executed with great promptness.

【Notes】 purchases 구입물

20. All that year the animals worked like slaves. But they were happy in their work; they grudged no effort or sacrifice, well aware that everything that they did was for the benefit of themselves and those of their kind who would come after them, and not for a pack of idle, thieving human beings. (*Animal Farm*)

【Notes】 grudge 아끼다

21. Stated in the simplest terms, science is but a sense of curiosity about life, religion is a sense of wonder at life, and art is a taste for life; philosophy is an attitude toward life, based on a greater or lesser, but always limited, comprehension of the universe as far as we know.

22. Aviation has lost its glamor - and its appeal for youth. College surveys show that bright young men, seeking exciting peacetime careers, now think of aviation as "old hat." Instead, they're interested in thrilling new fields like electronics and nuclear energy.

【Notes】 Aviation 항공(술) glamor 매력 appeal 호소력, 매력 nuclear energy 원자핵 에너지

23. My mother, whose name was Mary, had a sweet singing voice and knew by heart the arias from many operas and operettas. She loved dancing, which she taught me from an early age; and she was clever at making pretty things to wear and to decorate our little home.

24. There is a great deal of unnecessary prejudice against women students in Korea. Korean men must realize that we live now in a modern world where women have the same opportunities as men folk.

25. It is perhaps a natural impulse to view with horror and disgust all manners and customs different from those to which we are used.

【Notes】 impulse 충동 view 보다 horror 혐오 manners and customs 풍속과 관습

26. All of us belong to social groups and have contacts with other groups while at work. The type of clothing we wear, the kind of houses we live in, the type of recreation we enjoy, and the kind of food we eat, are the result of the influences of the groups to which we belong.

【Notes】 social group 사회 집단 while (we are) at work

27. Society is like a building, which stands firm when its foundations are strong and all its timbers are sound. The man who cannot be trusted is to society what a bit of rotten timber is to a house.

【Notes】 foundation 토대 timber 재목 trust 신뢰하다 bit 조각 rotten 썩은

28. His mother had no objection to making him whatever he was inclined to be - he did not want to take orders as his father intended him to, but he wanted to study architecture. Finally his father came to consider it beyond his power to influence him.

【Notes】 have no objection to~ ~에 반대하지 않다 whatever =anything that be inclined to~ ~하고 싶어 하다, ~하고 싶어지다 take orders 성직에 취임하다, 목사가 되다 architecture 건축[학] finally = at last beyond one's power~ ~할 수 없는 influence 영향[감화]을 주다, 좌우하다

29. Whoever is studious to make an outward show, to which no inward substance corresponds, is acting a lie, which may help him out of a difficulty perhaps for the occasion, but, like silvered copper, will be found out in due season.

【Notes】 be studious to~ 애써 ~하다 outward 외부의 substance 실체, 내용 correspond 상응하다, 일치하다 for the occasion 지금 당장에는 in due season 때가 되면, 얼마 안가서

30. Luck or the grace of Heaven may seem to take part in many happenings in life, but a little deeper looking into the causes of them reveals that one's own efforts were by far more responsible for them than most people imagine.

【Notes】 grace 은총 take part in ~에 참가하다 be responsible for ~에 책임이 있다

31. Whether a life is noble or mean depends, not on the profession which is adopted, but on the spirit in which it is followed.

【Notes】 mean 야비한, 저속한 adopt=choose

32. When the most insignificant person tells us we are in error, we should listen, and examine ourselves, and see if it is so. To believe it possible that we may be in the wrong, is the first step towards getting out of it.

【Notes】 insignificant 하찮은, 시시한 examine 조사하다 be in error 잘못이 있다 see if~ ~인지 어떤지 조사하다 be in the wrong=be wrong. get out of ~을 벗어나다, 모면하다.

33. I am deeply convinced that our peace of mind and the joy we get out of living depend not on where we are, or what we have, or who we are, but solely upon our mental attitude. Outward conditions have very little to do with it. (Dale Carnegie)

【Notes】 peace of mind 마음의 평화 solely=only mental attitude 심적 태도, 정신적 자세 have very little to do with ~과 별로 관계가 없다

34. Speaking of his ancestry Lincoln once humorously remarked, "I don't know who my grandfather was, but I am much more concerned to know what his grandson will be."

【Notes】 ancestry (집합적으로) 선조 be concerned to=be anxious to

35. England has been described as the paradise of the child; and certainly the English were the first people to realize that one of our first duties toward children is to give them an opportunity for having a happy time, and to let them have it in their own way.

【Notes】 in their own way 그들 좋을 대로

36. A man must be able to master himself, to master his own passions, and overcome his own weaknesses. This is what we usually mean when we speak of moral courage.

【Notes】 overcome 극복하다 moral courage 도덕적, 정신적 용기 moral courage는 physical courage(육체적 용기)에 대한 말 cf. moral victory 정신적 승리

37. Nothing in this world is more hopeless than aimlessness. It matters not how the individual is, or how favourable his surroundings are. If he has no purpose, he is destined to misery.

【Notes】 It matters not = It is not important. surroundings 환경 be destined to ~로 운명지어져 있다

38. Houses should be built so as to admit plenty of light as well as of fresh air. The former is not less necessary than the latter to a healthy condition of body. Just as plants, when deprived of light, become white in their stalks and leaves, so man becomes pale and unhealthy when he lives underground.

【Notes】 admit 들어오게 하다 plenty of=much. the former~, the latter… 전자는 ~, 후자는… (=the one~, the other…) deprive~of … ~로부터 …을 빼앗다 stalk(s) 줄기

39. Most people talk too much and old age is loquacious. Though I have always been more disposed to listen than to talk, it has seemed to me of late that I was falling into the defect of garrulity, and I no sooner noticed it than I took care to correct it.

【Notes】 old age 노인 loquacious 수다스러운 disposed=inclined. of late 최근에 defect 결함 garrulity 수다, 다변 take care to ~하도록 주의하다

40. We owe Edison our trams, moving pictures, and other things. He has given us a far greater number of useful inventions than has any other inventor in the whole history of mankind.

【Notes】 tram 전차 moving picture 영화 a great number of 대단히 많은 mankind 인류

41. The more things a man is interested in, the more opportunities of happiness he has and the less he is at the mercy of fate, since if he loses one thing he can fall back upon another. Life is too short to be interested in everything, but it is good to be interested in as many things as are necessary to fill our days.

【Notes】 at the mercy of fate 운명에 좌우되어 fall back upon~ ~에 의지하다 since=because if=even if

42. With most men the knowledge that they must ultimately die does not weaken the pleasure in being at present alive. To the poet the world appears still more beautiful as he gazes at flowers that are doomed to fade, at springs that come to too speedy an end. The loveliness of May stirs him the more deeply because he knows that it is fading even as he looks at it. It is not that the thought of universal mortality gives him pleasure, but that he holds the pleasure all the more closely because he knows it cannot be his for long.

【Notes】 with=concerning; in the case of ultimately 궁극적으로(=finally) gaze 응시하다 be doomed to~ ~할 운명에 있다(=be destined to ~) fade 시들다 come to an end 끝나다 loveliness 아름다움 universal 전자연계의, 보편적인, 만유의 mortality 죽을 운명, 죽음을 모면하지 못 함 closely 단단히

43. The only thing I can say in favor of giving pocket money freely is that it makes a child happy for the moment. I had an uncle who never sent a child to buy stamps without greeting it on its return with the blessed words "Keep the change."

【Notes】 in favor of~ ~에 유리하게, ~에 찬성하여 freely 아낌없이 on its return=when it returned blessed 행복한, 고마운 keep the change 거스름돈을 가지다

44. Birds are naturally the most joyous creature in the world. Not that when you see or hear them they always give you pleasure, but that they feel joy more than any other animal. The other animals commonly look serious and grave; and many of them even appear melancholy. But birds for the most part show themselves extremely joyous by their movements and by their aspects.

【Notes】 naturally 천성적으로 melancholy 우울한 for the most part 대개 (=mostly)

45. Not that his thoughts were of agreeable things; but he liked the sunshine and country quiet, and the sense of momentary independence.

46. They had not proceeded far before they perceived a bear making toward them with great rage.

【Notes】 perceive 알아차리다 bear 곰 with great rage 몹시 화를 내어

47. I find the great thing in this world is not so much where we stand, as in what direction we are moving. To reach the port we must sail sometimes with the wind and sometimes against it, -- but we must sail, and not drift, nor lie at anchor.

【Notes】 sail with[against] the wind 순[역]풍에 돛을 달다

48. Not all of us can become extremely strong or extremely clever; but all of us can, if we have ordinary bodies and brains, improve our strength and our memory by the same means --- practice.

【Notes】 extremely 극단적으로 ordinary 보통의 improve 증진시키다 strength 체력 means 수단 practice 연습 memory 기억력

49. My mother married at eighteen, but with eight children of her own she found ample scope for her talents. She did not teach us, I am sure, because she was dissatisfied with our village school. She taught us because she could not help it.

【Notes】 ample 넓은 scope 여지 talents 재능 found ample scope for her talents 그녀의 재능을 발휘할 여유가 충분히 있었다
I am sure~ ~라고 나는 확신한다 she could not help it = she could not help teaching

50. So great was felt to be the loss that nothing but the union of parties, which he had in vain desired during his lifetime, could fill up the gaps left by his death.

【Notes】 loss 손실 union of parties 당파의 연합 in vain 헛되이 fill up 채우다 gaps 틈

51. The notion that literary values are relative to literary periods, that the literature of a period is primarily an expression and a symptom of the time, is so natural to us now that we can hardly detach our minds from it.

【Notes】 notion 생각, 추상적 개념 be relative to~ ~과 관련 있다 symptom 징후, 징조 natural to us 우리에게 자연스러운

52. His sister is everything in his life, he says. They have always been together, and according to his account he has been a very lonely man with only her as a companion, so that the thought of losing her was really terrible to him.

【Notes】 everything 가장 중요한 것 according to~ ~에 따르면 account 이야기 as~ ~로서 companion 동료, 말상대

53. To his great surprise, he found the house quite neat and clean, and the tea things was laid out ready for him.

【Notes】 neat and clean 깨끗이 정돈되어 the tea thing 차 도구 laid out 가지런히 놓여 있었다

54. We should always lay by something, so that, in the event of our being unable to work from unemployment, sickness, or old age, we may not starve nor be compelled to ask charity from others.

【Notes】 lay by=save 저축하다 in the event of our being unable to work=when we are unable to work unemployment 실업 sickness 질병 compel 억지로 ~시키다 charity 자선(행위)

55. We are liable to say something rather amusing but perhaps rather unkind and our words leave a sting. The words may hardly have left our lips before we secretly wish we had not spoken in that way.

【Notes】 be liable to~ ~하기 쉽다(=be apt to~) amusing 재미있는 sting 바늘, 가시, 찌르는 듯한 아픔 secretly 남 몰래, 은밀히

56. Life is by no means always in as big a hurry to give us things as we are to receive them. We may imagine that the moment

we leave school the world will step aside and make way for us. Usually it does not. We have to learn to labour and to wait.

【Notes】 by no means=never in a hurry 서둘러 step aside 옆으로 비키다, 피하다 make way for~ ~에 길을 열다, 양보하다 labour 노력하다

57. My mother understood the fundamental principle of successful teaching; that in order to interest others, one must be oneself consumed with interest. No one and nothing could remain dull once she had touched and enlivened them with her magic.

【Notes】 fundamental principle 근본 원리 be consumed with~ 불타고 있다 remain dull 따분해 하고 있다 enliven 생기를 주다 magic 마술

58. Now that we have so many things to do, I think we ought to lay down a plan of operations: method is everything when work is to be done.

【Notes】 lay down a plan 계획을 세우다 operations 작업 method 방법 everything=very important thing work is to be done 일을 완수하려면

59. About a shilling in copper I gave to the people of the boat for my passage. At first they refused it, on account of my rowing; but I insisted on their taking it, a man being sometimes more generous when he has but a little money than when he has plenty, perhaps through fear of being thought to have but little.

【Notes】 copper 동전 passage 배 삯, 선박 요금 generous 활수의, 돈에 인색하지 않은 but = only

60. If I were a boy again, I would school myself into a habit of attention: I would let nothing come between me and the subject in hand.

【Notes】 school myself into~ 자신에게 ~을 가르치다

61. Knowing how light an insect is, you can imagine the staggering number of insects that are killed each year by man's tiny friend, the spider. If it weren't for the spiders, all those insects might have lived, many feeding on man's food supply, and causing a serious threat to human life.

【Notes】 Knowing~ = If you know~ staggering 깜짝 놀라게 하는 spider 거미 feed on~ ~을 먹고 살다 food supply 식량 serious threat 심각한 위협

62. There were too many kings in the world, Jefferson thought, and all new republics should support each other. If the new French Republic should fail, he said, America's new ideas of freedom and justice would lose their chief support.

【Notes】 republic(s) 공화국 freedom 자유 justice 정의 support 지지, 지주

63. The growth of the United States is a progress that has no precedent in the world's history; it is a new kind of thing. Such a community could not have come into existence before; and if it had, without railways it would certainly have dropped to pieces long before now. Without railways or telegraph it would be far easier to govern California from Peking than from Washington. (H. G. Wells)

【Notes】 growth 성장 progress 경과 precedent 전례, 선례 community 사회 come into existence 존재하게 되다, 성립하다 to pieces 산산조각으로 telegraph 전신, 전보

64. There is a danger that some people are, so to speak, getting too used to the present critical situation. They read of it daily in the newspapers, find it all very complicated, but feel that, somehow, sooner or later, things will come right again.

【Notes】 get used to~ ~에 익숙해지다 critical 위기의 complicated 복잡한 sooner or later 조만간

65. It rained very hard all the day; I was thoroughly soaked, and by noon a good deal tired; so I stopped at a poor inn, where I stayed all night, beginning now to wish that I had never left home. I cut such a miserable figure, too, that I found, by the questions asked me, I was suspected to be a runaway servant.

【Notes】 thoroughly 완전히 soak 흠뻑 젖게 하다 stop at~ ~에 유숙하다 cut a figure 모습을 띠다 miserable 비참한 suspect 의심하다

66. There are two virtues much needed in modern life if it is ever to become sweet. These virtues are honesty, and simplicity of life, and it must be noted that the practice of either of these virtues will make the other easier to us.

【Notes】 virtue(s) 미덕 sweet 기분 좋은 simplicity 간소, 순진 note 주의하다 practice 실행, 실천

67. "Bitterly cold this evening, isn't it? What if we use up our coal?" "What about dancing on and on together and keeping ourselves warm?"

【Notes】 bitterly 지독하게 use up 모두 소모하다 on and on 계속해서

68. It is no doubt a pleasant thing to have a library left you. But good as it is to inherit a library, it is better to collect one. Each volume then, however lightly a stranger's eye may roam from shelf to shelf, has its own individuality, a history of its own.

【Notes】 no doubt 의심할 바 없이 have a library left you 장서를 물려받다 inherit 물려받다 one=a library volume 책 roam 건성으로 보다

69. The more things a man is interested in, the more opportunities of happiness he has, and the less he is at the mercy of fate, since if he loses one thing he can fall back upon another.

【Notes】 opportunities 기회 at the mercy of~ ~에 좌우되어 fate 운명 fall back upon ~에 의존하다

70. The history of mankind is the history of man's activity, and so long as human nature and man's material conditions are what they are, so must economic and industrial factors have a potent influence in the course of political and social life.

【Notes】 activity 활동 material 물질적인 factor 요소 potent 강력한 influence 영향 course 진행

71. Our life is not short, but we make it so. Just as great wealth is scattered in a moment when it comes into the hands of a bad owner, while wealth, however small, if it is entrusted to a good keeper, increases by use, so our life is long enough for him who uses it properly.

【Notes】 scatter (금전을) 탕진하다 while 그런데(whereas; but) entrust 맡기다 properly 알맞게

72. It is with narrow-souled people as with narrownecked bottles: the less they have in them, the more noise they make in pouring it out.

【Notes】 narrow-souled 마음이 좁은(=narrow-minded) the less~, the more~. make much noise 큰 소리를 내다, 시끄럽게 떠들어대다 pour out 쏟아내다, 말을 발하다

73. It is with some stories as it is with many people — they become better as they grow older.

【Notes】 as they(=some stories) grow older 오래 될수록

74. There is no freedom save that which is based upon discipline. The chance to do as one please is not liberty, as so many people imagine; liberty involves knowledge, self-mastery, capacity for exertion, and power of resistance.

【Notes】 that which의 that는 freedom을 가리킴 be based upon ~에 의거하다, ~을 기초로 하다 chance = possibility self-mastery 자제 capacity 능력 exertion 노력 resistance 저항

75. There is a legend, quite without foundation, that I am fond of finding fault with society as it is, without having anything better to suggest in its place. I have my own vision of a happy future, which may be ours if we want it.

【Notes】 legend 전설 foundation 근거 finding fault 흠 찾기

76. Those with limited time at their disposal may well despair of gaining an adequate acquaintance with the many sights and treasures that London holds.

【Notes】 at one's disposal ~의 마음대로 하는 despair of~ ~에 절망하다 adequate 충분한

77. Friendship is a vase, which, when it is cracked by heat, violence, or accident, may as well be broken at once; it can never be trusted after. The more graceful and ornamental it was, the more clearly do we discern the hopelessness of restoring it to its former state.

【Notes】 crack 금가게 하다 violence 난폭한 취급 by accident 우연히 graceful 우아한 ornamental 장식적인 discern 분별하다 restore 회복하다

78. To be proud of having two thousand books would be absurd. You might as well be proud of having two overcoats. After your first two thousand difficulty begins, but until you have ten thousand volumes the less you say about your library the better.

【Notes】 absurd 우스꽝스러운, 불합리한

79. Not only through his books did he work for social good. He associated himself with every charitable scheme for improving the fate of those for whom the path of life was rugged.

【Notes】 for social good 사회를 위해서 associate oneself with~ ~에 찬동하다, ~을 지지하다, ~에 참가하다, ~에 관계하다 charitable 자선의 scheme 계획 improve 개선하다 path of life 인생행로 rugged 울퉁불퉁한, 곤란한

80. It is not likely that a mountain will be ascended without disappointment, if a wide range of prospect be the object, unless either the summit be reached before sunrise, or the visitor remain there until the time of sunset, and afterwards.

【Notes】 It is likely that~ 아마도 ~일 것이다 ascend 오르다 prospect 조망 summit 정상

81. A dog will bark more loudly and bite more readily when people are afraid of him than when they treat him with contempt, and the human herd has something of this same characteristic. If you show that you are afraid of them, you give promise of good hunting, whereas if you show indifference, they begin to doubt their own power and therefore tend to let you alone.

【Notes】 bark 짖다 bite 물다 readily 쉽게 with contempt = contemptuously 경멸하여 the human herd 군중 characteristic 특징 promise of good hunting 좋은 사냥감이 될듯하다는 가망

82. A knowledge of grammar can be of considerable help to us; for it will enable us to understand the reason why certain ways of expressing ourselves are right and others wrong, and to correct any errors we may have made.

【Notes】 considerable 고려할만한 가치가 있는, 상당한

83. Now I think that one has to distinguish between two forms of intelligence, that of the brain, and that of the heart, and I have come to regard the second by far the more important.

【Notes】 distinguish between~ ~을 구별하다 that of = the form of

84. No sooner had I come into contact with him than I determined to get to know him well. Never in my life have I been so strongly and immediately attracted to any man, before or since.

【Notes】 come into contact with~ ~와 접촉하다

85. He has never gone out except in a carriage, or with a servant; he does not know what to do by himself.

【Notes】 except 이 외에는 in a carriage 마차를 타고

86. It is seventeen years since I gave up teaching and started to live an independent life of the pen. I have never starved and never even felt poor, though my income for the first ten years was no better, and often worse, than it would have been if I had remained an elementary school teacher.

【Notes】 independent 독립적인 starve 굶주리다

제3부　장문 독해

(국가직 9급 7급 독해기출문제 풀어보기)

2013년 국가직 9급 영어 독해문제

문 11. 주어진 글 다음에 이어질 글의 순서로 가장 적절한 것은?

Year after year, a survey sponsored by Scotland's Centre for European Labour Market Research finds the same thing: If you want to be happy in life, be happy in your job. Okay, but what will make me happy in my job? Some researchers at the University of British Columbia in Canada have come up with an interesting way quantifying the seemingly unquantifiable. (A) For example, trust in management—by far the biggest component of job satisfaction—is worth as much in your overall happiness as a very substantial raise. Say you get a new boss and your trust in your workplace's management goes up a bit. (B) By analyzing life-satisfaction surveys that consider four key factors in job satisfaction, they have figured out how much each is worth when compared with salary increases. (C) Even that small increase in trust is like getting a thirty six percent pay raise, the researchers calculate. In other words, that will boost your level of overall satisfaction in life by about the same amount as a thirty six percent raise would.

① (A)-(B)-(C)　　② (B)-(A)-(C)

③ (C)-(A)-(B)　　④ (C)-(B)-(A)

【Notes】 come up with (해답 돈 등을) 찾아내다[내놓다]; …을 생산하다; 제시[제안]하다. quantify 수량화하다 seemingly 겉보기에, 외양상으로 unquantifiable 수량화할 수 없는 component (구성)요소, 부품 substantial 상당한, 실질적인 life-satisfaction surveys 삶의 만족도 조사 figure out 알아내다, 이해하다, 계산하다 calculate 계산하다 boost (사기, 기력 등을) 돋우다, (경기를) 부양하다 overall 전반적인

■ 밑줄 친 부분에 들어갈 가장 적절한 것을 고르시오. [문 12~문 14]

문 12.

It can sometimes feel as if South Korea, overworked, overstressed and ever anxious, is ____________ a national nervous breakdown, with a rising divorce rate, students who feel suffocated by academic pressures, a suicide rate among the highest in the world and a macho corporate culture that still encourages blackout drinking sessions after work. More than 30 Koreans kill themselves everyday, and the suicides of entertainers, politicians, athletes and business leaders have become almost commonplace.

① by virtue of ② as opposed to
③ in favor of ④ on the verge of

【Notes】 nervous breakdown 신경쇠약 divorce rate 이혼율 suffocate 숨이 막히게 하다 academic pressure 학업 압박 suicide 자살 macho (거칠게) 남자다움을 과시하는[으스대는] macho corporate culture 마초적인 기업문화 encourage 조장하다 blackout drinking sessions 정신이 나갈 정도로 술을 마시는 모임(회식자리) athlete 운동선수 commonplace 일상적인, 흔한 by virtue of ~덕분에 as opposed to ~에 반하여, ~와 다르게 in favor of ~을 지지하는, ~에 우호적인 on the verge of 막 …하려는[…하기 직전의] He was on the verge of tears. (그는 금방이라도 울음을 터뜨릴 것 같았다.)

문 13.

Strategic thinking can make a positive impact on any area of life. The first step in strategic thinking is to ______________________ ________________ so that you can focus on it more effectively. That's what automotive innovator Henry Ford did when he created the assembly line, and that's why he said, "Nothing is particularly hard if you divide it into small jobs." He also said, "Only one person in a million can juggle the whole things at the same time and think strategically to create solid, valid plans." He is well known for his habit of splitting tasks. Right before the beginning of each weekday, he would think about daily issues, prioritizing the issues for the weekday. He made a rule to deal with the issues only allotted for the day.

① make a habit of taking notes
② break down an issue smaller
③ deal with daily tasks without delay
④ think twice before setting to a work

【Notes】 strategic thinking 전략적 사고 positive impact 긍정적 영향 automotive innovator 자동차 혁신가 assembly line 조립라인 juggle 일을 곡예 하듯 하다, 일을 잘 처리하다, 요령 있게 다루다 solid, valid plan 견고하고 타당한 계획 split 나누다, 분리하다 prioritize 우선적으로 처리하다, 우선순위를 매기다 allot 할당하다, 분배하다 take notes 메모하다, 기록하다 break down 부수다, 분해하다, 나누다, 고장나다 set to 시작하다, 착수하다

문 14.

You as the parent must try to read their crying to be able to help them. This will also help you assess your children's perception of your discipline. In many cases, when a child feels that he has been punished wrongly, it is more difficult to console him. He cried pathetically. Others may receive the punishment in a defiant mood. ________________, when a child feels guilty and he is not punished or assured of forgiveness, he is likely to feel insecure and timid. In such a case when punished they may cry but quickly compose themselves and seek to attract love from the parent. Children usually want the crisp and clean punishment followed by fellowship rather than living with uncertainty.

① As a result　　② For example
③ In other words　　④ On the other hand

【Notes】 assess 평가하다 perception 인지, 인식, 지각 discipline 훈육, 훈련, 규율 console 위로하다 pathetically 애처롭게, 애절하게 defiant 반항적인, 도전적인 insecure 불안한 timid 소심한, 겁 많은 compose oneself 마음을 가라앉히다[가다듬다], 진정하다 crisp 단호한, 분명한, 아삭아삭한 fellowship 유대감

■ 주어진 글의 주제로 가장 적절한 것을 고르시오. [문 15~문 16]

문 15.

The space shuttle Challenger had just taken off for its tenth flight in January 1986 when it exploded in the air and killed all seven people inside. Millions of people around the world were watching the liftoff because schoolteacher Christa McAuliffe was on board. McAuliffe, who had been chosen to be the first teacher in space, was planning to broadcast lessons directly to schools from the shuttle's orbit around Earth. This Challenger disaster led NASA to stop all space shuttle missions for nearly three years while they looked for the cause of the explosion and fixed the problem. They soon discovered that the shuttle had a faulty seal on one of the rocket boosters. Unfortunately, the teacher-in-space program was indefinitely put on hold. So were NASA's plans to send musicians, journalists, and artists to space.

① Schoolteacher Christa McAuliffe's pioneering participation in the space program
② The reason why the American space program was put on hold
③ The importance of the space research and training of astronauts
④ A satire on the unsuccessful or tragic space missions

【Notes】 space shuttle 우주 왕복선 take off 이륙하다 explode 폭발하다 liftoff 이륙 broadcast lessons 수업을 방송하다 orbit 궤도 disaster 재난, 참사 fix the problem 그 문제를 해결하다 faulty 흠이 있는, 결함이 있는, 불완전한 seal 밀봉부문, 밀폐부분 rocket booster 로켓 추진체 indefinitely 무기한으로, 무한정으로 put on hold 보류하다, 연기하다 journalist 기자 astronaut 우주 비행사

문 16.

A team of researchers has found that immunizing patients with bee venom instead of with the bee's crushed bodies can better prevent serious and sometimes fatal sting reactions in the more than one million Americans who are hypersensitive to bee stings.

The crushed-body treatment has been standard for fifty years, but a report released recently said that it was ineffective. The serum made from the crushed bodies of bees produced more adverse reactions than the injections of the venom did. The research compared results of the crushed-body treatment with results of immunotherapy that used insect venom and also with results of a placebo. After six to ten weeks of immunization, allergic reactions to stings occurred in seven of twelve patients treated with the placebo, seven of twelve treated with crushed-body extract, and one of eighteen treated with the venom.

① A new treatment for people allergic to bee stings
② A more effective method of preventing bee stings
③ The use of placebos in treating hypersensitive patients
④ Bee venom causing fatal reactions in hypersensitive patients

【Notes】 immunize 면역력을 갖게 하다 venom 독 crush 으깨다 fatal 치명적인 sting reaction 벌침 반응 hypersensitive 과민한 a report released recently 최근에 발표된 보고서 serum 혈청 adverse reaction 역반응, 부작용 injection 주사 immunotherapy 면역요법 placebo 속임약, 위약 extract 추출물

문 17. 다음 글을 요약한 문장에서 빈칸 ㉠, ㉡에 들어갈 가장 적절한 것은?

Look at the following list of numbers: 4, 8, 5, 3, 9, 7, 6. Read them out loud and memorize that sequence. If you speak English, you have about a 50 percent chance of remembering that perfectly. If you're Chinese, though, you're almost certain to get it right every time. This is because pronouncing them in Chinese takes shorter time. In addition, the number-naming systems are in Western and Asian languages. In English, for example, they say fourteen and sixteen, so one might expect that they would also say oneteen and twoteen. But they don't. The number system in English is irregular. In contrast, Asians have logical counting systems. Those differences mean that Asian children learn to count much faster and perform basic functions better than Western children.

Being good at ㉠___________ may be rooted in the different ㉡___________ systems.

㉠	㉡
① pronunciations	counting
② mathematics	language
③ languages	name
④ logic	culture

【Notes】 sequence 순서 get it right 올바르게 하다 number-naming system 숫자에 이름을 붙이는 체계 in contrast 대조적으로

문 18. 다음 글의 요지로 가장 적절한 것은?

It's long been part of folk wisdom that birth order strongly affects personality, intelligence and achievement. However, most of the research claiming that firstborns are radically different from other children has been discredited, and it now seems that any effects of birth order on intelligence or personality will likely be washed out by all the other influences in a person's life. In fact, the belief in the permanent impact of birth order, according to Toni Falbo, a social psychologist at the University of Texas at Austin, comes from the psychological theory that your personality is fixed by the time you're six. That assumption simply is incorrect. The better, later and larger studies are less likely to find birth order a useful predictor of anything. When two Swiss social scientists, Cecile Ernst and Jules Angst, reviewed 1,500 studies a few years ago they concluded that "birth order differences in personality are nonexistent in our sample. In particular, there is no evidence for a firstborn personality."

① A firstborn child is kind to other people.
② Birth order influences a person's intelligence.
③ An elder brother's personality is different from that of his younger brother.
④ Birth order has nothing to do with personality.

【Notes】 folk wisdom 속설, 민중의 지혜 birth order 출생 순서 personality 인격, 성격 achievement 업적, 성취 claim 주장하다 radically 근본적으로 discredit 불신하다, 신용을 손상시키다 wash out 씻어 내다, 없애다 permanent 영원한 social psychologist 사회 심리학자 psychological 심리학의 assumption 가정, 전제 predictor 예측 변수 nonexistent 존재하지 않는 evidence 증거

문 19. 다음 글의 제목으로 가장 적절한 것은?

Late one night, Catherine Ryan Hyde was driving in Los Angeles. In a dangerous neighborhood, her car caught on fire. She got out. Three men ran toward her. She immediately felt afraid of them.

They didn't hurt her, though. They put out the fire and called the fire department. When she turned to thank them, they were gone. Years later, that event became the subject of her novel called Pay It Forward. She never forgot that event. In the book, a teacher asks his students to "think of an idea for world change and put it into action." A boy named Trevor suggested doing kind acts for others. They used his ideas. Trevor's idea works like this. Someone chooses three people and does something nice for each one. In return, the recipients of that favor must do favors for three more people. In 2000, the novel inspired a movie.

① The Kindness of Strangers
② A Trauma in Early Childhood
③ A Movie which Influences Real Life
④ An Unintended Violation of Someone's Idea

【Notes】 put out the fire 불을 끄다 fire department 소방서 put into action 실행하다 in return 보답으로 recipient 수혜자, 받는 사람 inspire 영감을 주다, 고무시키다 trauma 정신적 외상[충격] unintended 의도되지 않은 violation 침해, 위반

문 20. 주어진 문장이 들어갈 위치로 가장 적절한 것은?

[He knew, though, he would never become an Olympic runner, so he looked for other sports that he could play.]

Many people have faced great obstacles in their lives but have found ways to overcome and actually benefit from these obstacles. For example, Greg Barton, the 1984, 1988, and 1992 U.S. Olympic medalist in kayaking, was born with a serious disability. (A) He had deformed feet, his toes pointed inward, and as a result, he could not walk easily. Even after a series of operations, he still had limited mobility. (B) Even so, Greg was never defeated. First, he taught himself to walk, and even to run. Then, he competed in his high school running team. (C) Happily, he discovered kayaking, a perfect sport for him because it required minimal leg and foot muscles. Using his upper body strength, he was able to master the sport. (D) Finally, after many years of training and perseverance, Greg made the 1984 Olympic team.

① A ② B
③ C ④ D

【Notes】 face 직면하다 obstacle 장애물 overcome 극복하다 benefit 이득을 보다 disability 장애 deformed 기형의 toe 발가락 his toes pointed inward 그의 발가락들은 안쪽으로 굽었다 as a result 그 결과 operation 수술 mobility 기동성, 이동성 defeated 좌절한, 패배한 minimal 최소한의 perseverance 인내

정답

11 ②	12 ④	13 ②	14 ④	15 ②
16 ①	17 ②	18 ④	19 ①	20 ③

2012년 국가직 9급 영어 독해문제

■ 다음 글의 제목으로 가장 적절한 것을 고르시오. [문 11~문 12]

문 11.

Taking time to clear your mind through meditation can boost your spirits and your immunity. Psychologist, Richard Davidson, gave 40 people a flu vaccine. Half of them followed a regular meditation schedule for an hour a day, six days a week. The others just got the vaccine. After eight weeks, the meditators had higher levels of flu-fighting antibodies than those who didn't meditate. They were also better able to deal with stress and had increased activity in the area of the brain linked to good moods. "Meditation produces measurable biological changes in the brain and body," says Davidson. "It is safe and can be of great benefit."

① Relationship between Flu Vaccine and Antibody
② Process of Forming Immune System
③ Length of Meditation and Stress
④ Positive Effects of Meditation

【Notes】 take time 시간[짬]을 내다, 시간이 걸리다 clear mind 정신을 맑게 하다 spirits 정신, 활기 immunity 면역성, 면역력 meditation 명상 psychologist 심리학자 flu vaccine 독감 백신 meditator 명상하는 사람 flu-fighting antibody 독감과 싸우는 항체 deal with 다루다 measurable 주목할 만한, 눈에 띄는, 측정 가능한 biological change 생물학적 변화 of great benefit 크게 도움이 되는[이로운] immune system 면역체계 positive effect 긍정적인 효과

문 12.

Active listeners listen with their ears, their eyes, and their mind. They take in the objective information by listening to the literal words that are spoken. But every spoken message contains more than words. Speakers also communicate subjective information–their feelings and emotions–through other vocal sounds and nonverbal signals. These include verbal intonations such as loudness, emphasis, hesitations, voice movements, facial expressions, body posture, and hand gestures. By listening for feelings and emotions as well as for literal words, you can grasp the total meaning behind the speaker's message. Yet, no matter how good you become at listening for total meaning, there still remains the potential for misunderstanding. That's why the active listener verifies completeness by asking questions. The use of questions can uncover distortions and clarify misunderstandings.

① Methods of Good Listening
② Verbal Skills for Effective Listening
③ Importance of Asking Questions in Listening
④ Relationship between Listening and Emotions

【Notes】 active listener 적극적으로 듣는 사람 take in 받아들이다 objective information 객관적인 정보 literal 문자 그대로의, 과장이 없는, 사실에 충실한 subjective information 주관적인 정보 vocal 목소리의, 발성의 vocal sound 성음, cf. vocal music 성악 nonverbal signal 비언어적인 신호 verbal 언어적인 intonation 억양 emphasis 강조 hesitation 주저 voice movement 목소리의 변동 facial expression 얼굴 표정 posture 자세 hand gesture 손동작, 손짓 grasp 파악하다, 잡다 potential 잠재성, 가능성 verify 확인하다, 입증하다, 검증하다 uncover 드러내다 distortion 왜곡 clarify 분명하게 하다, 투명하게 하다

문 13. 다음 글의 요지로 가장 적절한 것은?

No matter how satisfying our work is, it is a mistake to rely on work as our only source of satisfaction. Just as humans need a varied diet to supply a variety of needed vitamins and minerals to maintain health, so we need a varied diet of activities that can supply a sense of enjoyment and satisfaction. Some experts suggest that one can start by making an inventory–a list of the things you enjoy doing, your talents and interests, and even new things that you think you might enjoy if you tried them. It may be gardening, cooking, a sport, learning a new language, or volunteer work. If you shift your interest and attention to other activities for a while, eventually the cycle will swing again, and you can return to your work with renewed interest and enthusiasm.

① 다양한 비타민 섭취를 통해 건강한 삶을 유지할 수 있다.
② 성공적인 직장 생활은 일 자체를 즐김으로써 이루어진다.
③ 만족스러운 삶을 위해서는 일 외의 다양한 활동이 필요하다.
④ 직장과 가정 생활의 조화가 업무 효율성을 높이는 지름길이다.

【Notes】 rely on 의지하다 varied 다양한 a variety of 다양한 as~, so… ~하듯이 (그렇게) …한다 As you sow, so shall you reap. (뿌린 것과 마찬가지로 거둘 것이다. 자업자득) As bees love sweetness, so flies love rottenness. (꿀벌이 단 것을 좋아하듯이 파리는 썩은 것을 좋아한다.) inventory 목록, 재고 목록, 물품 목록, 조사 일람표 shift 바꾸다, 전환하다 eventually 결국에는 swing again 다시 돌아오다 renewed 새로워진

■ 밑줄 친 부분에 들어갈 표현으로 가장 적절한 것을 고르시오. [문 14~문 16]

문 14.

Oscar Wilde once wrote, "In this world there are only two tragedies. One is not getting what one wants, and the other is getting it." He was trying to warn us that no matter how hard we work at being successful, success won't satisfy us. By the time we get there, having sacrificed so much on the altar of being successful, we will realize that success was not what we wanted. People who have money and power know something that you and I do not know and might not believe even when we are told. Money and power do not satisfy that unnameable hunger in the soul. Even the rich and powerful find themselves yearning for something more. We read about the family problems of the rich and famous, we see fictionalized conflicts on television, but we never get the message. Instead, we keep thinking that __________ __________________________________.

① if we had what they have, we would be happy
② the lives of the rich and powerful entirely depend on luck
③ though we have worked hard, we are not successful in life
④ money and power cannot replace valuable things in our life

【Notes】 sacrifice 희생하다, 희생시키다 altar 제단 unnameable 이름 붙일 수 없는 yearn 갈망하다 fictionalized conflict 허구로 만들어진 갈등 entirely 전적으로 replace 대체하다

문 15.

Farmland provides more than just crops for human and animal consumption. It provides raw materials used to make building materials, paper, and fuels. The lives of many people also revolve around farming, which gives them the driving force that keeps them alive. Farmland, however, has slowly been eliminated by urban sprawl, in which people in urban areas spread into and take over rural areas. In the near future, urban sprawl is going to leave us with a shortage of natural resources. We need to be aware of the potential risks in future years and ___________________.

① move from urban areas to rural areas for living in farmland
② start to restrict urban sprawl and unnecessary development
③ limit farming in rural areas and development in urban areas
④ accelerate the development of natural resources in a short period

【Notes】 farmland 농지 crop 농작물 consumption 소비 raw material 원료 building material 건축 자재 fuel 연료 revolve around ~주위에서 맴돌다 driving force 추진력 eliminate 제거하다 urban 도시의 sprawl 무질서한 확산, 무질서하게 뻗어 나간 도시 외곽 지역 rural 시골의 spread 퍼지다 take over 인수하다, 차지하다 shortage of natural resources 천연 자원의 부족 potential risk 잠재적인 위험 restrict 제한하다 accelerate 가속하다

문 16.

There's a company based in London, Great Britain, that offers a unique service: You can hire people to wait in line for you. Of course there's a fee. The "waiters" will queue up for anything from concert tickets, to passports, to a line for a driver's license.

The company says it has done some research showing that people in Britain spent about a year of their entire lives waiting in lines. Some people just don't want to spend time doing that. How much does the waiting service cost? Twenty nine dollars an hour. The company so far has eighty employees, most of them recruited from the long-term unemployed because "It's a job that doesn't require a lot of skill or experience." The one thing it does require is __________.

① creativity ② patience
③ practice ④ license

【Notes】 unique 독특한 wait in line 줄을 서서 기다리다 fee 요금 queue up 줄을 서다, 줄을 서서 대기하다 so far 지금까지 recruit 채용하다 the long-term unemployed 장기 실업자들

문 17. 다음 글의 내용과 일치하지 않는 것은?

Britain, the biggest single beneficiary of the first age of globalization, was unlikely to gain much from its end. In the 1920s the old and tested policies no longer seemed to work. Paying for World War I had let to a tenfold increase in the national debt. Just paying the interest on that debt consumed close to half of total central government spending by the mid-1920s. The assumption that the budget should nevertheless be balanced meant that public finance was dominated by transfers from income tax-payers to bondholders. The increased power of the trade unions during and after the war not only intensified industrial strife but also meant that wage cuts were slower than price cuts. Rising real wages led to unemployment: during the Depression year of 1932 nearly three million people, close to a quarter of all insured workers, were out of work.

① 영국은 세계화 초기에 가장 큰 수혜를 입은 나라였으나, 1920년대에 과거 정책들은 효과를 발휘하지 못했던 듯하다.
② 제1차 세계대전 당시 진 빚에 대한 영국의 이자지출은 1920년대 중반까지 중앙정부 예산지출의 약 10%를 잠식했다.
③ 전쟁 중 그리고 전쟁 후 노동조합의 커진 힘은 영국에서의 노동쟁의를 격렬하게 만들었다.
④ 대공황 해인 1932년에 영국의 실업자 수는 보험가입 노동자의 25%에 육박했다.

【Notes】 beneficiary 수혜자, 수익자 tested policies 검증된 정책들 tenfold 10배 national debt 국가의 부채[채무] consume 소모하다, 소비하다 assumption 가정 budget 예산 nevertheless 그럼에도 불구하고 public finance 공공 재정 dominate 지배하다 transfers 이전 income tax-payer 소득 납세자 bondholder 채권소지자 trade union 노동조합 intensify 강화하다 strife 투쟁 wage cut 임금 삭감 real wage 실질 임금 unemployment 임금 the Depression 대공황 insured worker 보험에 가입된 근로자 out of work 실직된

문 18. 다음 글에서 언급되고 있지 않은 것은?

Professor Taylor, who wrote "What are Children for?," believes that the status of fatherhood has been affected by modern life. "Fathers have moved farther away from their children than ever before," he says. "In the past, sons looked to their father, emulating his job and wisdom. Now, however, fathers have nothing for their children to inherit. The world is changing too quickly, and instead of sitting at their father's feet listening to stories about the world, children are closed up in their own rooms on the Internet, finding out about it first. It is difficult to redefine the role of father. There is nothing obvious for him to do or be."

① Modern life has influenced the role and the position of fathers.
② In the past, sons imitated their fathers' job, depending on their fathers.
③ Now fathers serve as a sole source of providing information for their sons.
④ These days fathers are not certain of what role to assume for their sons.

【Notes】 status 지위 fatherhood 아버지임, 아버지인 것, 아버지가 되어 있는 것 look to 의존하다, 기대하다 emulate 흉내 내다, 모방하다 inherit 상속받다 redefine 재정의하다 obvious 명백한, 분명한 sole 유일한 assume 맡다, 가정하다

문 19. 다음 문장이 들어갈 위치로 가장 적절한 것은?

[Not even the bedrooms were private.]

The growing individualism showed itself in a desire for privacy. (A) In the seventeenth century middle-class and wealthier families were served by servants, who listened to their conversation as they ate. (B) They lived in rooms that led one to another, usually through wide double doors. (C) But in the eighteenth century families began to eat alone, preferring to serve themselves than to have servants listening to everything they had to say. (D) They also rebuilt the insides of their homes, putting in corridors, so that every person in the family had their own private bedroom.

① A ② B
③ C ④ D

【Notes】 individualism 개인주의 privacy 사생활 serve oneself 스스로 하다 put in 설치하다 corridor 복도

문 20. 다음 문장 뒤에 들어갈 글의 순서로 가장 적절한 것은?

[Once, there was a little boy who had a bad temper. His father gave him a bag of nails and told him that every time he lost his temper, he must hammer a nail into the back of the fence.]

(A) The father took his son by the hand and led him to the fence. He said, "You have done well, my son, but look at the holes in the fence. The fence will never be the same. When you say things in anger, they leave a scar just like this one."
(B) He told his father about it and the father suggested that the boy now pull out one nail for each day that he was able to hold his temper. The days passed and the young boy was finally able to tell his father that all the nails were gone.
(C) The first day the boy had driven six nails into the fence. Over the next few weeks, as he learned to control his anger, the number of nails hammered daily gradually dwindled. Finally the day came when the boy didn't lose his temper at all.

① (B)–(A)–(C)　　② (B)–(C)–(A)
③ (C)–(A)–(B)　　④ (C)–(B)–(A)

【Notes】 temper 기질, 성질　nail 못　lose one's temper 화나다　hammer 망치질 하다　scar 상처　pull out 뽑다　hold one's temper 화를 참다　dwindle 줄어들다

정답

11 ④	12 ①	13 ③	14 ①	15 ②
16 ②	17 ②	18 ③	19 ③	20 ④

2011년 국가직 9급 영어 독해문제

문 11. 밑줄 친 부분에 들어갈 표현으로 가장 적절한 것은?

Some people give up the moment an obstacle is placed in front of them. Some people doggedly continue to pursue a goal even after years of frustration and failure. What is the difference between these two people? Those who feel they are not responsible for choosing their goals and pursing them tend to believe that results are arbitrary. To them, it does not matter how hard you try or how talented you are. Being successful is all a matter of luck. Those who persevere, __________ , recognize that they are ultimately responsible not just for pursuing their goals, but for setting them. To them, what you do matters, and giving up for no reasons does not seem very attractive.

① however ② moreover

③ likewise ④ therefore

【Notes】 obstacle 장애물 doggedly 완강하게, 악착같이 frustration 좌절 pursue 추구하다 arbitrary 임의적인 persevere 참다, 견디다 ultimately 궁극적으로 moreover 게다가 likewise 마찬가지로

■ 다음 글의 빈칸에 들어갈 적절한 것은? [문 12~문 13]

문 12.

If you are at the seaside, and you take an old, dull, brown penny and rub it hard for a minute or two with handfuls of wet sand, the penny will come out a bright gold colour, looking as clean and new as the day it was made. Now poetry has the same effect on words as wet sand on pennies. In what seems almost a miraculous way, it brightens up words that looked dull and ordinary. Thus, poetry is perpetually ______________________________.

① cultivating your mind
② recreating language
③ beautifying the nature
④ discovering the unknown universe

【Notes】 seaside 바닷가 dull 흐릿한, 지루한, 무딘 rub 문지르다 come out 드러나다 poetry 시 miraculous 기적적인 brighten up 빛나게 하다 perpetually 영원히 cultivate (교양 등을)함양하다, 세련되게 하다 recreate 재창조하다 beautify 미화하다

문 13.

One way to accelerate the flow of new ideas is to be put in difficult situations where you're likely to fail. When we fail to do something, we feel frustrated and we begin trying out other behaviors. Many ideas compete vigorously, greatly enhancing the creative process. Say you start to turn a doorknob that has always turned easily. It won't move. You turn the knob harder. Then you pull it up or push it down. Maybe you wiggle it. Eventually, you may shove or kick the door. These efforts from established behaviors will probably lead to new solutions. Creativity is an extension of ______________________.

① how long you think
② how you operate tools
③ what you already know
④ what your personality is

【Notes】 accelerate 가속화하다 try out 시도하다 compete 경쟁하다 vigorously 활기차게 enhance 향상시키다 doorknob 문의 손잡이 wiggle 이리저리 흔들다 eventually 결국, 마침내 established 기존의 solution 해결(책) creativity 창의성 extension 확장, 연장 personality 개성, 인격, 성격

■ 밑줄 친 부분에 들어갈 표현으로 가장 적절한 것은? [문 14~문 15]

문 14.

The white-tailed deer was one of the first animals to be protected by federal legislation. But as it turns out, unlike the passenger pigeon, white-tailed deer were not in much need of _____________. They have proven to be highly adaptable creatures, and their population has not diminished despite the loss of wooded areas. Like squirrels and robins, white-tailed deer have adapted quite nicely to life on the edge of suburbia. In fact, they are happy to supplement their regular diets with fruits and vegetables from gardens. In addition, many homeowners are fond of these gentle creatures and put out blocks of deer food that help the animals make it through harsh winters.

① evolution ② extinction
③ protection ④ habitat

【Notes】 white-tailed 흰 꼬리가 달린 federal 연방의 legislation 입법 passenger pigeon 나그네 비둘기 adaptable 적응력이 있는 population 개체수, 인구 diminish 감소하다 squirrel 다람쥐 robin 개똥지빠귀 adapt 적응하다 edge 가장자리 suburbia 교외 supplement 보충하다 blocks of deer food 사슴의 먹이 덩어리 make it through 견디다, 지내다 evolution 진화 extinction 멸종 habitat 서식지

문 15.

Fundamental happiness depends more than anything else upon what may be called a friendly interest in persons and things. The kind [of interest in persons] that makes for happiness is the kind that likes to observe people and finds pleasure in their individual traits, that wishes to afford scope for the interests and pleasures of those with whom it is brought into contact without desiring to acquire power over them or to secure their enthusiastic admiration. The person whose attitude towards ________ is genuinely of this kind will be a source of happiness and a recipient of reciprocal kindness. To like many people spontaneously and without effort is perhaps the greatest of all sources of personal happiness.

① others ② things
③ pleasure ④ happiness

【Notes】 fundamental 근본적인 make for ~을 향해 나아가다 trait 특성 afford 부여하다 scope 여지, 기회, 범위 acquire 획득하다 secure 확보하다 enthusiastic 열정적인 admiration 감탄, 찬사 genuinely 진정으로 recipient 수혜자, 수령자 reciprocal 상호적인 spontaneously 자발적으로

문 16. 다음 글의 제목으로 가장 적합한 것은?

As the weather changes, joggers, like some exotic species of bird, begin to molt. On frigid winter days, when the wind and snow sweep down from Canada, the joggers wear heavy layers of clothes. Ski masks cover their faces, woolen caps hide their hair, and heavy scarves are wrapped snugly around their necks. Gradually, however, the weather warms, and the bulky layers of clothes are peeled away. First, lightweight jogging suits in terry cloth, velour, and even plastic dot the paths in parks and along streets. As spring changes to summer, winter-pale legs and arms begin to appear, covered only partially by shorts and T-shirts.

① Fashionable clothes in Canada
② The latest fashion in jogging suits
③ How to choose a proper jogging suit
④ The effect of weather on joggers' fashion

【Notes】 jogger 조깅하는 사람 exotic 이국적인 species 종 molt (새가)털갈이하다 frigid 몹시 추운 sweep down 휩쓸며 내려오다 layer 층 layers of clothes 겹겹의 옷 wrap 감싸다 snugly 포근하게 bulky 부피가 큰 peel 껍질을 벗기다 terry cloth 테리직물(타월처럼 수분 흡수가 잘 되도록 짠 천) velour 벨루어(실크나 면직물을 벨벳처럼 만든 것) dot 여기저기 흩어져 나타나다 winter-pale 겨울 동안 창백해진 shorts 반바지 proper 적절한

문 17. 다음 글의 빈칸에 들어갈 가장 적절한 것은?

Many sports help to (A) one's reactions and dexterity. Sports can also improve one's process of thought. Be sure to judge whether or not the level of exercise activity is appropriate as you are participating in the sport. Being wise about the health benefits of sports will ensure a healthy lifestyle. Regular exercise will help one's personality to be positive. If you (B) what has been suggested, you will have favorable results.

	(A)	(B)
①	control	complement
②	enhance	complement
③	control	implement
④	enhance	implement

【Notes】 reaction 반응 dexterity 기민성, (손이나 머리를 쓰는)재주 appropriate 적절한 health benefit 건강상의 이점 ensure 보장하다 positive 긍정적인 favorable 우호적인, 이로운 complement 보충하다, 보완하다 enhance 높이다, 고양하다 implement 실행하다

문 18. 다음 글에서 전체적인 흐름과 관계없는 문장은?

According to government figures, the preponderance of jobs in the next century will be in service-related fields, such as health and business. ①Jobs will also be plentiful in technical fields and in retail establishments, such as stores and restaurants. ② The expansion in these fields is due to several factors: an aging population, numerous technical breakthroughs, and our changing lifestyles. ③ However, people still prefer the traditional types of jobs which will be highly-paid in the future. ④ So the highest-paying jobs will go to people with degrees in science, computers, engineering, and health care.

【Notes】 government figures 정부가 발표하는 수치들 preponderance 우세, 다수 plentiful 풍부한 establishment 업체, 회사, 설립 retail establishment 소매업체 expansion 확장, 팽창 be due to~ 때문이다, ~에 기인한다 aging population 노령화 인구, 고령인구 breakthrough 돌파, 획기적 발전 highly-paid 높은 임금을 받는 degree 학위, 정도 engineering 공학 health care 의료 서비스

문 19. 다음 문장이 들어갈 위치로 가장 적절한 것은?

[All you have to do is this: When you feel yourself getting angry, take a long, deep breath, and as you do, say the number one to yourself.]

When I was growing up, my father used to count out loud to ten when he was angry with my sisters and me. (A) It was a strategy he used to cool down before deciding what to do next. (B) I've improved this strategy by incorporating the use of the breath. (C) Then, relax your entire body as you breathe out. (D) What you are doing here is clearing your mind with a mini version of a meditation exercise. The combination of counting and breathing is so relaxing that it's almost impossible to remain angry once you are finished.

① A　　② B
③ C　　④ D

【Notes】 count out 숫자를 세다 strategy 전략 cool down 진정하다 incorporate 포함시키다, 연합하다 relax 이완시키다, 긴장을 풀다 breathe out 숨을 내쉬다 clear 제거하다, 없애다 clear one's mind 마음을 비우다 mini version 축소판, 소형 버전 meditation exercise 명상 훈련 combination 결합, 조합

문 20. 다음 글의 빈칸에 들어갈 가장 적절한 것은?

Character is a respect for human beings and the right to interpret experience differently. Character admits self-interest as a natural trait, but pins its faith on man's hesitant but heartening instinct to understand and support others. Character is allergic to tyranny, irritable with ignorance and always open to improvement. Character implies the ability to laugh wholeheartedly and weep unashamedly. Character is, above all, a tremendous humility before the facts — an automatic alliance with truth even when that truth is bitter medicine.
A quality of character not mentioned by the author is _________.

① freedom ② patience
③ sympathy ④ humbleness

【Notes】 character 인격, 성격, 특징 interpret 해석하다 self-interest 이기심, 자신의 이익 trait 특성 natural trait 천성, 타고난 특성 pin one's faith on~ ~을 믿다 hesitant 망설이는, 주저하는 heartening 용기를 북돋아 주는 instinct 본능 allergic to ~에 알레르기가 있는(싫어하는) tyranny 폭정, 폭압 irritable with ~을 참을 수 없는, ~에 화를 내는 open to ~에 개방적인, ~을 받아들이는 imply 암시하다 wholeheartedly 진심으로 unashamedly 부끄러워하지 않고 tremendous 거대한, 엄청난 humility 겸손 alliance 결합, 동맹 bitter 쓴 quality 특징, 특질 patience 인내 sympathy 동정, 공감 humbleness 겸손함

정답

11 ①	12 ②	13 ③	14 ③	15 ①
16 ④	17 ④	18 ③	19 ③	20 ②

2010년 국가직 9급 영어 독해문제

문 2. 다음 글에서 전체적인 흐름과 관계없는 문장은?

Some students make the mistake of thinking that mathematics consists solely of solving problems by means of formulas and rules. ① To become successful problem solvers, however, they have to appreciate the theory, recognizing the logical structure and reasoning behind the mathematical methods. ② To do so requires a precision of understanding the exact meaning of a mathematical statement and of expressing thoughts with accuracy and clarity. ③ However, this precision cannot be achieved without real appreciation of the subtleties of language. ④ In fact, anyone can advance much beyond mere problem solving tasks without manipulating mathematical formulas and rules. That is, superior ability in the use of language is a prerequisite to become successful problem solvers.

【Notes】 consist of ~으로 구성되다, ~으로 이루어지다 solely 오로지, 단지 by means of ~에 의해, ~을 사용하여 formula 공식 appreciate 이해하다, 인식하다, 감사하다 recognize 인식하다 clarity 명쾌함, 분명함 precision 정확, 정밀성 subtlety 미묘함 advance 진보하다, 나아가다 manipulate 조작하다, 교묘하게 다루다 prerequisite 필수요건, 전제조건

문 3. 다음 글의 밑줄 친 부분의 의미로 가장 적절한 것은?

An old woman came into her doctor's office and confessed to an embarrassing problem. "I fart all the time, Doctor Johnson, but they're soundless, and they have no odor. In fact, since I've been here, I've farted no less than twenty times. What can I do?" "Here's a prescription, Mrs. Harris. Take these pills three times a day for seven days and come back and see me in a week." Next week in upset Mrs. Harris marched into Dr. Johnson's office. "Doctor, I don't know what was in those pills, but the problem is worse! I'm farting just as much, but now they smell terrible! What do you have to say for yourself?" "Calm down, Mrs. Harris," said the doctor soothingly. "Now that we've fixed your sinuses, we'll work on your <u>other</u> sense!"

① oral ② sixth
③ visual ④ auditory

【Notes】 confess 고백하다 embarrassing 당혹감을 주는, 난처한 fart 방귀(를 뀌다)(break wind) odor 냄새, 악취 prescription 처방전 pill 알약 upset 화가 난, 속상한, 분노 march 행진하다, 행군하듯 걷다 terrible 고약한, 지독한 say for oneself 변명하다, 해명하다 soothingly 달래듯이, 진정시키듯이 sinus 코 안쪽으로 이어지는 구멍 work on ~에 대해 작업하다, 착수하다, 공들이다 oral 입의, 구두의 sixth sense 육감 visual 시각의 auditory 청각의

■ 다음 글의 제목으로 가장 적절한 것을 고르시오. [문 4~문 5]

문 4.

The sales talk of the old-fashioned businessman was essentially rational. He knew his merchandise, he knew the needs of the customer, and on the basis of this knowledge he tried to sell. To be sure his sales talk was not entirely objective and he used persuasion as much as he could; yet, in order to be efficient, it had to be a rather rational and sensible kind of talk. A vast sector of modern advertising is different; it does not appeal to reason but to emotion; like any other kind of hypnoid suggestion, it tries to impress its customers emotionally and then make them submit intellectually. This type of advertising impresses the customers by all sorts of means such as the repetition of the same formula again and again. All these methods are essentially irrational; they have nothing to do with the qualities of the merchandise, and they suppress and kill the critical capacities of the customers.

① Significance of the Sales Talk
② Change in Advertising Methods
③ Critical Capacities of the Customers
④ Importance of Emotional Advertising Slogans

【Notes】 sales talk 구매 권유, 판매를 위한 말 old-fashioned 구식의, 전통적인 방식의 essentially 본질적으로 rational 합리적인 merchandise 상품 entirely 전적으로 objective 목표, 객관적인 rather 꽤, 상당히, 오히려, 차라리 sensible 현명한 vast 엄청난, 막대한 hypnoid 최면의, 최면상태 submit 복종하다, 제출하다 suppress 억누르다, 억압하다 critical 중요한, 비평의 capacity 수용력, 능력, 역량 slogan 슬로건, 구호

문 5.

Many of the greatest economic evils of our time are the fruits of risk, uncertainty, and ignorance. It is because particular individuals, fortunate in situation or in abilities, are able to take advantage of uncertainty and ignorance, and also because for the same reason big business is often a lottery, that great inequalities of wealth come about. And these same factors are also the cause of the unemployment of labor, or the disappointment of reasonable business expectations, and of the impairment of efficiency and production. Yet the cure lies outside of the operations of individuals. I believe that the cure for these things is partly to be sought in the deliberate control of the currency and of credit by a central institution, and partly in the collection and dissemination of data relating to the business situation including the full publicity, by law if necessary, of all business facts which it is useful to know. Even if these measures prove insufficient, they will furnish us with better knowledge than we have now for taking the next step.

① Economic Evils and Money-oriented Society
② Economic Evils and Solutions to Them
③ Role of the Central Institution
④ Origins of Economic Evils

【Notes】 evil 악 uncertainty 불확실성 ignorance 무지 take advantage of ~을 이용하다 lottery 복권 inequality 불평등, 불균형 come about 발생하다 unemployment 실직, 실업상태 impairment 훼손, 손상, 장애 efficiency 효율 cure 치유, 구제책 deliberate 신중한, 고의의 currency 통화, 화폐 credit 신용, 증명 dissemination 배포, 보급, 파종 publicity 광고 measure 수단, 대책, 대책 insufficient 불충분한 money-oriented 돈을 지향하는 Central Institution 중앙기관

■ 다음 글의 빈칸에 들어갈 가장 적절한 것을 고르시오. [문 13~문 14]

문 13.

One custom that is common at weddings in the United States is throwing rice at the bride and groom as they leave the place where the wedding ceremony has just been held. No one knows exactly why people throw rice. One explanation is that the rice assures that the couple will have many children. If this is true, then the custom is not always a good one now because ________________.

① a lot of couples do not want many children
② many people are pleased about it
③ many couples go on honeymoon the next day
④ it is unreasonable to clear away rice after the ceremony

【Notes】 bride 신부 groom 신랑 wedding ceremony 결혼식 assure 보장하다 unreasonable 불합리한 clear away 치우다

문 14.

"There is a huge drive to deep right," the announcer cries. His voice shrills with excitement, "It's high, it's far, it's going, going ..., gone." As the batter triumphantly circles the bases, the crowd cheers politely. However, their suspicion is nearly as audible as their pleasure. Where did the muscles come from? Was the homer legitimate? Should it count in this particular game? And what about the sport's records? Due to the widespread use in sports of anabolic steroids, the lords of the game must accept that the very integrity of the game is ________________.

These steroids were developed originally to help cancer patients. They promote weight gain and increase muscle mass. In recent years, athletes have taken them hoping to improve their performance on the playing field. The problem with this is two-fold. First, steroid use gives one group of athletes an unfair advantage. Second, steroid users incur a great risk of psychological and physical side effects.

① under a ban ② in abundance
③ at stake ④ in control

【Notes】 huge 거대한, 엄청난 drive 강타, 숏, 샷 shrill 날카로운 소리를 내다 batter 타자 triumphantly 의기양양하게 circle 일주하다, 원을 그리며 돌다 crowd 군중 suspicion 의심, 혐의 audible 들을 수 있는 homer 홈런 legitimate 합법적인, 정당한 count 인정되다, 계산에 넣다 widespread 널리 퍼진 anabolic 동화작용의 integrity 진실성, 완전성, 청렴 mass 덩어리 athlete 운동선수 unfair 불공정한 incur 초래하다, 발생시키다 psychological 심리적인 physical 육체적인 side effect 부작용 ban 금지 under a ban 금지되어 있는 abundance 풍부 at stake 위험에 처한

■ 다음 글의 내용과 일치하지 않는 것을 고르시오. [문 17~문 18]

문 17.

In the late 20th century, the northern hemisphere experienced its most widespread warmth for 1,200 years, according to the journal Science. The findings support evidence pointing to unprecedented recent warming of the climate linked to greenhouse emissions.

University of East Anglia(UEA) researchers measured changes in fossil shells, tree rings, ice cores and other past temperature records. They also looked at people's diaries from the last 750 years. Timothy Osborn and Keith Briffa of UEA analysed instrument measurements of temperatures from 1856 onwards to establish the geographic extent of recent warming. Then, they compared this data with evidence dating back as far as AD 800. The analysis confirmed periods of significant warmth in the northern hemisphere from AD 890 to 1170 (the so-called "Medieval Warm Period") and for much colder periods from AD 1580 to 1850 (the "Little Ice Age").

① Researchers at UEA examined a variety of materials to check temperature changes.
② The Medieval Warm Period was shorter than the Little Ice Age.
③ The late 20th century is not the first in history that witnessed a temperature change.
④ Greenhouse emissions are considered to be the cause of the recent warming.

【Notes】 hemisphere 반구 northern hemisphere 북반구 unprecedented 전례가 없는 greenhouse 온실 emission 배출, 방출 fossil 화석 shell 껍데기, 조개, 포탄 tree ring 나이테 core 중심, 핵심, 핵 analyse 분석하다 instrument measurements 기계(도구)의 측정치들 geographic 지리학적인 extent 범위, 넓이 date back 거슬러 올라가다 confirm 확인하다 significant 중요한, 의미심장한 Medieval 중세의 Medieval Warm Period 중세 온난기 examine 조사하다 Little Ice Age 소빙기 witness 목격하다

문 18.

Ice wines are becoming increasingly popular across North America. While ice wines have always been fashionable in Western Europe, they were hard to find in North America and often ridiculously expensive. Ice wines are more expensive than other types of wine on account of the temperature requirements to make them. The grapes must be left on the vines until the first frost, after which they are harvested. If the first frost comes too late, the grapes will turn rotten, and the harvest will be lost. Add to that the cost of shipping the wines, and they become rather expensive. However, good quality North American ice wines, produced in California and British Columbia, have recently come onto the market, making ice wines more affordable.

① Specific temperature conditions are required to make ice wines.
② Ice wines used to be difficult to come by in North America.
③ The shipping costs contribute to the high prices of ice wines.
④ North America was well-known for its high quality ice wines.

【Notes】 increasingly 점점 fashionable 유행하는 ridiculously 우스꽝스럽게, 터무니없이 vine 포도나무 frost 서리 rotten 썩은 harvest 수확하다 shipping 선적 affordable 감당할 수 있는, 알맞은 come by 획득하다

문 19. 다음 글의 내용과 일치하는 것은?

The umbrella is so old that no one knows where it came from – it was invented before man learned how to write. But for thousands of years, the umbrella was used only for protection from the sun, rather than from the rain. The word ‘umbrella’, in fact, comes from the Latin word ‘umbra’, which means ‘shade’, and ancient slaves held umbrellas over their masters to give them shade. At the beginning, umbrellas were carried only by women, for they weren't considered ‘manly’ enough to be used by men. It wasn't until about 300 years ago that people began to use waterproof umbrellas in the rain.

① The umbrella was invented after man learned how to write.
② The umbrella was used mainly for protection from the rain.
③ At the beginning, umbrellas were carried only by men.
④ People began to use waterproof umbrellas about 300 years ago.

【Notes】 protection 보호 shade 그늘, 음영 manly 남자다운 waterproof 방수의

문 20. 다음 글을 읽고 아래 문장의 빈칸에 들어갈 가장 적절한 것은?

Euthanasia generally refers to mercy killing, the voluntary ending of the life of someone who is terminally or hopelessly ill. Euthanasia has become a legal, medical and ethical issue over which opinion is divided. Euthanasia can be either active or passive. Active euthanasia means that a physician or other medical personnel takes a deliberate action that will induce death. Passive euthanasia means letting a patient die for lack of treatment or suspending treatment that has begun. A good deal of the controversy about mercy killing stems from the decision-making process. Who decides if a patient is to die? This issue had not been established legally in the United States. The matter is left to state law, which usually allows the physician in charge to suggest the option of death to a patient's relatives, especially if the patient is brain-dead.

The article suggests that euthanasia should be ______________.

① primarily an ethical issue
② decided by physicians
③ determined by the federal government
④ a controversial issue not to be easily resolved

【Notes】 euthanasia 안락사 refer to 언급하다, 가리키다 mercy 자비 voluntary 자발적인 terminally 말기적으로, 불치병적으로 legal 법적인 ethical 윤리적인 active 적극적인 passive 소극적인 physician 의사 personnel 인력, 인원 medical personnel 의료종사자 deliberate 고의적인, 사려 깊은 induce 초래하다, 유도하다 treatment 치료, 처치 suspend 중지시키다 controversy 논쟁, 논란 stem from ~에서 생겨나다, 유래하다 decision-making 의사결정 establish 확립하다 in charge 담당하고 있는 relative 친척 brain-dead 뇌사한, 뇌사상태인 federal 연방의 controversial 논쟁적인 resolve 해결하다

정답

2 ④	3 ④	4 ②	5 ②	13 ①
14 ③	17 ②	18 ④	19 ④	20 ④

2009년 국가직 9급 영어 독해문제

문 6. 다음 문장에서 추론할 수 있는 것으로 가장 적절한 것은?

Illegible handwriting does not indicate weakness of character, as even a quick glance at the penmanship of George Washington, Franklin D. Roosevelt, or John F. Kennedy reveals.

① A person's handwriting reveals a lot about that person.
② The weakness of character is evident in illegible handwriting.
③ Washington, Roosevelt, and Kennedy all had weak characters.
④ Washington, Roosevelt, and Kennedy all had handwriting that was difficult to read.

【Notes】 illegible 읽기 어려운, 판독하기 어려운 handwriting 필체 character 인격, 성격, 특징 indicate 나타내다, 가리키다 glance 일별, 얼핏 봄 penmanship 필적, 필체 reveal 드러내다, 폭로하다

■ 글의 목적으로 가장 적절한 것을 고르시오. [문 12~문 13]

문 12.

Various fogs are essentially clouds that form at the earth's surface, produced by temperature differences and moisture in the air. As warm, moisture-laden air cools, the amount of moisture that air can contain decreases. Warm air can hold more water vapor than cold air. So if the air is cooled sufficiently it will reach the dew point, at which the moisture begins to gather together out of the air and form water drops, creating fog.

① To explain how fog is formed
② To describe various types of fog
③ To show when warm air affects the fog
④ To point out why moisture works in the air

【Notes】 fog 안개 surface 표면 moisture 습기 laden 잔뜩 실은, 가득한 moisture-laden 습기를 잔뜩 머금고 있는 decrease 감소하다 vapor 수증기 sufficiently 충분히 dew 이슬 dew point 이슬점 water drop 물방울

문 13.

Job-related stress can lead to symptoms of poor physical health such as weight gain, fatigue and illness. Both diet and exercise can contribute to the alleviation of these negative effects of stress. The first step is to eliminate junk food from the diet. Instead of soda or a candy bar, try a piece of fresh fruit. The next step is to make a habit of exercising every day. And you should aim for twenty to thirty minutes of exercise a day. The key is to find a form of exercise that you enjoy. That way, you are more likely to do it every day and will receive the maximum benefit. Both diet and exercise can help you maintain a healthy weight, keep you feeling energized, and protect you from sickness. Then you will be better equipped to deal with the sources of stress at your job.

① To prevent weight gain
② To explain the causes of stress
③ To announce why junk food is bad for the health
④ To explain how to ease the negative effects of stress

【Notes】 job-related 직업과 관련된 symptom 증상, 징후 weight gain 체중증가 fatigue 피로 diet and exercise 식이요법과 운동 contribute to ~에 기여하다, 공헌하다 alleviation 경감, 완화 negative effect 부정적인 효과 eliminate 제거하다 soda 탄산음료 candy bar 막대사탕 benefit 이익 energized 활력이 넘치는 equipped 준비된 ease 경감시키다, 완화하다

문 14. 글의 제목으로 가장 적절한 것은?

Dogs have long had special standing in the medical world. Trained to see for the blind, hear for the deaf and move for the immobilized, dogs have become indispensable companions for people with disabilities. However, dogs appear to be far more than four-legged health care workers. One Japanese study found pet owners made 30 percent fewer visits to doctors. A Melbourne study of 6,000 people showed that owners of dogs and other pets had lower cholesterol, blood pressure and heart attack risk compared with people who didn't have pets. Obviously, the better health of pet owners could be explained by a variety of factors, but many experts believe companion animals improve health at least in part by lowering stress.

① The friendliness of dogs
② The healing power of dogs

③ Dogs as health care workers
④ Japanese dogs for the disabled

【Notes】 special standing 특별한 지위 immobilize 움직이지 못하게 하다 the immobilized 움직이지 못하는 사람들 indispensable 필수 불가결한 companion 동반자, 반려자, 친구 disability 무능력, 신체장애 health care worker 의료요원, 건강관리 일꾼 blood pressure 혈압 heart attack 심장마비, 심근경색 obviously 명백하게 companion animal 반려[동반] 동물 friendliness 우정, 친절 healing power 치유 능력 the disabled 장애인들

문 15. 글의 요지로 가장 적절한 것은?

More and more people are turning away from their doctors and, instead, going to individuals who have no medical training and who sell unproven treatments. They go to quacks to get everything from treatments for colds to cures for cancer. And they are putting themselves in dangerous situations. Many people don't realize how unsafe it is to use unproven treatments. First of all, the treatments usually don't work. They may be harmless, but, if someone uses these products instead of proven treatments, he or she may be harmed. Why? Because during the time the person is using the product, his or her illness may be getting worse. This can even cause the person to die.

① Better train should be given to medical students.
② Alternative medical treatments can be a great help.
③ Don't let yourself become a victim of health fraud.
④ In any case, it is alright to hold off going to a doctor for several days.

【Notes】 turn away from ~로부터 등을 돌리다, 외면하다 unproven treatments 입증되지 않은 치료제들 quack 돌팔이 의사, 사기꾼 alternative medical treatment 대체의학 치료법[치료제] victim 희생물 fraud 사기꾼 alright=all right hold off 연기하다, 지체시키다

■ 빈칸에 들어갈 말로 가장 적절한 것을 고르시오. [문 16~문 18]

문 16.

For the Greeks, beauty was a virtue: a kind of excellence. If it occurred to the Greeks to distinguish between a person's "inside" and "outside," they still expected that inner beauty would be matched by beauty of the other kind. The well-born young Athenians who gathered around Socrates found it quite ______________ that their hero was so intelligent, so brave, so honorable, so seductive—and so ugly.

① natural ② essential
③ paradoxical ④ self-evident

【Notes】 virtue 미덕, 장점 excellence 탁월, 우수성 match 어울리다, 일치하다 well-born 명문 태생의, 양가 출신의 honorable 존경받는, 고매한 seductive 유혹적인, 매력적인 essential 본질적인, 필수적인 paradoxical 역설적인 self-evident 자명한

문 17.

We should behave towards our country as women behave towards the men they love. A loving wife will do anything for her husband except to stop criticizing and trying to improve him. That is the right attitude for a citizen. We should cast the same affectionate but sharp glance at our country. We should love it, but also insist upon telling it all its faults. The dangerous man is not the (A)__________, but the noisy empty (B)__________ who encourages us to indulge in orgies of self-congratulation.

	(A)	(B)
①	critic	patriot
②	citizen	leader
③	extrovert	introvert
④	Democrat	Republican

【Notes】 cast 던지다 affectionate 애정이 깃든, 자애로운 empty 텅 빈 encourage 격려하다 indulge in ~에 빠지다, 탐닉하다 orgy 난장판 파티, 법석대는 주연, 탐닉 self-congratulation 자축 critic 비평가, 비판가 patriot 애국자 extrovert 외향적인 사람 introvert 내향적인 사람 Democrat 민주당원 Republican 공화당원

문 18.

Thank you for inviting me to speak to you today. I'd like to take this opportunity to tell you about our Silver Service activities and why we believe it is important for everyone to be involved in helping the elderly in our community. Did you know that one in every six people over the age of 60 in this community needs some kind of help in his or her home? Those of us who have experience in this kind of work know that our small "investments" in time and effort are nothing compared to the kind of satisfaction and fulfillment we get in return.

The speech is delivered by a ___________.

① salesperson ② fund-raiser
③ pediatrician ④ social worker

【Notes】 be involved in ~에 연루되다, 종사하다 the elderly 노인들 investment 투자 fulfillment 성취 in return 보답으로 deliver a speech 연설하다 salesperson 판매원 fund-raiser 기금 모금자 pediatrician 소아과 의사 social worker 사회 사업가

■ 글의 내용과 일치하지 않는 것을 고르시오. [문 19~문 20]

문 19.

Fortunately, psychologists believe that books can serve as therapeutic tools — or at least as effective adjuncts to professional therapy — to help children come to terms with their parents' divorce. According to educator-counselor Joanne Bernstein, stories that confront life's problems with candor and credibility may provide insights, promote self-examination, and lead to changes in attitude and behavior. One way stories accomplish this is through identification. Reading about the grief and anxiety of others, she explains, can arouse sudden awareness as problems that have not been consciously or completely recognized are allowed to surface. Introduced to characters who share their difficulties, children may feel less alienated and thus freer to discuss and resolve their own plight.

① Children come to terms with their plight by reading.
② Stories are likely to alienate children from their parents.

③ Books are helpful for children whose parents are divorced.
④ Children identify themselves with characters while reading.

【Notes】 psychologist 심리학자 therapeutic 치료의 adjunct 부속물, 부가물, 보좌역 therapy 치료 come to terms with 감당하다, 타협하다 divorce 이혼하다 confront 직면하다 candor 솔직함, 정직 credibility 신용, 진실성 insight 통찰력 promote 증진시키다 self-examination 자기 성찰 accomplish 성취하다, 달성하다 identification 동일시, 일체화, 신분증명 grief 슬픔 anxiety 근심, 걱정 arouse 불러일으키다, 깨우다 consciously 의식적으로 surface 표면화되다, 겉으로 드러나다 alienate 소외시키다, 격리하다, 멀리하다, 소원하게 하다 plight 곤경, 곤란 identify 동일시하다

문 20.

International Import Company
100 East Houston St.
New York, NY 10053
U. S. A.

Farmers Fruit Ltd.
Aghia Paraskevi 19081
Athens, Greece

Dear Sirs,

In reply to your letter dated May 3rd, we thank you for allowing us a special discount. This makes it possible for us to place an order and to expect quite good sales. We have pleasure of enclosing our Order No. 813/BS, and would ask you to return the duplicate to us, duly signed, as an acknowledgement.

Yours faithfully,
Paul Hogan
Enc. Order No. 813/BS

① Order No. 813/BS is being enclosed.
② Paul Hogan is turning the order down.
③ Paul Hogan works for a company in New York.
④ The special discount makes possible an order for products.

【Notes】 place an order 주문하다 enclose 동봉하다 duplicate 사본, 복제물 duly 정식으로, 온당하게 acknowledgement 승인, 인정 Enc.=Enclosed(동봉된), Enclosure(동봉) turn down 거절하다

정답

6 ④	12 ①	13 ④	14 ②	15 ③
16 ③	17 ①	18 ④	19 ②	20 ②

2008년 국가직 9급 영어 독해문제

■ 다음 글의 빈칸에 들어갈 말로 가장 적절한 것을 고르시오. [문 6~문 7]

문 6.

There are two excellent television programs scheduled tonight, but I can see only one of them because they are ____________.

① indisputable ② concurrent
③ matchless ④ indispensable

【Notes】 excellent 탁월한, 뛰어난 indisputable 논란의 여지가 없는 concurrent 동시에 발생하는 matchless 무적의, 비길 데 없는 indispensable 필수불가결의, 없어서는 안되는

문 7.

Icelanders are individualists like Americans. The difference seems to be in a sense of community. Iceland, known as the land of "fire and ice," is about living with opposing forces. It is one of the most active volcanic countries on earth, but has 4,536 square miles of __________ — heat and cold, co-existing. No surprise then that its society can reconcile another set of opposing forces: individualism and the needs of the community.

① glacier ② prairie
③ desert ④ swamp

【Notes】 Icelanders 아이슬란드인들 individualist 개인주의자 a sense of community 공동체 의식 opposing 상반되는 volcanic 화산의, 화산활동의 the most active volcanic countries 화산 활동이 가장 활발한 나라들 co-existing 공존하는 No surprise then that=It is no surprise then that reconcile 조화하다, 화해하다 individualism 개인주의 glacier 빙하 prairie 초원 desert 사막 swamp 늪

문 11. 다음 글의 밑줄 친 부분의 뜻으로 가장 적절한 것은?

When Jesse and Rachel got married, they knew they wanted to live in a traditional nuclear family — mother, father, and biological children. Each of them had come from other family arrangements, and they had decided that a more traditional arrangement was what they wanted. Rachel had been born <u>out of wedlock</u>. Because her parents had never married, she had never met her biological father. Jesse's mother had been widowed. His father's early death made Jesse want to have a large family.

① rich ② illegitimate
③ divorced ④ handicapped

【Notes】 nuclear family 핵가족 biological children 친자식 arrangement 배열, 정돈, 협정, 타협 family arrangement 가족 구조[구성] wedlock 결혼, 결혼상태 out of wedlock 혼외의, 서출의 biological father 생부, 친아버지 widowed 미망인이 된, 홀아비가 된 illegitimate 불법적인, 서출의 divorced 이혼한 handicapped 장애의, 장애자

문 12. 다음 글의 Broom jumping에 관한 내용과 일치하지 않는 것은?

Broom jumping is most famous in the United States as an African-American wedding custom. The broom holds spiritual significance for many African people, representing the beginning of homemaking for a couple. The ritual itself in America was created during slavery. Because slaves could not legally marry, they created their own ways to honor their unions. Broom jumping is a ritual in which the bride and the groom, either at the ceremony or at the reception, signify their entrance into a new life and their creation of a new family by symbolically sweeping away of their former single lives, and jumping over the broom to enter upon a new adventure as wife and husband.

① It is a well-known African-American wedding custom.
② Its origin traces back to the period of slavery in America.
③ It was performed by the slaves who got legally married.
④ It signifies the union of the bride and the groom and their entrance into a new life.

【Notes】 broom 빗자루 wedding custom 결혼 관습 significance 의미, 중요성 homemaking 가정, 가사 ritual 의식 legally 합법적으로, 법적으로 bride 신부 groom 신랑 signify 의미하다, 나타내다 sweep away 쓸어내다, 일소하다 trace back to (유래, 출처, 원인 등이) ~까지 거슬러 올라간다

문 13. 다음 글의 내용과 일치하는 것은?

Upstate New York florist Patricia Woysher has been in the business for forty years. She's sold flowers to tens of thousands of folks in the area and even received one of the best assignments a florist could hope for, decorating the White House for the Christmas season. "I had to take a deep breath. I mean, you see pictures of the place all your life, then one day you're in the Oval Office." Despite the excitement, Patricia's focus remained on her day-to-day concerns. "Doing the White House was exciting and rewarding, but my job is to run my business. I want to have something here that will last forever, that I can pass on to my children."

① Patricia runs a flower shop in the White House.
② Patricia was invited to the White House for a party.
③ Patricia worked for the White House and forgot her daily routines.
④ Patricia hopes to turn her business over to her offspring.

【Notes】 upstate 주의 북부지방, 대도시에서 멀리 떨어진 florist 꽃집 주인 folks 사람들 assignment 임무, 과제, 할당된 일 the Oval Office (백악관의)대통령 집무실 day-to-day 매일 매일의, 일상적인 concerns 관심사들 rewarding 보람이 있는, 보답이 있는 run 운영하다 last 지속하다 pass on 전수하다, 물려주다 daily routines 일상적인 일과, 일상사 turn over 넘겨주다, 물려주다 offspring 자손

문 14. 다음 글의 빈칸 (㉠), (㉡)에 들어갈 말로 적절한 것은?

It is a great nuisance that knowledge cannot be acquired without trouble. It can only be acquired by hard work. It would be fine if we could swallow the powder of profitable information made palatable by the jam of fiction. But the truth is that, so made palatable, we cannot be sure that the powder will be profitable. I suggest to you that the knowledge the novelist imparts is (㉠) and thus (㉡) and it is better not to know a thing at all than to know it in a distorted fashion. If readers wish to inform themselves of the pressing problems of the day, they will do better to read, not novels but the books that specifically deal with them. I suggest to you that it is enough for a novelist to be a good novelist. It is unnecessary for him to be a prophet, a politician or a leader of thought. Fiction is an art and the purpose of art is to please.

(㉠)	(㉡)
① reasonable	believable
② naive	wholesome
③ biased	unreliable
④ impartial	realistic

【Notes】 nuisance 성가신 일, 짜증나는 것 acquire 획득하다 swallow 삼키다 palatable 입맛에 맞는 fiction 허구 impart 주다, 전하다, 알려주다 distort 왜곡하다 pressing 긴급한, 억누르는 prophet 예언자, 선지자 biased 편향된, 편견에 치우친 unreliable 믿을 수 없는, 의지할 수 없는 naive 순진한, 철없는 wholesome 건전한 impartial 공정한 realistic 현실적인

■ 다음 글의 빈칸에 들어갈 말로 가장 적절한 것을 고르시오. [문 15~문 16]

문 15.

Two men were dining together in a restaurant. The first man ordered the food. The second man, who was unaccustomed to eating out, said nothing. When the food arrived, the second man

_______ everything his friend did. When the first man took rice, so did the second. The first man ate a shrimp, and so did the second man. Finally, the first man took a toothpick, and his friend did the same. Later the first man asked his friend how he had enjoyed the meal. The second man answered, "Everything was perfect, except for the last bit. It tasted like bamboo."

① copied ② cursed
③ ignored ④ opposed

【Notes】 unaccustomed 익숙하지 않은 eat out 외식하다 shrimp 새우 toothpick 이쑤시개 bamboo 대나무 copy 모방하다, 복사하다 curse 저주하다 ignore 무시하다 oppose 반대하다

문 16.

A Western-style conversation between two people is like a game of tennis. If I introduce a topic, a conversational ball, I expect you to hit it back. If you agree with me, I don't expect you simply to agree and do nothing more. I expect you to add something — a reason for agreeing, another example, or an elaboration to carry the idea further. But I don't expect you always to agree. I am just as happy if you question me, or challenge me, or completely disagree with me. Whether you agree or disagree, _______.

① you'll be playing the wrong game
② your response will return the ball to me
③ you'll learn a new lesson from your experience
④ your conversation style will differ from the Western style

【Notes】 conversational 대화의 elaboration 정교하게 함, 공들임, 면밀함, 상세한 설명

문 17. 다음 글의 요지로 가장 적절한 것은?

A cause always has an effect, and an effect has a cause. Often, however, in searching for the cause or effect of an act, we jump to conclusions. If John Wilkins, who is big and strong, doesn't go out for the football team, some pupils say, "Wilkins has no courage." Perhaps the real reason is that his parents object, he is behind in his school work and can't afford the time, or he believes that football is not worth playing.

① Easy come, easy go.
② Don't be dejected, take courage.
③ Everybody has his own talent.
④ Don't make a hasty judgment.

【Notes】 effect 결과, 효과 jump to a conclusion 성급하게 결론을 내리다 be behind in one's school work 학업이 뒤처져 있다 afford the time 시간을 낼 여유가 있다 Easy come, easy go. 쉽게 얻으면 쉽게 잃는다. deject 낙담시키다

문 18. 주어진 문장으로 시작하여, 다음 글들을 문맥에 맞게 올바른 순서로 연결한 것은?

[The saying for which I had to find the meaning was: "People who live in glass houses shouldn't throw stones."]

(A) My first guess was that it was about a situation in which those who want to fight should first think about defending themselves from attack. Obviously, a person whose house is made of glass, which is easily broken, should be careful. If you throw a stone, the person at whom you threw the stone could throw it back and smash your house.
(B) I think this is good advice for anyone who is critical of other people.
(C) However, this saying, whose meaning I looked up in a dictionary of English idioms is not really about fighting. It means that you should not criticize others for faults similar to those you have.

① A–C–B ② A–B–C
③ B–C–A ④ C–A–B

【Notes】 smash 박살내다 critical 비판하는, 비판적인 look up (사전을) 찾아보다

문 19. 다음 주어진 문장이 들어갈 곳으로 가장 적절한 것은?

[Such variation, however, was common then with the spelling of many words, not just names.]

William Shakespeare is rightly regarded as one of the world's great writers; yet it would seem that he couldn't spell his own name! (㉠) Samples of his signature that have survived show his name spelled in several different ways. (㉡) Not until the eighteenth century when dictionaries came into use was a single spelling for each word accepted as correct. (ⓒ) A few words, however, escaped being standardized in this way; 'instill' (which can also be spelled 'instil') is one of them. (ⓓ) When a dictionary gives two different spellings of a word, the one given first is preferred.

① ㉠ ② ㉡
③ ㉢ ④ ㉣

【Notes】 variation 변이형, 차이 rightly 마땅히, 바르게, 정당하게 signature 서명 survive 살아남다 standardize 표준화하다 instill 주입하다, 서서히 스며들게 하다

문 20. 다음 글의 제목으로 가장 적절한 것은?

The term home schooling or home tuition, as it is called in England, means educating children at home or in places other than a mainstream setting such as a public or private school. There are many reasons why parents choose home schooling for their children. Some parents are dissatisfied with the quality of education in the public schools. Others do not want their children to have to worry about "peer pressure," or social pressure from friends. They say it may interfere with the child's studies. These parents fear this type of pressure will lead to negative behavior such as smoking, drinking alcohol, and taking drugs.

① Types of Pressure in Schools
② Pros and Cons of Home Schooling
③ Side Effects of Home Schooling
④ Reasons for Home Schooling

【Notes】 home schooling 재택 교육[수업] tuition 수업 mainstream 주류(의) setting 환경, 배경 peer 동료, 또래 interfere with 방해하다 drug 마약 pro 찬성하여, 찬성론(자) pros and cons 찬반양론, 장단점 side effect 부작용

정답

6 ②	7 ①	11 ②	12 ③	13 ④	14 ③
15 ①	16 ②	17 ④	18 ①	19 ②	20 ④

2013년 국가직 7급 영어 독해문제

■ 밑줄 친 부분에 들어갈 가장 적절한 것은? [문 13~문 15]

문 13.

Written and spoken texts have certain things in common: A person who wants something done uses language to get it done. The types of language that the speaker and the writer use, however, are different because distinct social activities are involved in the two types of texts. In the written text, wherein the writer has never met and will probably never meet the readers, the communication is one-way and consists to a large extent of neutral formulae. Thus, a distant and formal tone is appropriate for this kind of conventional exchange. ____________, the communication in the spoken text is a two-way process in which the interlocutors are necessarily engaged in some kind of personal interaction and thus a different type of language behavior is used to maintain a relationship.

① Meanwhile ② Similarly
③ Therefore ④ Otherwise

【Notes】 have A in common A를 공통으로 가지고 있다 distinct 별개의, 다른 be involved in ~에 관련되다 wherein [관계부사]거기에서, 그 점에서, 어디에서 one-way 일방적인 neutral 중립적인 formula 정형화된 문구, 공식 appropriate 적합한 interlocutor 대화자 be engaged in ~에 참여하다, 종사하다 interaction 상호작용 meanwhile 한편, 그동안에

문 14.

The simplest and most basic meaning of the symbol of Goddess is the acknowledgement of the legitimacy of female power as a beneficent and independent power. A woman who echoes Ntosake Shange's dramatic statement, "I found God in myself and I loved her fiercely," is saying "Female power is strong and creative." She is saying that the divine principle, the saving and sustaining power, is in herself, that she will no longer look to men or male figures as saviors. The strength and independence of female can be intuited by contemplating ancient and modern images of the Goddess. This meaning of the symbol of Goddess is simple and obvious, and yet it is difficult for many to comprehend. It stands ________________ to the paradigms of female dependence on males that have been predominant in Western religion and culture.

① in sharp contrast ② in passive obedience
③ at perfect ease ④ on its own

【Notes】 acknowledgement 인정 legitimacy 적법성, 정통성 beneficent 인정 많은, 선행을 하는, 유익한 fiercely 맹렬히 divine 신의, 신성한 sustain 지속시키다, 지탱하다, 존재하게 하다 savior 구원자 intuit 직관하다, 직관으로 알다 contemplate 숙고하다, 명상하다 comprehend 이해하다 paradigm (특정 시대 영역의 지배적인) 사고[이론]의 틀[체계], 모범 predominant 지배적인, 두드러진

문 15.

The globalization is a bit different. It has also one overarching feature — integration. The world has become an increasingly interwoven place, and today, whether you are a company or a country, your threats and opportunities increasingly derive from who you are connected to. This globalization system is also characterized by a single word: the Web. So in the broadest sense we have gone to a system increasingly built around integration and webs. This leads to many other differences between the globalization system and the Cold War system. The globalization system, unlike the Cold War system, is not frozen, but a dynamic ongoing process. That's why I define globalization this way: it is the inexorable ________________ of markets, nation-states and technologies to a degree never witnessed before — in a way that is enabling the world to reach into individuals, corporations and nation-states farther, faster, deeper than ever before.

① obliteration ② segregation
③ integration ④ perpetration

【Notes】 overarching 대단히 중요한 integration 통합 interweave 짜 넣다, 섞어 짜다, 뒤섞다 ongoing 진행중인 inexorable 거침없는, 멈출 수 없는, 용서[가차]없는, 냉혹한 obliteration 삭제, 소멸 segregation 분리, [인종, 성별]차별 perpetration 범행, 범죄

문 16. Katrina 이전의 모습으로 New Orleans를 재건하려는 것에 대한 필자의 시각은?

Residences and decision-making alike must move to higher ground regarding the future of New Orleans. Cool pragmatism must prevail over emotional attachment to place. Those who expect a return to pre-Katrina New Orleans life are selfishly myopic. Not only were residents' lives devastated by the tragedy, but emotional and other costs were also borne by families, friends, and fellow citizens throughout the country. Rescue workers put their lives and health in harm's way. Taxpayers bore the costs of the devastation and will be required to do so once again, inevitably. To rebuild the residential life of New Orleans is nothing less than reckless endangerment.

① affirmative ② optimistic
③ indifferent ④ negative

【Notes】 pragmatism 실용주의 prevail 우세하다, 만연하다 attachment 애착, 부착 myopic 근시의, 근시안적인 devastate 황폐화시키다, 완전히 파괴하다 inevitably 필연적으로 reckless 무모한 endangerment 위험에 빠뜨리기 affirmative 긍정적인 optimistic 낙관적인 indifferent 무관심한

문 17. 다음 글에 나타난 Dr. Westhoff의 생각과 일치하는 것은?

The new study, being published Monday in The American Journal of Obstetrics and Gynecology, finds that pregnant women who consume 200 milligrams or more of caffeine a day — the amount in 10 ounces of coffee or 25 ounces of tea — may double their risk of miscarriage. However, Dr. Carolyn Westhoff, a professor of obstetrics and gynecology, and epidemiology, at Columbia University Medical Center, had reservations about the study, noting that miscarriage is difficult to study or explain. Dr. Westhoff said most miscarriages resulted from chromosomal abnormalities, and there was no evidence that caffeine could cause those problems. "I think we tend to go overboard on saying expose your body to zero anything when pregnant. The human race wouldn't have succeeded if the early pregnancy was so vulnerable to a little bit of anything. We're more robust than that."

① Caffeine could cause chromosomal abnormalities, which eventually result in miscarriages.
② The early pregnancy is very vulnerable to even a little caffeine.
③ You should expose your body to zero caffeine when pregnant.
④ Most miscarriages are caused by chromosomal abnormalities.

【Notes】 The American Journal of Obstetrics and Gynecology 미국 산부인과 학회지 pregnant 임신한 miscarriage 유산 epidemiology 전염병학 reservation 의구심, 의혹, 보류, 예약 chromosomal 염색체의 abnormality 이상, 기형 go overboard on ~에 열중[열광]하다 vulnerable 취약한, 연약한, 상처받기 쉬운 robust 강인한, 튼튼한

문 18. 다음 글의 내용과 일치하는 것은?

Using biofuels made from corn, sugar cane and soy could have a greater environmental impact than burning fossil fuels, according to experts. Although the biofuels themselves emit fewer greenhouse gases, they all have higher costs in terms of biodiversity loss and destruction of farmland. The problems of climate change and the rising cost of oil have led to a race to develop environmentally-friendly biofuels, such as palm oil or ethanol derived from corn and sugar cane. The EU has proposed that 10% of all fuel used in transport should come from biofuels by 2020 and the emerging global market is expected to be worth billions of dollars a year.

① Fossil fuels have higher costs than biofuels in terms of biodiversity loss.
② Climate change has no bearing on the development of biofuels.
③ About 10 percent of all European cars should use biofuels by 2020.
④ Ethanol is one of the environmentally-friendly biofuels.

【Notes】 biofuel 바이오 연료, 생물 연료 sugar cane 사탕수수 soy 콩 impact 영향 fossil fuel 화석연료 emit 방출하다 biodiversity 생물 다양성 transport 운송, 수송 have no bearing on ~와 관련이 없다

문 19. 동물들이 단조로움을 극복하기 위해 하는 행동이 아닌 것은?

Observations have revealed that there are probably four main ways in which animals in confined spaces try to overcome their monotony. The first is to invent new motor patterns for themselves such as new exercises and gymnastics. They may also try to increase the complexity of their environment by creating new stimulus situations: many carnivores play with their food as though it were a living animal. Alternatively the animal may increase the quantity of its reaction to normal stimuli. Hypersexuality is one common response to this type of behavior. Finally, they may increase the variability of their response to stimuli such as food. Many animals can be seen playing, pawing, advancing, and retreating from their food before eating it. These observations of caged animals lead us to think how far studies of this sort can throw light on human behavior under similar conditions.

① Animals may increase the variety of their motor patterns.
② Animals may increase the quality of their reaction to stimuli.
③ Animals may increase the variability of their response to stimuli.
④ Animals may increase the complexity of their environment.

【Notes】 confine 제한하다, 한정하다 monotony 단조로움, 따분함 motor pattern 운동 패턴 gymnastics 체조 complexity 복잡성 stimulus 자극 carnivore 육식동물 alternatively 그 대신에, 대안으로, 그렇지 않으면 quantity 양 normal 보통의 hypersexuality 과도한 성욕, 성욕 과다 variability 다양성 paw 발로 건드리다[긁다] retreat 후퇴하다 throw[shed, cast] light on (문제 등에 대해) 해결의 실마리를 던져주다[이해를 돕는 사실을 보여주다]

문 20. 다음 글의 내용과 일치하지 않는 것은?

The fall of the Soviet Union has given Vietnam a practical usefulness to the U.S. that it never had during a war in which fifty-eight thousand American soldiers died. The Soviet Union's collapse has created a power vacuum in East Asia. The American withdrawal from the Philippines and the decrease of the U.S. military because of the end of the Cold War and economic troubles at home are also partially responsible for this power vacuum. This could be more of an illusion than reality because the U.S. still maintains both the air and naval capability to assert itself in East Asia. However, this illusion is very powerful and the Chinese have begun to perceive it. The Chinese are intent on filling the vacuum. In order to curb Chinese regional ambitions, the U.S. must strive to lift the economic embargo, open diplomatic relations, and support the cause of economic reform in Vietnam. The Vietnamese believe that the more involved American business is in Vietnam, the more

China will be discouraged to invade them. The constant threat from and fear of China encourages the Vietnamese to make peace with the U.S.

① The power vacuum is partly attributable to the dissolution of the Soviet Union.
② The end of the Cold War has resulted in the decrease of the U.S. military.
③ China remains a constant threat to the Vietnamese.
④ The power vacuum has led to economic troubles in the U.S

【Notes】 collapse 붕괴 vacuum 공백 withdrawal 철수, 인출 decrease 감소, 감축 illusion 환상, 허상, 환영 assert 주장하다 perceive 인지[인식]하다 be intent on ~에 열중하다 curb 억제하다 strive 애쓰다, 노력하다 embargo 통상금지, 출입항금지, 배포금지 diplomatic 외교의 reform 개혁 discourage 방해하다, 낙담시키다 invade 침입하다 make peace with 화해하다 attributable to ~에 기인하는, ~가 원인인 dissolution 해체, 붕괴, 소멸

정답

13 ①	14 ①	15 ③	16 ④
17 ④	18 ④	19 ②	20 ④

2012년 국가직 7급 영어 독해문제

■ 다음 글의 내용과 일치하는 것을 고르시오. [문 13~문 14]

문 13.

Most of the criteria used by anthropologists in determining racial categories have to do with physical characteristics that are of little or no consequence in human behavior. Skin color and certain other physical characteristics may be advantageous or disadvantageous in given environments but there is no evidence that skin color, hair, or other such features are in any way correlated with a particular kind of brain or with special qualities of mind and character. Unquestionably individuals come into the world with different potentialities but the evidence suggests that within any of the major racial groups the whole range of individual potentialities will be found. This does not necessarily mean that there are no statistically significant differences in specific innate abilities occurring in widely separated populations. It does mean that we do not now have any reliable way of determining whether such differences exist. Even if it were possible to determine that in some population there was a greater than average incidence of one kind of ability or another, we would still have to reckon with the various cultural factors involved. We would also be confronted with the fact that there are no objective criteria for deciding the relative superiority of mechanical aptitude, literary or artistic gifts, philosophical bent, and so on.

① No significant differences in specific innate abilities exist in widely separated populations.

② It is evident that such features as skin color are closely related to specific qualities of mind.

③ Many anthropologists appeal to physical characteristics in determining racial categories.

④ The relative superiority of artistic gifts can be easily determined by certain criteria.

【Notes】 criteria 기준, 표준 anthropologist 인류학자 racial categories 인종의 범주들 physical characteristics 신체의 특징들 of consequence 중요한 feature 특징 advantageous 유리한, 이로운 disadvantageous 불리한 be correlated with ~와 상관관계가 있다 potentiality 잠재력 statistically 통계적으로 innate 타고난 incidence 발생률 reckon 계산하다, 고려하다 be confronted with ~에 직면하다 mechanical 기계의, 기계적인 aptitude 적성 literary 문학의 gift 재능, 선물 bent 성향, 경향

문 14.

"No matter how much you invest in creating a premium experience, at the end of the day and especially through the night, if you don't get a comfortable sleep, the perception of service comes down a notch," Mr. Spurlock said. Among the findings that surprised him was how much the seat foam affects comfort. The density, thickness and contour that make a seat comfortable will make a bed uncomfortable. He said that research showed that passengers want soft seats that are not contoured to their body from the waist up. Virgin Atlantic solved the problem of making one piece of furniture serve two purposes with the touch of a button. The passenger stands up, presses the button and the seat back electronically flips to become a flat bed. The seat side is contoured and covered in soft leather; the reverse is built of firm foam.

① The level of comfort is influenced by the seat foam.
② Comfortable beds are contoured in the same way as comfortable seats are.
③ A comfortable seat must be equipped with a button.
④ Both sides of the seat developed by Virgin Atlantic are made of soft leather.

【Notes】 perception 인식 notch 등급, 눈금 come down a notch 한 등급 떨어지다 foam 발포제 density 밀도 contour 윤곽(을 이루다), 모양(을 이루다) electronically 전자적으로, 컴퓨터로, 자동적으로 flip 휙 젖혀지다, 확 뒤집히다 flat 편편한, 납작한 reverse 반대, 역 firm 단단한, 견고한, 확고한

■ 밑줄 친 부분에 들어갈 가장 적절한 것을 고르시오. [문 15~문 16]

문 15.

What if the good life isn't really all that good? What if the very things so many of us strive for–a high paying, powerful job; a beautiful house; a wardrobe of nice clothes in desirably small sizes; and a fancy education for our children to prep them for carrying on this way of life–turn out to be more trouble than they're worth? It's long been believed that the psychological burdens associated with being a 'low-status individual' grow lighter as people move up the social ladder. However, it turns out that's true only to a point. Once you get high enough, the mental and physical health benefits associated with greater __________________ fade away.

① ambiguity ② affluence
③ beliefs ④ burdens

【Notes】 what if~?(=what does it matter if~?; what would happen if~?) strive for ~을 위해 분투하다[노력하다] wardrobe 옷장 desirably 바람직스럽게 fancy 품질 좋은, 일류의, 고급의, 장식이 많은, 복잡한 prep 준비시키다, 준비하다, 자율학습, 예습, 예비의 turn out 드러나다, 판명되다 associated with ~와 관련된 low-status 낮은 지위의 ladder 사다리 move up the social ladder 사회적 사다리를 올라가다, 사회적 지위가 상승하다 only to a point 단지 어떤 지점까지만 health benefit 건강상의 이점[혜택] fade 사라지다 ambiguity 애매모호함 affluence 풍부, 풍요

문 16.

These men of the forest were equally unprepared for the impatient idealism that sought to convert them to Christianity and for the greed that clutched hungrily at their gold and their land. Because they were pushed back, despoiled, and exploited for three hundred years, their part in American literature is more a hint of what might have been than a record of what actually was. It seems to be a law of nature that any species will rapidly become extinct when confronted with a sudden change in environment or with a new foe whose ways it does not understand. The fact that the American Indian retreated and suffered is not necessarily an evidence of his __________________. He left an indelible stamp upon the imagination of his conqueror. To the white invaders he was an obstacle to be removed, but to their imaginations he often symbolized the nobility man could achieve by living openly with nature.

① inferiority ② deliberation
③ sumptuousness ④ perpetuity

【Notes】 impatient 조급한 idealism 이상주의 convert 개종시키다 greed 탐욕 clutch 움켜잡다 despoil 약탈하다, 빼앗다 exploit 착취하다 species 종 extinct 멸종한 foe 적 retreat 퇴각하다 indelible 지워지지 않는 stamp 낙인, 소인, 흔적, 우표 conqueror 정복자 invader 침입자 obstacle 장애(물) remove 제거하다 nobility 고귀함 inferiority 열등 deliberation 심사숙고 sumptuousness 화려함, 호화, 고가임 perpetuity 영속, 영원

■ 다음 글의 내용과 일치하지 않는 것을 고르시오. [문 17~문 18]

문 17.

In the 1920s, there were many ingenious machines in the world such as locomotives, assembly lines, telephones, airplanes, and so on. But each did only one thing. Everyone accepted the idea that to get a different task done, you needed to build a different machine. Everyone was wrong. Alan Turing was the man who first showed in persuasive detail how it would be possible to change that. His life ended in tragedy, for although he conceived a perfect, clearly describable computer, and although the new insights about how electrons can leap or seemingly stop might have allowed him to construct it, the technology remained elusive. New ideas in science don't automatically produce new machines. He would be lauded in death, but not while he lived.

① In the 1920s, it was generally believed that a machine could only perform one task.
② Alan Turing was the first to manufacture a multipurpose computer.
③ The technology Turing conceived was difficult to understand at that time.
④ Scientific ideas do not necessarily lead to the production of new machines.

【Notes】 ingenious 기발한, 재간이 많은 locomotive 기관차 assembly line 조립라인 persuasive 설득력 있는 conceive 구상하다, 상상하다, 임신하다 describable 설명될 수 있는, 묘사될 수 있는 insight 통찰(력) electron 전자 leap 펄쩍 뛰다 seemingly 외견상으로, 겉보기에 elusive 교묘히 피하는, 알기 어려운 laud 칭송하다 multipurpose 다목적의

문 18.

All propaganda is a systematic effort to persuade. Thus the issue is not the truth or falsehood of what is said. The propagandist gives a one-sided message, emphasizing the good points of one position and the bad points of another position. One of the most widely used forms of propaganda in the 20th century is the political speech. Politicians running for office try to project the best possible image of themselves while pointing out all the flaws of their opponents. Propaganda uses the media of mass communication–radio, television, newspapers, and magazines–to reach a mass audience. Such an audience cannot argue back; it can simply show approval or disapproval. The propagandist is not interested in a reasoned response but only in making converts to a point of view. Propaganda can be compared to other attempts to persuade large audiences. Among them are advertising, public relations, and teaching. Advertising is designed to sell products, services, and entertainments. The task of public relations is to create for the public an image of an individual or institution. The image is not necessarily false, but one that omits all flaws and faults. Teaching may become propaganda if it turns into indoctrination. Religious schools often teach doctrines and traditions.

① The ideas that propagandists try to deliver are mostly biased.
② The image created by public relations is expected not to contain flaws.
③ Propagandists usually aim to receive logical responses from the public.
④ Teaching might become propaganda if it tries to make converts to a point of view

【Notes】 propaganda (허위의, 과장된)선전 persuade 설득하다 falsehood 거짓, 허위 propagandist 선전자, 선동가 position 입장 run for office 공직에 출마하다 project 보여주다, 투영하다, 계획하다, 과제, 계획된 일 flaw 결함 opponent 상대방 argue back 반박하다 approval 찬성, 승인 disapproval 반대, 불인정 reasoned 이유를 갖춘 reasoned response 합리적인 반응 convert 전향자, 개종자, 전향하다, 개종하다 point of view 관점 public relations 홍보 institution 기관 omit 생략하다 indoctrination 교의[교리] 주입 doctrine 교리, 교의, 신조, 정책 biased 편향된

■ 다음 글을 읽고 물음에 답하시오.

Harry Truman, from Missouri, was a different kind of President. A measure of his greatness may rest on what he did after he left the White House. Historians have written the only asset he had when he died was the house he lived in, which was in Missouri. When he retired from office in 1952, his income was a US Army pension reported to have been $13,507.72 a year. Congress, noting that he was paying for his stamps and personally licking them, granted him an 'allowance' and, later, a retroactive pension of $25,000 per year. When offered corporate positions at large salaries, he declined, stating, "You don't want me. You want the office of the President, and that doesn't belong to me. It belongs to the American people and it's not for sale."

문 19. Why did Truman turn down the offers of corporate positions?

① Because he was legally not allowed to accept them as a former president.

② Because the American people did not want him to work for private companies.

③ Because he thought the companies wanted his influence as a former president.

④ Because he believed his pension would suffice for his life after retirement.

【Notes】 measure 척도, 기준 rest on ~에 있다 historian 역사가 asset 자산 retire from office 공직에서 물러나다(은퇴하다) pension 연금 congress 의회 lick 혀로 핥다 grant 주다, 허가하다 allowance 수당, 용돈, 보조금 retroactive 소급적인 corporate 기업의, 법인 조직의 turn down 거절하다 legally 법적으로 suffice 충족시키다, 충분하다

문 20. 밑줄 친 부분에 들어갈 가장 적절한 것은?

The Renaissance painter Giotto imitated nature so accurately that his teacher swatted at a painted fly on one of Giotto's works. Is this not an insuperable artistic achievement? If so, the artist's object was mimesis. Beginning during the Renaissance, mimesis was considered the pinnacle of artistic achievement. However, modern art focuses not only on depicting the world of surfaces, but also the inner world of abstract thoughts and feelings. Modern art focuses on the way the elements in the work of art interact and what feelings these elements evoke. A quick glance at art produced over the past century reveals that ____________________

① artistic achievement in modern art depends solely on the imitative description of objects.
② abstract thoughts and feelings are ignored in modern art.
③ mimetic skills allow artists to interact with inner feelings.
④ the importance of mimesis has decreased in modern art

【Notes】 swat 찰싹 때리다 insuperable 이겨내기 어려운, 무적의 mimesis 모방, 모사 pinnacle 최고 정점 depict 묘사하다 interact 상호작용하다 evoke 불러내다, 환기시키다 mimetic 모방의, 모사의

정답

13 ③	14 ①	15 ②	16 ①
17 ②	18 ③	19 ③	20 ④

2011년 국가직 7급 영어 독해문제

문 6. 밑줄 친 부분에 들어갈 가장 적절한 것은?

The Buddha did not intend his ideas to become a religion; in fact, he discouraged following any path or advice without testing it personally. His dying words, as it's told, were: "You must each be a lamp unto yourselves." __________, within several hundred years of his death, the Buddha's teachings had taken strong hold. Today, with 379 million followers, Buddhism is the world's fifth largest religion.

① Thus
② Moreover
③ Nevertheless
④ Accordingly

【Notes】 discourage 말리다, 단념시키다, 용기를 잃게 하다 personally 개인적으로 dying words 유언 take strong hold 강력해지다, 강력한 장악력을 갖다 moreover 게다가 nevertheless 그럼에도 불구하고 accordingly 따라서

문 12. 다음 글의 요지로 가장 적절한 것은?

Teaching is supposed to be a professional activity requiring long and complicated training as well as official certification. The act of teaching is looked upon as a flow of knowledge from a higher source to an empty container. The student's role is one of receiving information; the teacher's role is one of sending it. There is a clear distinction assumed between one who is supposed to know and another, usually younger person, who is supposed not to know. However, teaching need not be the province of a special group of people nor need it be looked upon as a technical skill. Teaching can be more like guiding and assisting than forcing information into a supposedly empty head. If you have a certain skill, you should be able to share it with someone. You do not have to get certified to convey what you know to others or to help them in their attempt to teach themselves. All of us, from the very youngest children to the oldest members of our cultures, should come to realize our own potential as teachers. We can share what we know, however little it might be, with someone who has need of that knowledge or skill.

① It is difficult to be a good teacher.
② Every person has a potential to be a good teacher.
③ Teaching is a professional activity requiring special training.
④ Teaching is the flow of knowledge from a higher source to an empty container.

【Notes】 be supposed to ~인 것으로 생각되다, ~하기로 되어 있다 professional 전문적인 complicated 복잡한 certification 증명서 be looked upon as ~로 간주되다 distinction 구별 assume 가정하다, 추정하다 province 영역, 분야, 지방 supposedly 아마도, 이른바 get certified 자격이 갖추어지다, 자격증을 취득하다 convey 전달하다 teach oneself 독학하다 potential 잠재력

문 13. 다음 글에 묘사된 실험의 목적으로 가장 적절한 것은?

An experiment was conducted first by Dr. Ash in the United States. What happens in this experiment is this: Someone is asked to join a group who are helping to study the discrimination of length. The victim, having agreed to this seemingly innocent request, goes to a room where a number of people—about half a dozen—and the experimenter are seated. Unbeknown to our victim, none of the other people in the room is a volunteer like himself; they are all in league with the experimenter. A pair of cards is produced; and everyone in turn is asked which of the three lines on the second card is equal to the line on the first. They all, without hesitation, pick—as they have been told to pick—the same wrong line. Last of all comes the turn of our volunteer. In many cases the volunteer, faced with this unanimity, denies the plain evidence of his senses, and agrees.

① To test how to learn the concept of length
② To test the role of the pressure to conform
③ To test the role of motivation in voluntary work
④ To test how to improve the capacity of human senses

【Notes】 conduct 수행[실행]하다 discrimination 구별, 차이, 차별 victim 희생자 innocent 순수한, 순진한, 무죄의 unbeknown to ~에 눈치 채이지 않고 volunteer 자원자 in league with ~와 협력하는 experimenter 실험자 in turn 차례로 hesitation 주저 last of all 최후에, 최후로 faced with ~에 직면하여 unanimity 만장일치 deny 부정하다 plain 명백한, 쉬운, 평이한 conform 순응하다, 따르다 motivation 동기, 동기부여 capacity 능력

■ 밑줄 친 부분에 들어갈 가장 적절한 것을 고르시오. [문 14~문 15]

문 14.

Poland is the largest of the eastern European countries. ____________________ Someone will immediately start quibbling that "eastern" Europe doesn't exist. That will start a long argument about whether "east central Europe" or "central Europe" is the best way of describing the ex-communist region. "Largest" is dodgy too—not least because it may prompt a discussion about the fragile and tragic foundations of Poland's eastern and western frontiers. Ukrainians and Russians will be quick to ask, justifiably, why they have been excluded from this notional category.

① How successful is its economy, then?
② Is it a safe enough statement, however?
③ At least it was, during its communist days.
④ It has always been one, despite its complex history.

【Notes】 quibble 트집 잡다 ex-communist region 과거 공산권 지역 dodgy 의심스러운, 교활한 prompt 촉발시키다 fragile 깨지기 쉬운 foundation 토대, 기반 frontier 국경 justifiably 정당하게 exclude 배제하다 notional 개념의, 개념적인 category 범주 communist days 공산주의 시절

문 15.

People exercise their bodies daily, yet they neglect to exercise their feelings and emotions. Young men are taught to hide and deny emotions. Women are reluctant to seek help in coping with their depression, anxiety, or distressed relationship. The same fitness fanatic who exercises daily, eats right and has two physicals a year will neglect the mind until a crisis is reached. Emotional problems don't just happen, but are cumulative and they can be avoided at times with the same daily fitness and annual physical approach we use when caring for our bodies. Just like it's better to maintain a healthy heart than recover from a heart attack, ___________.

① it is better to hide emotions than make them known
② people need to be aware of the development of disease
③ exercising regularly is more important than seeing a physician
④ dealing with emotional issues is easier before the chaos of a crisis breaks

【Notes】 neglect 소홀히 하다 deny 부정하다, 부인하다 reluctant 꺼려하는, 주저하는 cope with 다루다, 대처하다, 처리하다, 극복하다 depression 우울, 불경기 anxiety 걱정 distressed 고통스러운 fitness fanatic 신체단련에 광적인 사람 physical 신체검사, 건강검진 crisis 위기 cumulative 축적적인 annual 해마다의, 연례의 care for 돌보다 heart attack 심장마비 chaos 혼란, 혼돈, 무질서 break 사건이 터지다, 갑자기 발생하다

■ 다음 글의 내용과 일치하지 않는 것을 고르시오. [문 16~문 17]

문 16.

The traditional art of Africa plays a major part in African society. African art consists mainly of sculptures, paintings, masks and fetishes. Sculptures are considered to be the greatest achievement for African art. A majority of the sculptures are mainly done in wood but are also made of metal, stone, mud, and other materials. They are found in many parts of Africa but mainly in western and central Africa. Many ancient rock paintings have been found in southern and eastern Africa. These paintings are believed to be attributed to the Bushman people. Masks and fetishes are often used to scare off bad things such as evil spirits, witches or ghosts. They are also used to bring about a desired end, break a bad habit, or kill a natural or supernatural enemy.

① Rock paintings are believed to be done by the Bushman people.
② Masks and fetishes are used to drive out evil spirits and break a bad habit.
③ In western and central Africa, sculptures are mainly made of stone and mud.
④ Sculptures, paintings, masks and fetishes are among the major elements of African art.

【Notes】 play a major part in ~에서 중요한 역할을 하다 sculpture 조각 fetish 주술 도구, 맹목적 집착[숭배], 숭배의 대상 achievement 성취, 업적 be attributed to ~의 것으로 여겨진다, ~의 덕분이다, ~에 기인하다 scare off 겁을 주어 쫓아내다 evil spirits 악령들 witch 마녀 ghost 유령 bring about 초래하다, 유발하다 break a bad habit 나쁜 습관을 타파하다 supernatural 초자연적인 drive out 몰아내다

문 17.

Cyprus is the third largest island in the Mediterranean, strategically situated off Turkey and Syria. Despite its situation, and its rule by the Ottoman Empire from 1571, it was overwhelmingly inhabited by Greeks. It was occupied and administered by the British from

1878, and formally annexed by them at the beginning of World War I. A British Crown Colony from 1925, it served as an important military base during World War II and the Suez Crisis. In the 1950s the movement against foreign rule and for union with Greece picked up momentum, against the background of decolonization worldwide. A second movement started a violent campaign against British rule in 1955. Britain was eager to retain some influence on the strategically important island, so that in 1959 it offered independence and membership of the Commonwealth instead of union with Greece.

① The history of Cyprus is marked by foreign invasion and occupation.
② The geographical location of Cyprus explains why it is predominantly populated by Greeks.
③ During the 1950s Cyprus was no exception to the global move to strive to achieve independence.
④ Because of the strategical importance of Cyprus, Britain disallowed it from unifying with Greece in the 1950s.

【Notes】 strategically 전략적으로 overwhelmingly 압도적으로 inhabit 거주하다 administer 통치하다 formally 공식적으로 annex 합병하다 British Crown Colony 영국 직할 식민지 serve 역할을 하다 military base 군사기지 movement 움직임, 운동 foreign rule 외국의 지배[통치] union 통합, 연합 pick up momentum 탄력[가속력]을 얻다 decolonization 탈식민지화 worldwide 전세계적으로, 전세계적인 campaign 운동 eager 열망하는 retain 유지하다 offer 제안하다 independence 독립 membership 회원자격 the Commonwealth 영연방 be marked by ~에 의해 특징지어 지다, ~가 특징이다 invasion and occupation 침입과 점령 geographical location 지리적 위치 predominantly 압도적으로 populate 거주시키다, 이주시키다 exception 예외 global move 세계적인 움직임 strive 애쓰다, 노력하다 disallow 허락하지 않다 unify 연합[통합]하다

문 18. 다음 글의 제목으로 가장 적절한 것은?

The Harry Potter series of novels have been the subject of a number of legal proceedings, largely stemming from claims by the American religious groups that the magic in the books promotes witchcraft among children. Vatican City's official newspaper, L'Osservatore Romano said that Harry Potter, who promotes witchcraft and occult, was the wrong kind of hero and poses a danger to children around the world. Various religious conservatives have claimed that the books promote witchcraft and are therefore unsuitable for children, while a number of critics have criticised the books for promoting various political agendas. Rowling's revelation that the character Dumbledore was a homosexual has increased the political controversies surrounding the series.

① Controversies over the Harry Potter Series
② Various Themes of the Harry Potter Series
③ The Cultural Impact of the Harry Potter Series
④ The Effects of the Harry Potter Series on Magic

【Notes】 legal proceedings 소송절차 stem from ~에서 유래하다, 기인하다 promote 증진시키다, 조장하다 witchcraft 마술, 마법 occult 주술 pose 제기하다 conservative 보수주의자 unsuitable 부적합한 critic 비평가 agenda 의제, 안건 revelation 폭로, 게시 controversy 논란 impact 영향, 여파

■ 다음 글을 읽고 물음에 답하시오. [문 19~문 20]

The nucleus of the population is the local businessmen, whose interests constitute the municipal policy and control its municipal administration. The local businessmen are such as the local bankers, merchants of many kinds and degrees, real estate prompters, local lawyers, local clergymen... The businessmen, who take up the local traffic in merchandising, litigation, church enterprise and the like, commonly begin with some share in the real estate speculation. This affords a common bond and a common ground of pecuniary interest; which commonly masquerades under the name of local patriotism, public spirit, civic pride, and the like. This pretense of public spirit is so consistently maintained that most of these men come presently to believe in their own professions' worth. Pecuniary interest in the continued growth of the town, hence any creditable misrepresentation of the town's volume of business traffic, population, tributary farming community, or natural resources, is rated as serviceable to the common good. And any member of this business-like community will be rated as a meritorious citizen in proportion as he is serviceable to this joint pecuniary interest of these "influential citizen."

문 19. 위 글에서 필자가 언급하고 있는 '영향력 있는 사람들'은 누구인가?

① those who are blinded to facts by their patriotic spirit
② those who are fully serviceable to the welfare of the community
③ those who deceive themselves into thinking they are altruistic
④ those who look upon the welfare of their community as of paramount importance

문 20. 위 글의 어조로 가장 적절한 것은?

① satirical ② didactic
③ eulogistic ④ reflective

【Notes】 nucleus 핵, 핵심 local 지역의 constitute 구성하다 municipal 지방 자치체의, 시[읍, 군]의 administration 행정 real estate prompter 부동산업자 clergymen 성직자 take up 차지하다 traffic 거래 merchandising 상품판매 litigation 소송 enterprise 기업 and the like 기타 등등 share 몫 real estate speculation 부동산 투기 afford 제공하다 bond 유대 ground 토대 pecuniary 금전적인 masquerade 가장하다, 가면 무도회에 참가하다, 가면으로 가리다, 가면 무도회, 가장, 은폐 local patriotism 애향심 public spirit 공공의 정신 civic pride 시민적 긍지 pretense 가장, 구실 consistently 일관되게, 지속적으로 presently 곧 profession 직업 hence 따라서 creditable 신용할 만한, 칭찬받을 만한, 명예로운 misrepresentation 그릇된 설명[표현], 허위 진술 volume of business traffic 사업 거래량 tributary 공물을 바치는, 보조적인, 공헌하는, 지류의, 속국, 지류 farming community 농업공동체 natural resources 천연자원 rate 평가하다 serviceable 도움이 되는, 쓸 만한, 이바지하는, 도모하는 common good 공통의 이익, 공익, 공통의 선 meritorious 칭찬할 만한, 공로가 있는, 공로가 인정되는 in proportion as ~에 비례하여 joint 공동의, 연합의 influential citizen 영향력 있는 시민 patriotic spirit 애국적 정신, 애국심 welfare 복지 deceive 속이다 altruistic 이타적인 paramount 최고의 satirical 풍자적인 didactic 교훈적인 eulogistic 찬양[찬미]하는 reflective 사색적인

정답

6 ③	12 ②	13 ②	14 ②	15 ④
16 ③	17 ②	18 ①	19 ③	20 ①

2010년 국가직 7급 영어 독해문제

문 3. 다음 글의 제목으로 가장 적절한 것은?

One of the most famous houses in the United States is Monticello. It was the home of Thomas Jefferson, the third President of the United States. Located on a hill near Charlottesville, Virginia, it has a beautiful view of the surrounding countryside. The house is famous, first of all, because it belonged to a president. It is also a fine example of early 19th century American architecture. Jefferson designed it himself in a style he had admired in Italy. Many American buildings of that time, in fact, imitated European styles. But while most were just imitations, his Monticello is lovely in itself. Furthermore, the design combines a graceful style with a typical American concern for comfort and function.

① A View from Monticello
② Why Is Monticello Famous?
③ Thomas Jefferson, the Greatest President
④ American Architecture in the 19th Century

【Notes】 located 위치한 surrounding countryside 주변의 시골지역 architecture 건축, 건축양식 admire 칭찬하다, 감탄하다 imitate 모방하다 imitation 모방, 모조품 in itself 그 자체로 combine 결합하다 graceful 우아한 typical 전형적인 concern 관심, 관심사, 걱정 comfort and function 안락함과 기능

■ 다음 글의 주제로 가장 적절한 것을 고르시오. [문 4~문 5]

문 4.

According to interviews in a Ms. magazine with women who have undergone breast implant surgery, many women felt effects like crippling fatigues, joint pain, and irritable skin which leads to skin rashes. For some it was as serious as being infected with inflammatory rheumatoid arthritis, burning lungs, seizures, and axonal polyneuropathy, a condition that prevents brain signals from reaching the nerves.

① The popularity of breast implant
② The enormous price of breast implant
③ The negative impacts of breast implant
④ The merits of breast implant

【Notes】 Ms. magazine 여성잡지 undergo 겪다, 경험하다, (수술을) 받다 breast implant surgery 유방 이식[확대] 수술 crippling 불구로 만드는, 큰 손상을 입히는 fatigue 피로 joint pain 관절 통증 irritable 민감한, 화를 잘 내는, 염증성의 rash 발진, 뾰루지 infected 감염된 inflammatory 염증을 일으키는 rheumatoid arthritis 루마티스성 관절염 seizure 발작, 체포 axonal (신경세포의)축색돌기의 polyneuropathy 다발성 신경장애 condition 질환, 증상, 상태, 조건 brain signal 뇌 신호 nerve 신경 enormous 거대한, 엄청난 impact 영향 merit 장점, 가치

문 5.

Even now, ancient India is still visible and accessible to us in a very direct sense. At the beginning of the twentieth century, some Indian communities still lived as all our primeval ancestors must once have lived, by hunting and gathering. The bullock-cart and the potter's wheel of many villages today are much the same as those used 4,000 years ago. A caste-system whose main lines were set by about 1,000 B.C. still regulates the lives of millions, and even of some Indian Christians and Moslems. Gods and goddesses whose cults can be traced to the Stone Age are still worshipped at village shrines.

① The economic system of ancient India
② Religious cults for gods in Indian villages
③ Indian communities regulated by a caste-system
④ The old-fashioned way of life in India

【Notes】 visible and accessible 볼 수 있고 접근 가능한 primeval 원시시대의, 태고의 ancestor 조상 hunting and gathering 사냥[수렵]과 채집 bullock 거세한 소, 송아지 bullock-cart 소달구지 potter's wheel 도자기 만들 때 사용하는 돌림판, 도공용 물레 caste-system 카스트 제도 main line 주된 골격, 본줄기, 간선 regulate 통제하다, 규제하다 Moslem 이슬람교도 cult 숭배(의식), 유행 be traced to ~까지 소급되어 올라가다 worship 숭배[예배]하다 shrine 사당 old-fashioned 구식의

문 6. 다음 글의 요지로 가장 적절한 것은?

Should we be concerned that the Copenhagen Climate Change Conference is not going to produce a concrete plan to reduce greenhouse-gas emissions? Lots of people clearly are. Indeed, while activists prepare to unfurl protest banners, politicians are scrambling for a face-saving way to declare the summit a success. They should all save their energy. The failure of the summit may be a blessing in disguise, because when it comes to dealing with climate change, the last thing we need right now is yet another empty agreement and yet more moral posturing.

① The summit to deal with climate change was a real success.
② Politicians are not taking any effective measure to reduce greenhouse effects.
③ Getting the politicians involved is the first step to deal with climate change.
④ Politicians are keen on setting concrete moral standards with respect to greenhouse-gas emission.

【Notes】 be concerned that ~을 걱정하다 Climate Change Conference 기후변화 회의 concrete 구체적인 reduce greenhouse-gas emission 온실가스 배출을 줄이다 activist 활동가, 행동대원 unfurl 펴다, 전개하다 protest 항의(하다) banner 현수막 scramble 앞다투다, 쟁탈전을 벌이다, 스크램블 face-saving 체면을 세워주는 declare 선언하다 summit 정상회담 a blessing in disguise 전화위복 blessing 축복 disguise 위장, 변장 when it comes to ~에 관한 한 empty agreement 공허한 협정, 알맹이 없는 협정, 무의미한 협정 posture 자세를 취하다, ~인 척하다, 자세 moral posturing 도덕적 허식[가식, 자세] take measures 조치를 취하다 greenhouse effect 온실효과 involve 관여시키다, 포함시키다 be keen on ~을 열망하다 with respect to ~에 관련하여

문 7. 밑줄 친 부분에 들어갈 말로 가장 적절한 것은?

Man is always left with a crisis in decision. The main test before him involves his __________ to change rather than his ability to change. That he is capable of change is certain. For there is no more mutable or adaptable animal in the world. We have seen him migrate from one extreme clime to another. We have seen him step out of backward societies and join advanced groups within the space of a single generation. This is not to imply that the changes were necessarily always for the better; only that change was and is possible. But change requires stimulus; and mankind today needs to look no further for stimulus than its own desire to stay alive. The critical power of change, says Spengler, is directly linked to the survival drive. Once the instinct for survival is stimulated, the basic condition for change can be met.

① will
② freedom
③ knowledge
④ imagination

【Notes】 be left with (감정 따위를) 계속 지니다; (책임 따위가) 맡겨지다 a crisis in decision 결정을 함에 있어서의 위기 mutable 변화할 수 있는, 변덕스러운 adaptable 적응할 수 있는, 융통성이 있는, 개조할 수 있는 migrate 이주하다 extreme 극단적인 step out of ~에서 빠져나오다 backward society 후진 사회, 낙후된 사회 join advanced groups 선진 집단들에 합류하다 within the space of a single generation 한 세대 내에서 imply 암시하다 stimulus 자극 critical 중요한 linked to ~에 연관되어 있는 survival drive 생존욕구 instinct 본능 stimulate 자극하다 meet 충족시키다 will 의지, 유언장

문 8. 주어진 글 다음에 이어질 내용을 문맥상 가장 자연스럽게 배열한 것은?

Popcorn was discovered thousands, if not hundreds of years ago. Movie theaters didn't appear on the scene until the early 1900s. Nevertheless, the two intersected, and movies became associated with popcorn.

(A) They'll sit and watch an entire movie without eating anything. Others will munch on pretzels or candy or rice cakes, or download heavier fare such as pizza.

(B) It was fate, and eating popcorn while watching movies became a tradition. But some of your fellow citizens insist on thumbing their noses at this tradition.

(C) Don't be one of them. Popcorn is the only acceptable snack to consume while watching a movie. Not only is it satisfying, it's also high in fiber and low in calories.

① A–C–B
② B–A–C
③ C–A–B
④ C–B–A

【Notes】 appear on the scene 현장[무대]에 나타나다 intersect 교차하다 munch 우적 우적 씹어 먹다, 간식을 먹다 pretzel 프레첼(짭짤하고 딱딱한 비스킷) rice cake 떡 download 이송[전송]하다, 다운로드하다 heavy 소화가 잘 안 되는 fare 음식물, 식사 fate 운명 thumb one's nose at ~을 비웃다 snack 간식 consume 먹다, 소비하다 fiber 섬유질

■ 다음 글을 읽고 물음에 답하시오. [문 9 ~ 문 10]

It is a common prejudice that whales live only in the cold, open water of the oceans, and most of my fellow countrymen from Greece are not aware of the fact that bottlenose whales live right in front of their noses. A close relative of the northern bottlenose, the elusive Cuvier's beaked whale, can be found throughout the warm and heavily trafficked waters of the Mediterranean Sea. In 1996 I had an unfortunate encounter with a dead Cuvier's beaked whale. Probably struck by a ship's propeller, the animal was a sad reminder of mankind's negative effects on our marine environment. Douglas Chadwick's article and Flip Nicklin's photographs gave me a rare glimpse into a world close by yet so far away.

문 9. 윗글의 내용과 일치하는 것은?

① Whales live only in the cold and open water of the oceans.
② As Greeks know, bottlenose whales live in the Mediterranean Sea.
③ The Cuvier's beaked whale is at odds with the usual notion about whales' habitat.
④ Cuvier's beaked whales live only in the warm waters of the Mediterranean Sea.

문 10. 윗글에서 "a dead Cuvier's beaked whale"이 언급된 이유로 가장 적절한 것은?

① To give another example of bottlenose whales that live in the warm ocean.
② To show how mankind can affect the sea environment.
③ To point out the danger that whales can give to the ship.
④ To tell how impressive Flip Nicklin's picture of the whale was.

【Notes】 prejudice 편견 open water 개빙(開氷)구역(부빙(浮氷)이 수면의 10분의 1 이하) bottlenose whale 병코 고래 elusive 잡히지 않는, 피하는 Cuvier's beaked whale 민부리 고래 heavily trafficked waters 교통량이 많은 바다 the Mediterranean Sea 지중해 encounter 우연한 만남 reminder 상기시켜 주는 것 marine 바다의 article 기사, 물품, 조항, 관사 glimpse 흘끗 봄, 잠시 들여다 봄 is at odds with ~와 일치하지 않다, ~와 상충하다, ~와 다투다 notion 관념, 개념 habitat 서식지

정답

3 ②	4 ③	5 ④	6 ②
7 ①	8 ②	9 ③	10 ②

2009년 국가직 7급 영어 독해문제

■ 다음 글의 제목으로 가장 적절한 것을 고르시오. [문 6~문 7]

문 6.

Competition in sports, it has been argued, is ethically defensible when it involves participants in a mutual quest for excellence. In effect, competitors should view themselves as under a moral obligation to their opponents. Each competitor is obligated to try his or her best, so that opponents can develop their own skills and be genuinely tested. In this view, sports are absorbing to spectators and participants alike precisely because they involve both our minds and bodies so fully in meeting a challenge, a challenge worth meeting for its own sake.

① Demerits of Competition
② Moral Obligations in Competition
③ Methods of Winning in Competition
④ Side Effects of Competition

【Notes】 argue 주장하다 ethically 윤리적으로, 도덕적으로 defensible 방어할 수 있는 involve 관련[참여, 연루]시키다, 포함[수반]하다 participant 참여자 mutual 상호간의 quest 추구, 탐구 excellence 장점, 우월, 탁월(성) in effect 사실상, 실제로 obligation 의무 opponent 상대방, 적수 obligate 의무를 지우다, 강요하다 genuinely 진정으로, 정말로 absorb 흡수하다, 몰두시키다 absorbing 몰입하게 [빠져들게] 만드는 spectator 관중 precisely 정확하게 meet a challenge 도전에 직면하다 for its own sake 그것 자체를 위해서 demerit 단점 side effect 부작용

문 7.

There are over 30,000 different kinds of spiders in the world. Spiders live in all different kinds of climates and environments from blazing deserts to damp caves and towering mountain tops. What enables spiders to survive in such diverse environments? Silk. Every spider is born with the ability to produce silk. This wondrous tool of survival is used by spiders to catch their dinner and escape from danger. Spiders adapt the use of their silk according to the situation they find themselves in. For example, to catch an insect in a web, they make the web out of two different kinds of silk. The outer part of the web which is attached to a tree, flower or pole is rigid and strong so it does not break. On the other hand, the middle part of the web is flexible so that when an insect flies into it, it will stretch rather than break. This center silk can stretch up to four times its original length. When spiders are in danger, they can escape by flying through the air at the end of an instantly made silk dragline. The dragline is sticky and easily attached to a solid surface.

① Spiders' Silk for Survival
② The Life Cycle of Spiders
③ The Danger of Spiders
④ The Types of Spiders

【Notes】 blazing desert 타는 듯한 사막 damp cave 습기 찬 동굴 towering mountain top 우뚝 솟은 산꼭대기 diverse 다양한 adapt (상황에)맞추다, 적응[순응, 조화]시키다, 개작[개조, 번안]하다 insect 벌레 web 거미줄 attach 붙이다, 첨부하다 pole 막대기, 장대, 기둥 rigid 단단한 flexible 유연한 stretch 늘어나다 instantly 즉시 dragline 유도 밧줄, 끄는 밧줄 sticky 끈적거리는 solid 딱딱한, 견고한 life cycle 생애 주기

문 13. 다음 글의 주제로 가장 적절한 것은?

When the media report on cloning in the news, they are usually talking about only one type called reproductive cloning. There are different types of cloning, however, and cloning technologies can be used for other purposes besides producing the genetic twin of another organism. A basic understanding of the different types of cloning is the key to taking an informed stance on current public policy issues and making the best possible personal decisions. The following three types of cloning technologies will be discussed: recombinant DNA technology or DNA cloning, reproductive cloning, and therapeutic cloning.

① Understanding different types of cloning
② History of cloning technologies
③ Legalization of cloning
④ Various public issues of cloning

【Notes】 cloning 복제 reproductive 재생의, 번식의, 생식의 genetic 유전적인 twin 쌍둥이 organism 유기체, 생명체 informed 학식이 있는, 지식이 풍부한 stance 자세 current public policy issues 현재의 공공 정책 문제들, 공공정책의 현안들 recombinant 재조합형의 therapeutic 치료의, 치료상의 legalization 법제화

문 14. 의미상 밑줄 친 부분에 들어갈 가장 적절한 것은?

You have probably heard the proverb that "Blood is thicker than water." But it is not necessarily better than water. Many friends are more helpful, kind, and generous than family and you need to connect to them. Even when you have a wonderful family, or one that has not been fraught with divorce, abuse, or indifference, the great gains you get from creating a family of choice — a close circle of friends — decreases your chances of getting the blues. We treat our circle of friends like good brothers, sisters, fathers, or mothers; they are there for us when our own family is ____________________ because of geography or an unwillingness to help.

① nearby ② commensal
③ jubilant ④ unavailable

【Notes】 proverb 속담 generous 관대한 connect 연관[연결]되다, 관계되다 fraught with ~로 가득한, ~투성이인 abuse 학대 indifference 무관심 of choice 최고의, 고급의, 상등품의, 탁월한, 특선의, 특선품 a close circle of friends 가까운 친구들의 모임 decrease 감소시키다 the blues 우울증 unwillingness to help 자발적으로 도와주려 하지 않음 commensal 공생하는, 식사를 같이 하는 [친구들], 공생 생물 jubilant 환호하는, 기뻐하는 unavailable 이용할 수 없는

■ 밑줄 친 부분에 들어갈 가장 적절한 것들로 짝지어진 것을 고르시오. [문 17~문 18]

문 17.

If high technology is the unstoppable force, here is the immovable object: Cattle subsist largely on grass. Cows need to be led to where the grass is ㉠__________. To achieve that requires no more and no less than an individual on horseback, accompanied by a rope and maybe a decent stock dog or two — all set on a landscape detached from urban ㉡__________, not to mention cell phone service.

	㉠	㉡
①	ample	serenity
②	scanty	clamor
③	ample	clamor
④	scanty	serenity

【Notes】 subsist 생존하다, 존재하다, 살아가다(on) accompany 동반하다 decent 어지간한, 쓸만한, 품위 있는 stock dog 가축몰이 개 landscape 풍경 detach 분리하다 urban 도시의 ample 풍부한 serenity 고요함 scanty 빈약한, 불충분한 clamor 소란

문 18.

Over two million years ago, primitive human beings took up stones and began transforming them into ㉠____________. What were once nothing more than pieces of debris were deliberately reworked into tools to be used to strip the bark from wood and roots, or to slice the tough outer hide from a dead animal. Although perhaps not as impressive a feat as space travel, the creation of these humble tools marks a turning point in human evolution. No other species has been as ㉡____________ as the human has in adapting nature to serve its purpose.

	㉠	㉡
①	decorations	genuine
②	implements	versatile

③ monuments memorable
④ buildings destructive

【Notes】 primitive 원시의 transform 변형하다 debris 암석부스러기, 파편, 쓰레기, 잔해 deliberately 심사숙고하여, 계획적으로, 신중히, 찬찬히, 의도적으로 rework 재가공하다, 재생하다 strip 벗기다 bark 나무껍질 slice 얇게 베어내다 tough 거친 hide 짐승의 가죽 feat 묘기, 재주, 위업, 공적 space travel 우주여행 humble 소박한, 겸손한 mark 표시하다 turning point 전환점 evolution 진화 adapt 개조하다, 적응시키다 decoration 장식 genuine 진짜의, 참된 implement 도구 versatile 다재다능한 monument 기념비 memorable 기억할 만한 destructive 파괴적인

■ 다음 글을 읽고 물음에 답하시오. [문 19~문 20]

Though couched in indirect terms, Barack Obama's inaugural address was a stark repudiation of the era of George W. Bush and a vow to drive the United States into "a new age" by reclaiming the values of an older one. It was a delicate task, with Mr. Bush and the former vice president, Dick Cheney, sitting feet from him as he described the false turns and the roads not taken. In his words, Mr. Obama blamed no one other than the country itself—"our collective failure to make hard choices" and a willingness to suspend national ideals "for expedience's sake." Yet every time Mr. Obama urged Americans to "choose our better history," to make decisions according to science instead of ideology, to reject a "false choice" between safety and American ideals, to recognize that American military power does not "entitle us to do as we please," he signaled a commitment to pragmatism not just as a governing strategy but as a basic value.

문 19. According to his inaugural address, how can Obama's evaluation of George W. Bush's era be characterized?

① infusive ② negative
③ sympathetic ④ roborant

문 20. Which of the following is not true of the passage?

① Dick Cheney attended Obama's inaugural ceremony.
② Obama seems to believe that Bush's government made easy choices.
③ Americans have made decisions based on science rather than ideology.
④ Pragmatism appears to be Obama's basic value.

【Notes】 couch 표현하다, 긴 의자 indirect term 간접적인 용어 inaugural address 취임 연설 stark 적나라한, 완전한, 준엄한 repudiation 부인, 거부, 반대, 결별, 의절 era 시대 vow 맹세 drive 만들다, 몰아가다, 추진시키다 reclaim 되찾다, 환원하다, 재생[갱생]시키다, 교정하다, 개선하다 delicate 섬세한, 조심스러운, 정교한, 다루기 어려운 describe 설명하다 false turn 잘못된 방향전환 our collective failure to make hard choices 힘든 선택들을 우리 모두가 하지 않은 것 suspend 보류하다, 정지하다, 매달다 expedience 편의, 편익, 편리 urge 촉구하다 recognize 인식하다 entitle 자격[권리]를 부여하다 as we please 우리가 원하는 대로, 우리가 하고 싶은 대로 signal 신호를 보내다, 시사[암시]하다, 표시하다 commitment 헌신, 전념, 언약, 공약, 책임 pragmatism 실용주의 governing strategy 통치 전략 evaluation 평가 infusive 고무하는 sympathetic 공감하는, 동정하는 roborant 힘을 북돋우는, 강장제, 보약

정답

6 ②	7 ①	13 ①	14 ④
17 ③	18 ②	19 ②	20 ③

2008년 국가직 7급 영어 독해문제

■ 다음 글의 주제로 가장 적절한 것을 고르시오. [문 11~문 12]

문 11.

First, in the colonial era, the main goal of education was to train people for religious and moral purposes, and to promote good behavior. Later on, reformists such as Horace Mann called for public education for all, and professional training for teachers. As opposed to educators of the colonial period, later educators wanted this public education to be free from religion. Later in the 19th century, John Dewey began teaching the theory of 'learning by doing.' Even more importantly, he stressed that school was not just a period preparing for life, but was a period of life itself. Lastly, in the 20th century, the shift in population from the countryside to the cities made schools more concerned with social problems.

① schools in the colonial era
② the contributions of reformists
③ changes in educational philosophy
④ the most effective strategy of education

【Notes】 colonial 식민지의 promote 장려하다, 증진시키다, 승진시키다 reformist 개혁가 call for 요구하다 public education 공교육 professional training 전문적 훈련[교육] as opposed to ~와는 반대로[대조적으로] stress 강조하다 shift 변동, 변화, 교체, 교대(조) countryside 시골 concerned with ~에 관심을 갖는 contribution 공헌 strategy 전략

문 12.

Agriculture is responsible for providing food for a growing population and as it becomes clear that yields cannot continue to rise without limit, the sustainability of agricultural practices becomes an increasingly important question. Crop rotation is one of the most important management practices in a sustainable agriculture system, both as a means of conserving soil and of maintaining its fertility. A well-thought-out crop rotation is worth seventy-five percent of everything else that might be done, including fertilization and pest control. Crop rotation is by no means confined exclusively to organic farming, although much of what is considered in planning a rotation sequence encompasses the concerns of the organic farmer.

① crop rotation for sustainable agriculture
② challenge of organic farming
③ providing more food for more people
④ fertilization and pest control for crop rotation

【Notes】 agriculture 농업 yield 생산량, 산출량 sustainability 지속가능성 agricultural practices 농업의 관행 crop rotation 윤작 management practices 관리법, 경영 업무 sustainable 지속가능한 conserve 보존하다 fertility 비옥, 다산, 풍부, 번식력 well-thought-out 심사숙고된, 면밀한, 잘 계획된 fertilization 비옥화 pest control 해충 방제 confine 제한하다 exclusively 배타적으로, 독점적으로 organic farming 유기 농업 sequence 순서, 차례, 연속(물), 연쇄, 연달아 일어남 rotation sequence 윤작의 (일련의)순서 encompass 포함하다, 포위하다 concerns of the organic farmer 유기 농업을 하는 사람들의 관심사

■ 밑줄 친 부분에 들어갈 가장 적절한 것을 고르시오. [문 15~문 16]

문 15.

The current financial turmoil shows that most Asian economics are like ______________________, dependent not on their own intrinsic strength but on the wind and the string.

① fearful eagles
② high flying kites
③ strong-winged airplanes
④ automatically-driven rockets

【Notes】 financial 재정의, 금융의 turmoil 혼란, 소동, 법석 current financial turmoil 현재의 재정[금융] 혼란 intrinsic 고유의, 본질적인, 본래의 fearful eagle 무서운 독수리 kite 연 strong-winged airplane 날개가 튼튼한 비행기 automatically-driven rocket 자동조종 로켓

문 16.

Unlike ordinary parks, botanical gardens and arboretums are laid out with more than just the beauty of the landscape in mind. Although trees and shrubs may be interspersed throughout the area to enhance the pleasant surroundings, ______________________ ______________________________. Often there are small, special gardens, such as rose gardens, rock gardens, or wildflower gardens contained within the larger botanical gardens. Many have sections devoted to plants of particular geographic origins, such as a tropical plant section, or an aquatic plant section.

① a botanical garden is not always judged by its origin and history
② plants are usually grouped according to their scientific relationships
③ many kinds of plants need certain climatic conditions at certain seasons
④ their maintenance requires good techniques and practices of cultivating plants

【Notes】 ordinary park 일반 공원 botanical garden 식물원 arboretum 수목원 lay out 배열하다, 설계하다 landscape 풍경, 전망, 조경술 shrub 관목 intersperse 산재시키다, 흩뿌리다, 사이에 배치하다 enhance 높이다, 고양시키다, 강화하다 tropic 열대(지방)의, 회귀선의 tropical plant section 열대식물 구역 aquatic 수생의, 물속에 사는, 물의 aquatic plant section 수생식물 구역 maintenance 유지 cultivate 재배하다, 경작하다

■ 다음 글의 내용과 일치하는 것을 고르시오. [문 17~문 18]

문 17.

Afterwards, of course, there were endless discussions about the shooting of the elephant. The owner was furious, but he was only an Indian and could do nothing. Besides, legally I had done the right thing, for a mad elephant has to be killed, like a mad dog, if its owner fails to control it. Among the Europeans opinion was divided. The older men said I was right, the younger men said it was a damn shame to shoot an elephant for killing a coolie, because an elephant was worth more than any coolie. And afterwards I was very glad that the coolie had been killed by the elephant; it put me legally in the right and it gave me a sufficient pretext for shooting the elephant. I often wondered whether any of the others grasped that I had done it solely to avoid looking like a fool.

① It was an Indian who shot the elephant.
② The writer was angry with the death of the elephant.
③ The death of the coolie gave the writer a pretext for shooting the elephant.
④ The younger Europeans were worrying that they couldn't stop the elephant from killing the coolie.

【Notes】 furious 격노한 damn 저주스런, 지독한 coolie (인도나 중국의)하급 노동자, 막일꾼 it put me legally in the right 그것은 나를 법적으로 정당하게 해주었다 sufficient 충분한 pretext 구실, 핑계 grasp 이해하다, 붙잡다

문 18.

Simple playthings like balls, jump ropes, hula hoops and riding toys do more for encouraging physical activity than swings, jungle gyms and other stationary playground equipment, according to a new report in the January issue of the American Journal of Preventive Medicine. Kids were far more likely to be active at centers that scheduled more playtime, both inside and outdoors, and offered physical activity training and education for staff and students. Children in centers that had more portable playground toys and other characteristics showing support for active playtime reported about 80 more minutes of moderate to vigorous physical activity and 140 fewer minutes of sedentary activity each week compared to centers that were viewed as less supportive of physical activity.

① Children benefit from sedentary activity.
② If you want your child to be more active, try throwing him a ball.
③ Children were more likely to be active in places with slides and swings.
④ If you support your child's physical activity, he or she will come to like stationary playground equipment.

【Notes】 plaything 노리개, 장난감 swing 그네 jungle gym 정글짐(철골로 만든 놀이 시설) stationary 정적인, 정지된, 움직이지 않는 stationary playground equipment 고정된 놀이터 장비[기구] Preventive Medicine 예방의학 physical activity training and education 신체 활동 훈련과 교육 portable playground toy 휴대용 놀이터 장난감 moderate 적당한, 온건한 vigorous 격렬한, 원기 왕성한, 강력한, 활동적인, 활기찬 moderate to vigorous physical activity 적당한[온건한] 신체활동에서 격렬한 신체활동에 이르기까지의 신체 활동 sedentary 앉아 있는, 앉아서 일하는 supportive 격려하는, 뒷받침하는 benefit 이득을 보다 slide 미끄럼틀

문 19. 주어진 문장에 이어질 글의 순서로 가장 적절한 것은?

[Cancer is a group of diseases characterized by the uncontrolled growth and spread of abnormal cells.]

(가) For certain types of cancers, treatment with chemotherapy and radiation therapy may be used instead of or in combination with surgery. New therapies include inactivating damaged genes and boosting the immune system's ability to destroy cancerous cells.

(나) The most effective way to lower the number of deaths, however, is to prevent cancer from developing by eating healthy, exercising regularly, and early screening.

(다) The treatment for cancer usually depends on the stage the disease has reached. Surgically removing tumors can be successful if the cancer has not yet spread to the vital parts like the lymph nodes.

① (가)-(나)-(다)
② (가)-(다)-(나)
③ (다)-(가)-(나)
④ (다)-(나)-(가)

【Notes】 cancer 암 abnormal cell 비정상적인 세포 treatment 치료 chemotherapy 화학요법 radiation therapy 방사선요법 in combination with ~와 결합[병행]하여 surgery 수술 inactivate 비활성화하다 gene 유전자 boost 증대시키다, 밀어 올리다, 북돋우다, 신장시키다 immune 면역의 immune system 면역체계 cancerous 암에 걸린 cancerous cell 암세포 lower 낮추다 screen 검진하다 early screening 조기검진 surgically 수술로 remove 제거하다 tumor 종양 vital 중요한, 생명유지에 필수적인, 활기찬, 치명적인 lymph node 림프절

문 20. 다음 글의 제목으로 가장 적절한 것은?

If you ask people what animals they hate or fear most, chances are you will hear the following: skunks, bats, snakes and rats. But some of these animals are gaining new respect. The skunk is feared by most people because of its awful smell. But recently people have begun to rethink their ideas about skunks. "Skunks are very useful animals," says Dr. Briggs. "They catch rats, mice and beetles. They are great for pest control." Many people are also terrified of bats. Lately, however, bats have become more popular because they eat mosquitoes. "Bats are an environmentally friendly way to get rid of mosquitoes," says Prof. Austin.

① Environmentally Friendly Ways of Animal Keeping
② Inviting Animals into a New Perspective
③ Kinds of the Most Beloved Animals
④ Getting Rid of Hated Creatures

【Notes】 chances are (that) ~ 아마 ~일 것이다, 가망성은 ~이다 bat 박쥐 awful 끔찍한, 지독한 beetle 딱정벌레 pest control 해충방제 be terrified of ~을 두려워하다 mosquito 모기 environmentally friendly 환경 친화적인 get rid of 제거하다 animal keeping 동물 기르기 invite 안내하다, 초대하다 perspective 관점, 전망, 시각

정답

11 ③	12 ①	15 ②	16 ②
17 ③	18 ②	19 ③	20 ②

정재문

서울대학교(문학사)
원광대학교 대학원(문학박사)
브리티시 콜럼비아 대학교(UBC) 객원교수
현재 군산대학교 영어영문학과 교수

저서

셰익스피어 영어의 문법,
College English for Beginners & Pre-Intermediate Students,
College English for Intermediate Students 외 다수

English Reading Comprehension

(영어독해의 초석 다지기 & 영어독해에 이르는 지름길)

초판 1쇄 발행 _ 2014년 2월 28일

저 자 • 정 재 문
발 행 인 • 정 현 걸
발 행 • 신 아 사
인 쇄 • 예지인쇄
출판등록 • 1956년 1월 5일 (제9-52호)
주 소 • 서울특별시 은평구 녹번동 28-36번지 2F
전 화 • (02)382-6411 • 팩스 (02)382-6401
홈페이지 • www.shinasa.co.kr
E-MAIL • shinasa@daum.net

ISBN: 978-89-8396-849-4 (93740)

정가 15,000 원